Sir John Fortescue's
The Trying of Souls

Sir John Fortescue's
The Trying of Souls
The British Army during the American War of Independence

J. W. Fortescue

LEONAUR

Sir John Fortescue's The Trying of Souls
The British Army during the American War of Independence
by J. W. Fortescue

FIRST EDITION

Text taken from *A History of the British Army*

Leonaur is an imprint of Oakpast Ltd

Copyright in this form © 2016 Oakpast Ltd

ISBN: 978-1-78282-493-0 (hardcover)
ISBN: 978-1-78282-494-7 (softcover)

http://www.leonaur.com

Publisher's Notes

Contents

CHAPTER 1

A Matter of 'Tax'

While Bouquet's operations were yet in progress in the backwoods of America, the Ministry in England was beginning to attack the question of Imperial defence in earnest, (April 1763). Bute, on his resignation, had been succeeded as First Lord of the Treasury by George Grenville, an able, upright, and resolute man, but straitened by a mind of that academic type which is of all least fitted for the government of men. Overtures were made to Pitt to join the Ministry, but without success; and Grenville, who was esteemed a master of finance, was left, unchecked by a statesman's tact, to prosecute his own designs.

Careful scrutiny of the working of the Acts of Trade and Navigation quickly revealed to Grenville the fact that they had been systematically violated in America, and that the revenue derived from the custom-houses in the thirteen provinces was not only trifling in itself, but insufficient to pay as much as one-third of the cost of collection. He resolved that this failing should be remedied forthwith; and accordingly not only were stringent measures devised for enforcing the Acts, but by a statute of new duties were imposed in addition to those already existing. The severity of the new enactment was, however, tempered by the grant of additional bounties and by removal of some of the earlier restrictions, while the terms of the Act expressly reserved the revenue raised under its provisions to defray the cost of protecting the Colonies.

In the same session Grenville carried a resolution in favour of the imposition, by Act of the British Parliament, of certain stamp-duties in the Colonies, as a further contribution to the cost of colonial defence. These measures all formed part of a scheme for quartering ten thousand British troops permanently in America, who should be paid, in whole or in part, by the Colonies themselves.

That such a garrison was by no means in excess of the requirements of the long Atlantic coast-line and the equally extensive western boundary of the Mississippi can, I think, be contested by no reasonable man. Even if the French had been removed, the Spaniards still
held New Orleans and Louisiana, with nominal sovereignty over the
whole of the territory west of the Mississippi; while recent experience had shown that the Americans could not be trusted to defend
themselves even against Indians. Again, whatever the power of the
British Navy for protection, a fleet requires naval bases, and naval bases
require garrisons. Nor was the demand upon the Colonists excessive,
for the American Colonies had gained more than any other portion
of the Empire from the great defeat of France.

It is true that in America they had furnished forces exceeding the
Imperial troops in number for the expulsion of the French; but in
urging this point they conveniently ignored the fact that the sixty
thousand men, all paid by England, under Ferdinand of Brunswick,
and the British fleets in the Channel and the Mediterranean, had quite
as much to do with the conquest of Canada as the squadrons of Hol-
mes and Saunders and the armies commanded by Amherst and Wolfe.

At the first conclusion of peace thoughtful Americans probably
foresaw some such scheme as Grenville's; and it is certain that at the
beginning of 1764 Benjamin Franklin, the strongest intellect to be
found at that time in the whole Anglo-Saxon race, looked upon the
quartering of British troops in America as reasonable, and welcomed
the prospect for its promise of security not only against foreign invasion but against intestine disorder, (Franklin, *Works*, iv.).

It is more than likely that Grenville also saw an advantage in the
presence of disciplined men to enforce the law in a new country,
where the people, from long habits and traditions of self-dependence,
were extremely impatient of any restraint; but it is beyond question
that nothing was further from his thoughts than injustice to the Colonies. Far from hurrying the Stamp Act forward, he candidly told the
agents of the various provinces that he was not wedded to any particular form of tax, that he wanted no more than a contribution to the
defence of the empire, and that he would be quite willing to accept
any method of raising it that the Americans might prefer.

It is even said that he appealed to the Americans privately through
their friends in London, to bear their share of the burden and to save
him from resorting to legislation, but was met by a most uncompro-
mising refusal. (Speech of Lord Temple, *Parl. Hist.* xix.). Be that as it

may, in February 1765 he expressed to the agents his willingness to accept a voluntary contribution voted by the Colonial Assemblies, putting only the pertinent question whether the provinces were likely to agree on the proportion that should be paid by each. The agents were silent, for it was written in the history of the Colonies, beyond all denial, that it was hardly possible for any two of them, much less for thirteen, to agree on the simplest and least controversial of measures. The Stamp Act was accordingly introduced and passed almost without comment. It provided for the raising of £100,000 annually, or rather less than a shilling a head on the white population of the North American Colonies, with an express stipulation that every penny of it should be spent in America for defraying the cost of its defence.

Such a measure presents at first sight no visible appearance of oppression; but the year's warning before its final enactment had given time for the manufacture of an agitation, which the strict enforcement of the Acts of Trade made the Colonists only too ready to welcome. The profits of smuggling had been grievously curtailed; ships had been seized, condemned, and forfeited; and angry merchants were asking with indignant sarcasm whether, under the new regulations, there were any form of trade which was not reckoned smuggling.

The king's ships had been actively employed on the preventive service, and, once welcomed as symbols of British protection, had come to be loathed as engines of tyranny. Loud and bitter were the complaints of arbitrary and violent proceedings on the part of the king's officers, and of their ignorance of the law, which, in all probability, they knew inconveniently well. In all this there was nothing new, for every attempt from the very beginning to enforce the Acts of Trade had been met with the same outcry, and indeed with something more than outcry.

There were probably old men still living in Baltimore and in Boston, who could recall how a governor of Maryland had shot a revenue-officer dead with his own hand in cold blood, and how a governor of Massachusetts had brutally assaulted a captain of the Royal Navy, when the unfortunate officer was still disabled by a wound received in action against the French. The mob of Boston had long ago learned to meet any unpopular measure with lawless violence, and their congregational ministers to search the Scriptures for their encouragement. The trade of Boston was already on the wane, and the town was full of able and ambitious lawyers, panting for a wider sphere of activity and influence, who had carefully laid their train for a violent explosion at the favourable moment.

The Stamp Act set the match to this train; and the populace of Boston rose, wrecked the house of the Commissioner of Customs, attacked and rifled the Custom-house, sacked and burned that of the Chief Justice, who had dared to proclaim his resolution to uphold the law, and released some few of their number, who had been arrested, from the gaol. To stay the riot was impossible, for the only force at the disposal of the executive was the militia, and the whole of the militia were already employed as rioters. In New York also there were violence and intimidation; and though the rest of the Colonies expressed their feelings by legitimate resolution or remonstrance, there was everywhere a simultaneous manifestation of resentment.

The news of the tumult in Boston was received in England with profound dismay. The Colonies, hitherto submissive to the authority of the British Parliament, had rejected it with contumely, and that on so vital a matter as contribution to Imperial defence. To excuse the inconsistency of their long acquiescence in the Acts of Trade with their present attitude towards the Stamp Act, the opponents of that Act drew distinctions between external taxation for regulation of commerce and internal taxation for purposes of revenue.

This subtle definition was embraced to the end by Pitt, accepted for a time by Franklin, and maintained or controverted through a wilderness of pamphlets; but it was rejected from the first by Burke, and was soon discarded by the majority of sensible men as meaningless and futile. Nevertheless the Colonists carried their point. Grenville's Ministry had fallen in July 1765; and after vain endeavours to persuade Pitt to form a government, a weak administration had been brought together under Lord Rockingham. Pitt, in the Commons, warmly espoused the contention of the Colonies, pleading their cause with an intemperance of rhetoric which strengthened the hands of the agitators beyond all estimation, he said:

> I rejoice that America has resisted. Three millions of people so dead to all the feelings of liberty as voluntarily to submit to be slaves, would have been fit instruments to make slaves of the rest.

Wherein the Acts of Trade, to which the Americans had submitted for a century, and to which he himself was indissolubly wedded, were less enslaving than the Stamp Act, he did not pause to explain; but Pitt was guided by passion rather than reason. Had he used his vast influence towards a remodelling of the entire commercial code, to which course he was bound by the logic of such an utterance as that quoted above, he might have done much to heal the breach between the Mother Country and the Colonies. By acting as he did he contributed more than any man to the widening of it. However, the Stamp Act was repealed, and the wounded pride of England was salved by a Declaratory Act, whereby the authority of Parliament over the Colonies was upheld without any reservation whatever.

A little later Rockingham's Ministry, after useless efforts to secure the adhesion of Pitt, fell from power; and Pitt at last consented to place himself at the head of affairs, though at the same time greatly impairing his influence by accepting a peerage as Earl of Chatham. Always on his guard against the possibility of an attack by France and Spain, he attempted, as one of his first measures, to form an alliance of the Northern powers of Europe; but Frederick the Great, the most important power of all, refused to accede to it, and the negotiations ended in absolute failure.

Meanwhile the problem of Imperial defence still clamoured for solution, and Chatham had not the remotest idea how to deal with it. Convinced even to bigotry that the commercial prosperity of England depended on the Acts of Trade, he would gladly have seen things revert to their former condition of 1763. But this was now impossible; and, in view of the agitation begun by Otis against the Acts of Trade in 1761, and of the losses caused to the Colonies by the Indian insurrection, it would have been impossible, even if the Stamp Act had never been passed. The movement against the commercial code in America had never ceased. Otis quite logically said that if Parliament had a right to impose the Acts of Trade on the Colonies, it had an equal right to expect obedience to the Stamp Act; wherefore if the latter enactment were unconstitutional, so also were the others; and he boldly told the merchants of Boston that they were fools to submit to any Imperial restrictions on their trade whatever. (Governor Bernard to Secretary of State, 18th August 1766).

The situation was one of extreme difficulty, which was increased by the factious and intemperate language of the Opposition in Parliament, and above all by the resistance, violent beyond all proportion to the provocation, of the Colonists. To do nothing, which was the policy of Chatham and Burke, was no remedy. The Colonists had enjoyed Free Trade under the guise of smuggling for over a century, and had no intention of parting with it. Nothing less than entire recasting of the commercial code would have satisfied them; but there were only two wise, men—Burke and Governor Pownall—who would have welcomed such a reform, while Chatham would have raved against it with his dying breath.

Apart from this deadlock on the commercial question, there were troubles of another kind even more intimately connected with the question of Imperial defence. The Americans cherished all the prejudice of their race against a standing army; and it was made a principal grievance by the agitators that the money to be extorted from them by Act of the British Parliament was to be expended on the maintenance of a permanent force.

Such a force, they urged, could be needed only for the abridgment of their liberties; and therewith the story of Pontiac's invasion was conveniently forgotten, and a stream of trash about chains and slavery, hirelings of oppression, brutal instruments of tyranny, and so forth, flowed inexhaustibly from the tongues of orators and the pens of pamphleteers. Even before the Stamp Act there had been refusals to recognise the validity of the Mutiny Act in the Colonies, except in respect of such clauses as contained specific mention of British dominions beyond sea; and when the Act was amended to meet this difficulty, the Assembly of New York persistently evaded the whole of its provisions. Concurrently the practices of seducing soldiers from the service, of harbouring deserters, and of buying their arms and clothing, were unchecked by the American magistrates; while if an officer arrested a deserter, the man was claimed from him as an indentured servant, and he himself was prosecuted and fined.

★★★★★★

Even at a time of deadly peril both for America and England, when William III. with great difficulty sent a few hundred men to New York in response to the wailing of the Colonies, the first thing that the Colonists did was to seduce them to desertion, to gain the advantage of their labour. *Cal. S. P. Colonial.* New York, 1694.

★★★★★★

Officers were even prosecuted and imprisoned for occupying the quarters allotted to them; while magistrates made captious difficulties over granting sites for military storehouses, and were even suspected, in one case, of inciting a mob to destroy a storehouse and to pillage its contents. Georgia followed New York in raising persistent obstacles against the working of the Mutiny Act; and the obstruction rose to such a height that, in 1767, Parliament passed an Act prohibiting all legislation of any kind in the province of New York until provision should have been made for the king's troops. This sharp measure quickly brought the colony to reason; and it is noteworthy that on this occasion Chatham condemned New York's protest against the Mutiny Act as "improper, absurd, excessive in pretension and grossly fallacious in reasoning," uttering not a word about chains and slavery. (Gage to Halifax, 23rd January, 2 1st December 1765; 22nd February, 11th November, 23rd December 1766; 17th April 1767. *Chatham Correspondence*, iii.).

Notwithstanding the animosity displayed against the troops in America at this time, they were anything but idle; for the provincial governments were by no means too proud to utilise their services when it suited their purpose. In 1766, when the outcry against the Mutiny Act was at its loudest, there were riots at Albany and elsewhere in New York over a dispute as to the ownership of certain lands. The British troops were at once called out, and, having received the fire of the rioters, dispersed them with a single volley and drove them away in flight to the border of Massachusetts, where, amusingly enough, an armed force under a sheriff of that State was waiting to protect the rioters and to fight the British troops if they should cross the frontier. (Gage to Secretary of State, 26th August 1766).

The secret of this mysterious action lay of course in the passionate jealousy of rival provinces; and indeed in the heat of their wrangles over their boundaries, the Colonies took no account of the constitutional principle for which they professed such zeal in their controversy with England. Even in 1770, when that controversy had become inflamed to violent heat, the government at Philadelphia made no scruple of asking for British troops to secure some land that was in dispute between Pennsylvania and Connecticut; a request which was answered by the biting retort that when the courts of law had determined which party was in the right, then, but not till then, the general would, if invited by the civil power, send troops to enforce their decision. (*Ibid.* 24th April 1770).

Again, endless trouble was made by the back settlers of Virginia and Pennsylvania, who, despite the terrible warning written in the blood of hundreds during Pontiac's invasion, returned almost immediately to their evil practices of encroachment and outrage on Indian territory. The officer at Fort Ligonier was compelled to remove a number of these lawless ruffians from the Monongahela River lest they should provoke a fresh onslaught of Indians; but they only returned in larger numbers, the provincial governments being afraid to cope with them. Finally, when the Pennsylvanian government sent a commissioner to conciliate the Indians, the settlers threatened to shoot him, and the general was entreated to provide him with a military escort. (*Ibid.* 13th June, 10th October 1767; 21st January 1768).

In truth, so contemptibly weak and cowardly was the executive in all the provinces, that the people could do, and very often did, only what was right in their own eyes; and England was hated as the protectress of native races and as the upholder of law and order.

The most trying time of all for the unfortunate British soldier was now close at hand. Soon after taking office Chatham fell so ill of suppressed gout that he became unfit to transact any business whatever, and can hardly be said to have been of sound mind. Though he remained in name at the head of the government, the supreme direction of public affairs passed into the hands of the Chancellor of the Exchequer, Charles Townshend, a man of great cleverness, great eloquence, and no principles.

Townshend approached the American question exactly in the spirit that might have been expected from a spoiled darling of the House of Commons. Seizing hold of the American acknowledgment of England's right to impose external taxation, he levied duties on tea and on certain other articles which had hitherto been free, and assigned the proceeds of these new duties, estimated at £40,000 annually, not to the defence of the Colonies, but to the formation of a civil list for payment of the governor and of the judges in each province.

Thus the strong foundation of Imperial defence, on which England so far had based her claims, was abandoned; and everything was sacrificed for the passing gain of a petty controversial triumph. Townshend died a few months later, but, young though he was, he had already lived for a year too long. His foolish trifling with a great problem set all America seething once more; and since Massachusetts was rightly held to be the centre of discontent, General Gage was ordered, in June 1768, to send to Boston a force sufficient to assist magistrates and revenue-officers in enforcing the law generally, and in particular the Acts of Trade.

Accordingly, on the 30th of September, Colonel Dalrymple with the Fourteenth and Twenty-Ninth Foot and one company of Artillery with five guns arrived at Boston from Halifax. He was met by a prompt refusal of the local authorities to provide quarters, on the ground that there were barracks on an island in the harbour which must first be filled before quarters could be granted. The plea was strictly legal, and Gage, who was himself on the spot, bowed to the inevitable and quartered the men at the king's expense.

Such a beginning promised no easy duty to the troops in carrying out their instructions. Since the passing of the Stamp Act there had been practically no government in Boston but that of the populace. The machinery of municipal administration permitted the assembling of mobs under the name of town-meetings, whenever the agitators might require them; and by dint of wrecking houses, tarring and feathering unsympathetic persons, and the like methods, the revolutionists had intimidated the party of law and order into silence. Yet so admirably was the agitation conducted, so cunningly were its measures chosen to preserve apparent compliance with the letter of the law, and so skilfully were the manifestoes of its leaders drawn up to represent the revolutionists as injured innocents and the party of order as traitors in league with the oppressor, that even shrewd men, unacquainted with the methods of Boston, might well have been misled by them.

For there was, I repeat, nothing new in these methods; one and all of them had been in practice almost from the foundation of the city. The state-papers and remonstrances, many of them very ably drafted, with their pretence of humility and submission, their grave and ceremonious insolence, and their frequent shameless perversion of facts; the ready connivance of the magistrates with the violence of the rabble, and their equally ready abuse of legal forms for the perversion of justice and the persecution of persons obnoxious to them; the unblushing partiality of juries, and the inflammatory discourses of congregational ministers all these things by long tradition came quite naturally to the people of Boston. The student passing from the records, say, of 1683 or 1689 to those of 1775, might well think that he had turned the page, not of three-quarters of a century, but of a single week.

Nor is this matter for surprise, since the settlers of Massachusetts had left England originally as an irreconcilable faction, deeply imbued with the doctrines of republicanism and independence. They had enjoyed something hardly distinguishable from independence during the great Civil War; they had spared no effort of lying and subterfuge—the natural weapons of the weaker party—to retain it after the Restoration. They had made a bold stroke for it by force in 1689; and I have little doubt that, if Sir William Phips had succeeded in taking

Quebec, they would have dictated their own terms to King William. Now, with the French expelled from Canada, they had raised the old issue once more, and the British Government had resolved, as in 1684, to meet it by force.

Without entering into any discussion as to the right or expediency of resorting to coercion at Boston, it is certain that, if troops were to be employed at all, they should have been employed in sufficient strength and with sufficient powers. Two weak battalions, together barely numbering eight hundred men, were not an adequate force; and even though these were augmented in January 1769, by the arrival of the Sixty-Fourth and 1769. Sixty-Fifth, yet they still remained powerless to act until called in by the civil power. To invoke their aid was more than any magistrate's life was worth; yet the Government in England, though perfectly aware of the fact, gave no instructions to the general to proclaim martial law. The result was that the troops were laid absolutely at the mercy of the mob of Boston. In July the Sixty-Fourth and Sixty-Fifth were removed from the town, and Major-general Mackay wrote to Gage words of significant warning:

> Whatever troops are left in the town must be ruined in a year. They will be seduced to desert, or driven to desertion by the oppression of the magistrates. A soldier was lately confined to gaol for some petty theft, tried by the justices, condemned to pay damages to the amount of (I think) seventy pounds, and for not paying has been indented as a slave and sold for a term of years.—Enclosure in Gage to Secretary of State, 2nd July 1769.

The reader may be incredulous, but it is an incontrovertible fact that the practice of selling white men into servitude, though condemned by one of the earliest governors of Massachusetts more than a century before, was still in full usage in this land of liberty.

This was but one of many outrages against the troops. The soldiers were daily accosted by such endearing names as "lobster scoundrel," "red herring," and "bloody back," this last term alluding of course to the results, soon to be experienced by American soldiers under Washington, of a flogging at the halberts. The troops, having strict orders never to strike an inhabitant, whatever the provocation, endured these insults with a forbearance which speaks volumes for their discipline; but this did not save them from most violent and barbarous assaults.

Such was the brutality of the worst ruffians of Boston that they would attack a sick man when hardly able to hobble out of hospital;

and when reviling the soldiers they always encouraged each other by the words, which were unfortunately too true, "They dare not fire." Once at least the populace tried to break into the guard-room, attacked the relief on its way thither with sticks and stones, and only desisted, though then with precipitation, on the firing of a shot into the air. But the magistrates behaved even worse than the mob. On one occasion a constable came round to the barracks and arrested a soldier who was not named in his warrant; but when his officers appeared on his behalf in court, they were indicted for riot and rescue, and fined.

Officers and men were frequently arrested upon frivolous charges and required either to find heavy bail, which when produced was generally refused for no reason whatever, or to go to gaol; then, when the case came up for trial, the prosecution disappeared and the accused was instantly acquitted.

******

This again was an old and common trick in Boston. The most notable instance is that of Sir Edmund Andros, the governor, who was imprisoned by the revolutionists in 1689 and accused of a number of terrible crimes by the Revolutionary Government. A certain number of false affidavits were collected in support of them; but when the case came before the Privy Council, the accusers, of whom one was a minister of the Gospel, dared not sign the charges, whereupon the case, in the default of prosecutors, was dismissed.

******

In one such case the accuser offered a private two hundred dollars to bear false witness against his officer. Again, one justice openly threatened an officer from the bench with the vengeance of the populace, while another encouraged the rabble in court to hail an officer as a "bloody-back rascal." It was small wonder that under such oppression soldiers should have deserted, especially as the mob was always ready to rescue them if arrested; and it is significant that temptations of another kind were also made to seduce men from their colours, one of the garrison confessing that he had received an offer of fifty pounds a year to go into the country and teach the people their drill.

But violence and persecution were the usual measure meted out to the soldier; and matters reached at length such a pitch that, on the application of two privates to General Mackay for redress after a murderous assault upon them, the general was fain to give them half a guinea apiece, and advise them to abandon the prosecution of their assailants, since, however good their cause, there was no redress for soldiers in Boston.

★★★★★★

Gage to Secretary of State, 4th December 1769; 12th November 1770. I have been careful to give these details, since Mr. Fiske, generally an impartial writer, has written that "any manifestation of brute force in the course of a political dispute was exceedingly disgusting and shocking" to the Americans. *American Revolution*, i. .

★★★★★★

Such a state of things, notwithstanding the extraordinary patience of the troops, could not continue for ever. On the 4th of March 1770, there was an angry altercation between a few soldiers and some ropewalkers, the latter as usual giving the provocation; and on the following day there was a general rising against the troops, who were attacked in the streets with sticks and snowballs.

An officer passing by at once ordered the men back to barracks, and the mob then turned upon a sentry before the Custom House, raised a cry of "Kill him," and began to pelt him. Captain Preston hurried down with a sergeant and twelve men to rescue the sentry, and was at once attacked and pelted, the rabble pressing close to the party with ironical shouts of "Fire, fire!" while Preston in advance of his men entreated the assailants to go quietly home. At length one of the soldiers, receiving a violent blow on the arm, either voluntarily or involuntarily fired his musket, though with no effect; and the mob, thinking that the soldiers were loaded with powder only, grew bolder and more violent, till at last, either in desperation or in bewilderment at the eternal cry of "Fire!" all round them, seven of the men did fire without orders, killing four men outright and wounding seven more, two of them mortally. Thus at length the rabble of Boston received a lesson which it needed sorely.

The blame for the bloodshed rests wholly with the magistrates of Boston; and, considering the shameful treatment of the troops during eighteen long months, the populace escaped with very light punishment. Yet still, from sheer weakness of authority, the troops were kept under the heel of the mob. Preston and his party were at once committed to gaol; and Samuel Adams, the leading spirit of the revolutionary party, by threat of a general insurrection actually awed Lieutenant-Governor Hutchinson into withdrawing both battalions to the barracks at Castle William, on an island in the harbour. Had there

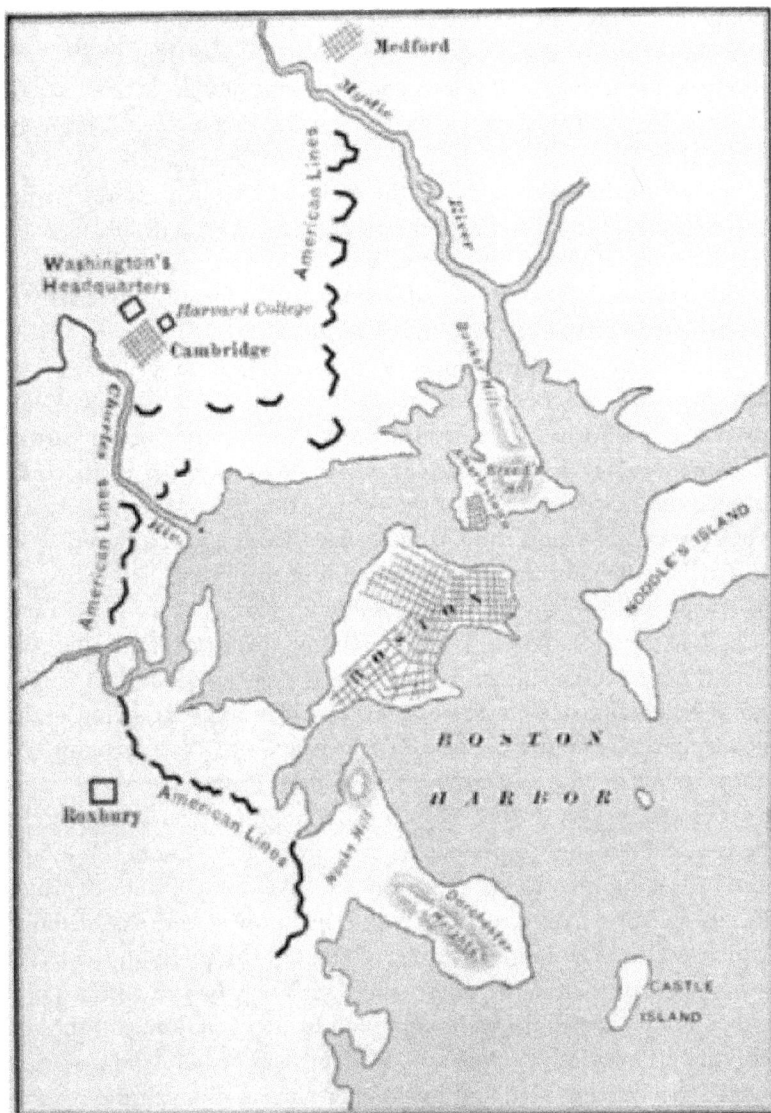

MAP OF THE SIEGE OF BOSTON, SHOWING THE IMPORTANCE OF BREED'S HILL,
DORCHESTER HEIGHTS, AND NOOK'S HILL

been, as there ought to have been, five thousand troops in Boston, Hutchinson could have defied Adams; and indeed the populace would never have dared to provoke them. Now, however, the mischief was done. The affray was at once dubbed the Boston Massacre, and sensational reports of it, full of falsehoods, were at once sent to England to regale the friends of the insurgents at home and the British public at large. (A good specimen is in the *London Evening Post*, 21st April 1770).

However, the magistrates and the mob were so plainly in the wrong that two of the revolutionary leaders came forward to defend Preston and his men, of whom all but two were acquitted, and those two but lightly punished. It should be added that thenceforward this trial was always paraded as a specimen of the impartiality of American justice.

Meanwhile, affairs in England were going from bad to worse. Chatham had resigned owing to ill-health in 1768, and the Duke of Grafton, who had been really premier during the greater part of Chatham's reign, resigned also in 1770. No power on earth could induce the hostile sections of the Whig party to work together; and Grafton was the third Prime Minister who had resigned in seven years. It may have been blameworthy, but it is not surprising that, with a set of drivers whose only care was to elbow each other from the box-seat, the king should have taken the reins of government into his own hands. Lord North succeeded Grafton as chief minister, and almost immediately initiated a new policy of conciliation by removing all the new American import-duties except that upon tea, and pledging the government to raise no further revenue from America.

The reservation of the duty on tea, though no grievance, was the height of folly, for, while gathering practically no money into the Treasury, it afforded to the revolutionary party a pretext for continuing its agitation. Moreover, the whole question of Imperial defence, which was the real point at issue, was still left studiously in the background. Nevertheless, the new policy was not wholly without good effect. For a short time there was a lull in the agitation; and the old commercial relations between the Mother Country and, the Colonies, which had been interrupted by voluntary associations of the Americans against the import of English goods, were in great measure resumed.

Throughout the years of which I have so far treated, the army had suffered little apparent change. Ligonier remained as commander-in-chief until 1767, though in 1763 he was shamefully ousted from

THE BOSTON MASSACRE.

the post of Master of the Ordnance for political ends, in order to make room for Lord Granby, who in due time succeeded him also as commander-in-chief. Mr. Welbore Ellis continued as Secretary of War until 1765, when he gave place to Lord Barrington, who had enjoyed long experience of the office. The numerical establishment remained practically unaltered on paper from the strength assigned to it in 1763; though in 1769 an important reform was effected by permanently raising the Irish Establishment from twelve thousand to rather over fifteen thousand men, which enabled regiments in Great Britain and in Ireland to be maintained at the same strength. Yet there were troubles and difficulties in the military administration which threatened to become serious. In the first place, there had been reversion to the evil system of employing military penalties to punish officers for political indiscipline.

Thus in 1764 Generals Conway and A'Court were deprived of their regiments and Colonel Barr of all his military appointments, because they voted against the Ministers on some matter concerning the arrest of the notorious John Wilkes. In the second place, recruits were so scarce that, although the king rightly judged the army to be of dangerous weakness and worked his hardest to keep it up at any rate to its attenuated establishment, it was found impossible to fill the ranks with effective men. So great was the cost of obtaining recruits, that officers were loath to part with old soldiers, however inefficient, so long as they could crawl. Strict orders were issued to remedy this evil, but with so little effect that two years later no fewer than eighty men were peremptorily discharged from a single weak battalion on the day after inspection, as unfit for further service. (General Harvey to Secretary at War, 8th December 1767, 19th April 1769).

The dearth of recruits was due not to any new distaste for the service, but to a raising of the general standard of comfort and luxury in all callings except that of the soldier. In a word, the pay of the private soldier was too small; but it was hopeless in the prevailing temper of the House of Commons to expect that it should be increased.

Several causes conspired to make the paucity of recruits of dangerous consequence. French officers had been at work in England all through 1767 and 1768, surveying the southern coast and taking note of the country and of the best military positions inland; and there were even traces of a joint design of France and Spain to surprise and burn the dockyards at Portsmouth and Plymouth. (Mahon, *History of England*, v.).

PAUL REVERE'S ENGRAVING OF THE BOSTON MASSACRE

Again, sickness made heavy drains upon the West Indian garrisons, while Pensacola, Mobile, and the posts on the Illinois promised to be as unhealthy as any West Indian island.

★★★★★★

The garrison of Pensacola within six weeks after landing had lost 3 officers, 95 men, and 45 women and children. At Fort Chartres but 19 men out of four companies were fit for duty. Gage to Secretary of State, 3rd February 1769.

★★★★★★

Finally, in 1770, a Spanish attack upon the British settlements in the Falkland Islands threatened to bring about immediate war. An augmentation of twelve thousand men was at once ordered for the army; but such was the difficulty of raising even a fraction of them, that, although it was undesirable to enlist Protestants in Ireland and illegal to enlist Papists, recruiting parties were sent into Leinster, Munster, and Connaught to gather in whatever material they might. (*Cal. H.O. Papers,* 11th January 1771).

The difference with Spain was composed without war; but already there was another cloud on the horizon. In the newly annexed Island of St.Vincent there was a fierce race of men known as the Black Caribs, bred of the Yellow Caribs, indigenous to the Archipelago, and of negro slaves who had escaped, or, as tradition goes, had been wrecked on the coast and had taken refuge in the forest. They were not numerous, little exceeding fifteen hundred souls in all; but they were by nature warlike and ferocious, and were secretly encouraged to insubordination by Jesuit missionaries and French agents. They claimed two-thirds of the best and richest land in the island—whether with or without justice I cannot pretend to decide—and were consequently a great obstacle to settlement.

After much restlessness they at last, in 1771, took advantage of the transfer of a part of the garrison to Dominica to capture a surveying party, together with its escort of forty men. Attempts were made to conciliate them, to which their only response was an appeal to the French in Martinique and St. Lucia for arms and ammunition, which were covertly though abundantly supplied. In view of the urgent representations of the governor, the Ministry decided in April 1772 that the Caribs must be suppressed by force of arms; and orders were sent to General Gage to detach two battalions from America to join those already in the West Indies and others to be embarked from England, for the service.

24

The operations were begun in October; but it would serve no purpose to trace the movements of several tiny columns through the forest of St. Vincent. Suffice it to say that the Caribs, using every artifice of savage warfare, made a brave and stubborn resistance; that the difficulties and suffering of the troops were very great and the impediments to the transport of supplies almost insuperable; but that on the 27th of February 1773 the Caribs were finally forced to submission. Two thousand five hundred men, including six whole battalions and parts of two more, (6th, 14th, 31st, 32nd, 50th, 68th, six companies of 2/60th, detachments of 70th), besides artillery and marines, were employed on this petty but troublesome expedition, at the close of which one hundred and fifty men had been killed and wounded, over one hundred more were dead of sickness, and close upon four hundred men lay in hospital, from which doubtless the majority were carried to their graves. (The documents treating of the expedition will be found in the Record Office. Board of Trade, Grenada, 1, 3, 5. America and West Indies, 8).

Throughout 1771 and the earlier months of 1772 the reports of the commander-in-chief in America were decidedly encouraging. The alarm of war with Spain seems to have revived the old feelings of loyalty. All the provincial Governors, even those of Rhode Island and Connecticut who were elected by the people, gave assurance of every possible help to the King's recruiting parties; while three regiments, which actually began to enrol recruits, met with such success that Gage felt no doubt of raising the whole of his battalions to their full strength, if occasion should require it. The disputes with the Assemblies of New York and New Jersey as to the quartering of troops also came to an end; and on the removal of a battalion from New Jersey in the ordinary routine of service, many of the people protested with unexpected warmth that their capital ought never to be left without a regiment in garrison. (Gage to Secretary of State, 2nd April, 6th November 1771; 2nd January, 5th February 1772).

In North Carolina, indeed, there was a rising of some bands of lawless settlers on the western border; but this being no more than a defiance of all constituted authority, such as is common among remote settlers in a new country, was of no Imperial significance, and the insurrection was crushed by the provincial militia in a fierce pitched battle, without the aid of Imperial troops. The whole situation was in fact improved; and it is, I think, probable that a great opportunity was lost, at the close of the dispute with Spain, for removing the tea-duty as a graceful concession to the loyal spirit shown in America, and inviting the colonial agents to a general conference on the subject of Imperial defence.

But in 1772 the old mischief sprang up afresh from the enforcement of the Acts of Trade, which, it cannot be too often repeated, were the true root of all the troubles in America. Rhode Island had long been notorious for smuggling, every man from the governor downwards having an interest in the traffic; and as far back as in 1763 one of the batteries had actually fired upon a king's ship which was in pursuit of a smuggling craft. (Admiral Montague to the Admiralty, 18th April 1772; Governor Bernard to Secretary of State, 14th December 1764).

The king's ship *Gaspee*, commanded by one Lieutenant Duddington, had been particularly active, and, according to American accounts, wantonly predatory in suppressing this illicit trade; and on one night in June she had the misfortune to run aground while in chase of an American ship. On the following night she was attacked by eight boats full of armed men, captured after a smart fight in which Duddington was severely wounded, and burned to the water's edge. All efforts to obtain redress were fruitless; the outrage remained unpunished; and yet another triumph was won by the party of violence.

A few months later the agitation in Massachusetts found fresh fuel in a Royal Order that the judges in the province should henceforward be paid by the Crown and should hold office during the Royal pleasure. This measure was doubtless due to the shameful denial of justice to the troops while quartered in Boston, and was designed to secure the legal rights of the loyal as well as of the disloyal in Massachusetts. Obviously, however, it lay open to a different interpretation, while from its purpose it could not but be obnoxious to the revolutionary party; and Samuel Adams was speedily at work. He now made a masterly addition to the existing machinery of rebellion by the institution of committees of correspondence, in order to guide not only every town within the province, but the whole of the provinces together, towards united action.

This was in fact the first step towards American Union; and it is a tribute to Adams's genius for organisation that these committees of correspondence soon found imitation in Europe. The efficiency of the arrangement was soon tested. Vast stores of tea belonging to the East India Company lay at this time unsold in its warehouses, and, since the Company was in extreme financial difficulty, it obtained permission to export this tea directly to the Colonies. As fate ordained it, Boston was the first port to be entered by the tea-ships.

A gang of forty or fifty men, disguised as Indians, under the immediate direction of Samuel Adams, boarded these ships on the 16th of December, and threw the whole of the tea overboard. The magistrates as usual took not the least notice, the troops remained unsummoned at Castle William, and the heroic action (Fiske i),—for such appears to be the American view of it—went forward without the slightest risk of interruption. The other Colonies quickly followed this example, and from Boston to Charleston the landing of the tea was prevented by force.

The news of this outbreak was received with not unnatural indignation in England. On the 7th of March 1774, a Royal Message brought the whole matter before Parliament, which proceeded in due course to pass a series of coercive measures directed against Massachusetts. By these the port of Boston was closed, until peace should be restored and the East India Company indemnified for the destruction of its property. Further, the government of the province was altered so as to confer much additional power on the Crown, though with abridgment of no privilege of the Lower House beyond that of electing the Council.

Lastly, power was given to the governor to transfer to England the trial of any magistrate, revenue-officer, or soldier indicted on a capital charge in Massachusetts, if in the interests of justice he should deem it necessary. Gage, who was in England on leave, was appointed governor of the province, and empowered by a new Act to quarter soldiers on the inhabitants.

It is noteworthy, as a sign of the intense irritation aroused in England by the violent behaviour of Boston, that the Act for closing the port was approved even by such warm partisans of America as General Conway and Colonel Barre. Burke, however, took a different line, reviewing the whole dispute in his celebrated speech on American taxation, a discourse full of profound wisdom in itself, but offering no suggestion except a return to the relations with the Colonies that existed in 1763. For all practical purposes he might as profitably have urged a return to the relations that existed at the time of the flood.

There was yet another Act of this session which, though eminently statesmanlike, provoked greater controversy than any of the preceding, namely, the Quebec Act for fixing the boundaries and regulating the government of Canada. The Ministry, looking to the religion, the traditions, the prejudices, and the expressed wishes of the majority of the Canadians, very wisely determined for the present to abstain from the introduction of representative institutions, trial by jury, or any popular system whatever. The Act also enlarged the boundaries of Canada so as to include outlying districts, not regularly settled, but inhabited chiefly by Frenchmen and controlled by the commanders of military posts; and finally, it to all intent established the Roman Catholic religion, which was that of more than ninety-nine in every hundred of the population.

This last provision woke all the bigotry dormant in the British character. Insular prejudice stood aghast at the thought of a people which could prefer to submit its causes to a skilled judge rather than to twelve unskilled men, who, as experience had repeatedly shown, were not always to be trusted for either honesty, integrity, or moral courage. Orators, pamphleteers, and scribblers raved with voice and pen against the measure, and no one raved more loudly and less intelligently than Chatham.

The Colonies, having early information of all that was going forward, made their own preparations accordingly. A circular was issued from Boston to the various provinces to concert united action; and at the suggestion of the revolutionary party at New York, a Congress, to which every colony except Georgia sent delegates, assembled at Philadelphia on the 5th of September 1774. It was a curious body, and, to judge by its first action, not a very straightforward one. After drawing up a declaration of rights, Congress issued addresses to the people of Great Britain, of the Colonies, and of Canada.

Of these the two first contained, among other matters, a violent attack on the Quebec Act as designed to overthrow the liberty of the Colonies by the pressure of a vast influx of Catholics; while the third artfully insinuated to the Canadians that this same Quebec Act was a danger and a snare to them, and that their only hope of salvation lay in joining with the English Colonies. These productions, though on the face of the matter not admirable even as specimens of lying, are remarkable as indications of the early hunger of the Americans after Canada.

In Massachusetts the coercive Acts proved a complete failure, from the absence of sufficient means to enforce them. The whole working of the new government was defeated by intimidation of every official appointed by the Crown, and by the setting up of a rival government, which was omnipotent everywhere except under the shadow of British bayonets. Gage found himself helpless, though he had four battalions in Boston, a force which might possibly have saved the situation in 1769, but was now far too small. The troops were encamped on a common just outside the town; and, since the revolutionists were busier than ever in the encouragement of desertion, Gage placed a guard on Boston Neck, the narrow isthmus which connects the town with the mainland. This innocent action was promptly magnified by the agitators into a design to reduce Boston by famine, and July went near to bring about a collision with the country-people.

Matters grew rapidly worse and worse. Relentless intimidation of the loyalists continued; the insurgents began to collect ammunition and military stores, and the young men to assemble to learn their drill; so that at the beginning of the autumn Gage judged it prudent to remove the contents of outlying magazines to Castle William, and to fortify Boston Neck. It was indeed high time, for a provincial congress of Massachusetts had already resolved to raise twelve thousand men, and to invite Connecticut, Rhode Island, and New Hampshire to increase that number to twenty thousand. Gage wrote on the 30th of October:

> If force is to be used at length, it must be a considerable one; for to begin with small numbers will only encourage resistance and not terrify.

A fortnight later he issued a proclamation warning the inhabitants against obedience to the revolutionary government; whereupon the populace in Rhode Island rose and seized forty cannon, which were mounted for the protection of Newport harbour. In New Hampshire likewise a small fort in Piscataqua harbour was taken and a large quantity of stores with it. Though no blood had yet been spilt, it was now plain that the quarrel could not be settled without war.

CHAPTER 2

The Fatal Hill

At the close of 1774 General Gage was in Boston with the people of Massachusetts drilling all round him, and with the news arrived from New Hampshire and Rhode Island that the king's fort and cannon had been seized by the populace. Meanwhile the British Parliament had met on the 29th of November, and, after passing certain additional coercive Acts, had voted to increase the troops in Boston to ten thousand men. Chatham, on the other side, brought forward the draft of a bill "for settling the troubles in America," which is remarkable only as evidence of his total misapprehension of the situation. Burke likewise moved resolutions in favour of conciliation, wise enough in themselves, but quite inadequate to meet the case.

Whatever the American party in England might think, the revolutionary leaders in Boston had long been working for independence, would be satisfied with nothing less, and were quite prepared to fight for it. At least one shrewd observer, the historian Robertson, had detected this from the first, while there was another very able writer, no very friendly critic of America, who advocated the concession of independence; but this was a length to which Burke could not go, while the bare thought of it would have made Chatham furious. The only alternative seemed to be force; but with the exception of a few who, like Lord Sandwich, talked with blind and insolent ignorance of the Americans yielding at the sound of the first cannon, there was not a man in England, least of all the king himself, who desired war. Faction was too busy, the memory of the last war too fresh, the debt bequeathed by it too grievous, the disturbance of trade already too distressing, the issue of a struggle with America too problematic, for any thinking man to desire to plunge lightly into such a conflict.

The British Government therefore tried hard to avert war by

blinking facts. Gage had written that a policy of coercion would mean the reconquest of New England and would require twenty thousand men. Lord Dartmouth wrote almost hysterically:

It is impossible without putting the army on a war-establishment; and I am unwilling to think that matters have come to such a pass yet.—Dartmouth to Gage, 27th January 1775.

No effort, therefore, was made to comply with the recommendation of the general on the spot; but a new measure of conciliation was passed, bringing back the dispute to its original issue by the promise to exempt from Imperial taxation any province which would of its own accord make a proper contribution to the common defence of the empire, and a fixed provision for the support of the civil government. This proceeding was of course violently denounced by the Whigs, though it was far more practical than anything that had been suggested by Burke or Chatham; but before the new proposal could reach the Colonies the first blood had already been shed.

In February the Provincial Congress, which had assumed the functions of government in Massachusetts, met in session at Cambridge, issued an inflammatory address exhorting the militia to perfect themselves in discipline, and passed resolutions for the collection and manufacture of arms. This example was presently followed all over the country. Seeing what he must expect, Gage on the 18th of April despatched the flank companies of his garrison to Concord, some twenty miles from Boston, to seize a quantity of military stores which had been amassed there by the agents of the Provincial Congress.

Boston being full of spies and the revolutionists' system of intelligence very perfect, all egress from the town was forbidden on that night, and the troops moved off with all possible silence and secrecy at ten o'clock. Rowing across the harbour to Charles River, they followed that stream upward for some distance, when they landed and pursued their march through the darkness. They had not proceeded many miles before the ringing of bells and firing of guns warned them that the alarm had been given. Colonel Smith, who was in command, at once pushed forward six companies under Major Pitcairne in order to secure the bridges on the other side of Concord; and this advanced detachment on arriving at Lexington at about five o'clock found a body of American militia drawn up for drill on the village green.

Pitcairne ordered them to disperse, whereupon they moved off; but, as they retired, several shots were fired from behind a wall and from adjacent houses, which wounded one man and struck Pitcairne's horse in two places. Some of the British Light Infantry answered by a volley, by which eighteen of the Americans were killed and wounded and the remainder effectually broken up.

★★★★★★

It is only fair to give the American version as stated by Mr. Fiske, namely, that Pitcairne, on the militia refusing to disperse, ordered his men to fire, and that his men declined to do so until he set the example by firing his pistol. Colonel Smith in his report says expressly that the British did not fire until fired upon, that Pitcairne's troops had not loaded until they found armed men formed to oppose them, and that his own detachment had not loaded at all. Whether this be true or not (and I see no reason for doubting its truth), the proved good discipline of the British makes it absolutely incredible that the soldiers should have refused to fire when ordered; so on this ground alone, if on no other, I must reject Mr. Fiske's story. Pitcairne's pistols are shown in the town library of Lexington as having fired the first shot of the war, which sufficiently accounts for the rise of this legend. The matter is really of trifling importance.

★★★★★★

Pitcairne's detachment was, however, detained by this incident sufficiently long for Smith's party to join it, when the whole body moved on together to Concord. As they approached it they found another body of militia drawn up in their front, which, however, retired across a river on the further side of the town without resistance. The bridges over this river were then occupied by the Light Infantry, while the grenadiers destroyed such of the stores as had not been concealed or carried off. While they were thus employed, the American militia, reinforced to a strength of some four hundred men, attacked the Light Infantry at one of the bridges, and after a sharp exchange of fire carried the passage by sheer weight of numbers, driving the British back upon Concord. Though for the present they refrained from pressing their advantage further, Smith speedily realised that it was high time for him to retreat.

Then the day's work began in good earnest. The entire population had turned out in arms, and along the whole line of march a continual fire of musketry rained on the British troops from an invisible enemy concealed in houses or behind walls and trees. Not Braddock's column itself was in a more desperate situation. It was useless to attempt a counter-attack; and the men were weary after fourteen hours afoot and a march of twenty miles without food. As far as Lexington Smith's soldiers were driven along like a flock of sheep, and, but for the fact that a few of the dead and wounded had been scalped by some rough Americans at the bridge, it is probable that they would not have struggled even as far as Lexington. There, however, a party of about fourteen hundred men, (eight companies each of the 4th, 23rd, 47th, and Marines), with two guns, which had been despatched under command of Lord Percy to their support, was awaiting them; and Percy forming a hollow square received the survivors of the detachment, who threw themselves down on the ground in utter exhaustion.

Having refreshed them, Percy resumed the retreat, harassed for fifteen miles by the same incessant, irregular fire from front, flanks, and rear. The numbers of the enemy increased at every point on the road, and it was only by great energy, considerable skill, and some good fortune that Percy saved his force from annihilation, and at sunset brought it, quite worn out with fatigue, into Boston.

The casualties of the eighteen hundred men who took part in this disastrous expedition amounted to nineteen officers and two hundred and fifty men killed and wounded.(Flank-companies of the 5th, 10th, 18th, 23rd, 38th, 43rd, 52nd, and 59th. The whole of the 4th, 23rd, 47th, and ten companies of Marines). The loss of the Americans, who for the most part were in the happy position of giving without receiving fire, did not exceed ninety; and all that can be said of the affair is that, bad though it was, it might easily have been far worse.

To blame Gage for attempting the enterprise and Smith for not abandoning it when he found that the alarm was given, is mere wisdom after the event. The whole incident was a revelation to the British, and a sufficiently unpleasant one, since it showed the nature of the warfare that was to be expected, and the efficiency, for short and sudden effort, of the levies of the New England townships. The Americans were naturally much elated by their success; and within a very few days from sixteen to twenty thousand men from the several provinces of New England were drawn round Boston from north to south, holding Gage and his eleven weak battalions in strict blockade. There was nothing further for him to do but to await reinforcements from England.

The effect of the skirmish at Lexington made itself felt far beyond New England. In New York, where there had been symptoms of a return to loyalty, the populace seized the magazines and two provision-

RETREAT OF THE BRITISH FROM CONCORD

ships, erected a Provincial Congress, and began to arm and organise a military force. In Philadelphia and New Jersey the same spirit was at work, and the conciliatory proposals of Lord Dartmouth were everywhere rejected. And meanwhile New England, not content with defensive measures, resolved with great promptness, while the British were still weak, to make a sudden attack upon the British posts on the Lakes.

Benedict Arnold, a man of inborn genius for war who had lately joined the American Army before Boston, was the person who suggested this stroke and received a commission to deliver it; but the same idea had occurred also to the Government of Connecticut, which, after carefully proposing to Gage a cessation of hostilities, had already sent Ethan Allen of Vermont to surprise Ticonderoga.

Allen characteristically refused to serve under Arnold; and since few of Arnold's men had yet joined him, Arnold accompanied Allen's force as a volunteer. Early in May the little party, numbering but eighty-three men in all, arrived before Ticonderoga. The garrison counted but forty-eight men; and Allen had observed that its commander was incompetent, its discipline relaxed, and the most ordinary precautions unobserved. With great cunning he paid an innocent visit to the officer in command, borrowed twenty men of him for certain heavy work on the lake, made every man of them drunk, and on the same night captured the post without firing a shot. Over one hundred and twenty cannon, besides large stores of ammunition, which were sorely needed by the Americans, thus fell into their hands. Crown Point having neither guard nor soldiers, was of course taken without trouble; and Arnold, seizing the one British vessel on Lake Champlain, sailed at once to St. John's, where he quickly overpowered the garrison.

General Carleton, who was in command at Montreal, presently sent a force to recover it, but Arnold, ascertaining that the entire British force for the defence of Canada consisted only of the Seventh and Twenty-Sixth Foot, both of them weak battalions, speedily conceived a scheme for the reduction of the whole province. Meanwhile the preparations in England had gone forward very slowly, chiefly owing to the extreme difficulty of obtaining recruits. The Highlands of Scotland had hitherto been a recruiting-ground that had never failed; but in recent years the Americans had offered such inducements to emigrants as had tempted large numbers to the New World, and not all the measures of the British Government could keep emigrant ships from entering every creek on the western coast and carrying off whole families. (*H. O. S. P. Scotland*, 47. Lord Justice Clerk to Secretary of State, 14th August 1775. Nearly four thousand emigrants had sailed since the beginning of 1774).

Seven battalions of infantry and one regiment of light dragoons were ordered to embark from Ireland and England during January and February, but all were so weak that they could only be raised to passable strength by heavy drafts from other corps. The Seventeenth Light Dragoons, even after receiving one hundred drafts, embarked less than three hundred strong. From this and from other causes the embarkation was long delayed; and Captain Delancy, who had been sent forward to New York to buy horses for the dragoons, found the city in the hands of the revolutionary party and was compelled to abandon his mission.

Thus it came about that the reinforcements did not arrive at Boston until late in May. With them came three officers in particular, of whom we shall see much. General William Howe, younger brother of Lord Howe, was the senior of them, being the same man who, as Colonel Howe, had led the forlorn hope up the cliffs to the Plains of Abraham. General John Burgoyne also we have seen before in Portugal with the Sixteenth Light Dragoons, since which time he had made himself conspicuous chiefly by ornate speeches in the House of Commons and by violent attacks on Lord Clive. General Henry Clinton had served with distinction in the Seven Years' War, and had been *aide-de-camp* to the Hereditary Prince of Brunswick. The subsequent narrative will show the quality of their military talent.

During this interval the American Continental Congress had met and had adopted the troops before Boston as a Continental Army. It was rather a remarkable force. A great number of the men had seen service against the French, and the majority were, through the nature of their life, good marksmen trained in the excellent school of sport. Their equipment, however, was deficient, and their discipline very faulty indeed. Several companies, owing to a quarrel with their commissaries, had threatened to march home even while the British transports were entering Boston harbour, and had only with difficulty been kept to their duty. (Johnson, *Life of Greene*, i.).

Their officers were of varying merit; but in command of the Rhode Island contingent there was one who, though untrained except by books and by constant study of the British regiments in Boston, was brave, far-seeing, single-minded, and skilful, by name Nathaniel

Greene. The object of the Americans was to drive the British from Boston; but, though they had already given Gage much trouble to collect supplies, they could only dispossess him by seizing some of the hills which commanded the town.

The situation of the two armies, dictated of course by the configuration of the ground, was somewhat peculiar. The Americans occupied a line of heights in a semicircle from north to south, with the curve to westward, around the inner harbour; while the British held the peninsula of Boston, which forms, roughly speaking, the southern half of the base of that semicircle. There were two eminences from which Boston could be commanded by artillery: one called Dorchester Heights to the south-eastward, the other in the peninsula of Charleston, which forms the northern half of the base of the semicircle, called Bunker's Hill. The latter, being the nearer, was the more important of the two; and Gage, soon after the arrival of the reinforcements, resolved to occupy it.

So perfect was the American system of intelligence that every design of the British was known at once at their headquarters; and thus it came about that on the evening of the 16th of June a strong party of Americans stole out with entrenching tools, not to Bunker's Hill but to Breed's Hill, a height on the same range still nearer to Boston, where with great industry they threw up a strong redoubt on the summit of the hill, and a line of trenches reaching for a hundred yards from this redoubt to the water on the northern side. So silently was the work done that no sound of it was heard in the transports and men-of-war that surrounded the peninsula; and when the day broke Gage found that he had been forestalled, and that the entrenchment was well-nigh completed.

He was in luck if ever a general was—only less lucky than Abercromby when Montcalm resolved to stand his ground at Ticonderoga. The water all round the peninsula was navigable for vessels of light draught, and the command of that water lay with him, so that he could land troops wherever he would in the flanks or rear of the entrenchment, or, simpler still, he could either occupy the neck of Charleston peninsula, which was not two hundred yards wide, or station a gunboat on each side to rake it with cannon. In a word, the American detachment on Breed's Hill lay practically at his mercy.

The vessels of war in the harbour soon opened a lively fire on the entrenchment, but with little effect owing to the extreme elevation; and as the Americans still stuck with creditable pertinacity to their work with the spade, Gage after much discussion decided, with a contempt which was quite unwarranted by previous exploits of the Americans, to make a frontal attack. Accordingly, twenty companies of the Grenadiers and Light Infantry of the army under General Howe, together with two battalions under General Pigot, were landed at the extreme east of the Charleston peninsula and to the north of Charleston.

These officers reconnoitred the position and decided, before attacking, to ask for a reinforcement of two battalions more. The whole detachment was drawn up in three lines; the Grenadiers, Fifth, and Fifty-Second in column of battalions forming the left wing under Howe, and the Light Infantry, Thirty-Eighth, and Forty-Third the right wing under Pigot.

The action then opened with a sharp cannonade from eight British field-pieces and howitzers, directed chiefly but ineffectually against the redoubt, under cover of which fire the infantry slowly advanced. The day was intensely hot, the grass rose up to the men's knees, the ground was broken by a succession of fences; and yet the men were burdened by their heavy packs and by three days' provisions, which, supposing that they were needed at all, had much better have been conveyed by water. During the advance of about six hundred yards the regiments deployed, and the plan of attack developed itself; the Light Infantry being directed against the extreme left of the Americans, while the Grenadiers, Fifty-Second, and Fifth, with the Thirty-Eighth and Forty-Third in support, were turned against the entrenchment and redoubt, to the left of the Light Infantry.

It should seem, indeed, that the advance against the redoubt was designed to be more or less of a demonstration, the British commanders really counting for success on the turning of the enemy's left. In this case a vessel of light draught might have raked the American left from end to end without need to employ any infantry whatever.

Be that as it may, the attack was delivered with equal strength or weakness against the entire American front; and the fire of the British—a very rare fault with them was opened at too great a range. The Americans, with the good judgment of old soldiers, as indeed many of them were, held their fire until the British were within fifty yards, and then poured it into the scarlet ranks with the greatest effect. Groups of riflemen had been specially detailed to pick off the officers, whose glittering gorgets made an excellent target; and the best of the American marksmen were supplied with a succession of loaded weapons, so that they should do the greatest possible execution.

Siege of Charleston

The fire was so terrible that the British, after a gallant attempt to reload and return it, gave way, broken to pieces by their losses, and fell back out of range, when they quickly rallied and reformed for a second attack.

The left wing having been galled during its advance by a flanking discharge of musketry from the houses of Charleston, a heavy fire had been poured into the town from a battery on the outskirts of Boston; and the houses being thus kindled burned fiercely, sending up columns of smoke, which were borne by the wind straight into the eyes of the British. But on the field the British guns were silent, because, through mere carelessness, shot of the wrong calibre had been sent from Boston, while the officers declared it impossible to advance their pieces within range of grapeshot owing to a patch of swampy ground. None the less Howe led a second attack, exactly similar to the first, though it seems that the battalions were now extended from end to end of the American line, the Light Infantry as before holding their place on the extreme right of the British, with the Grenadiers, Fifty-Second, Forty-Third, Thirty-Eighth, and Fifth aligned with them in order as named.

Once again the same scene was repeated. The British advanced with all possible gallantry over the bodies of their fallen comrades, only to be swept down by the same rain of bullets. A brick-kiln, with some other obstacles within a hundred yards of the redoubt, kept the Fifty-Second in particular exposed to the worst of the fire; and the second attack, like the first, was driven back with very heavy loss.

But neither Howe nor his troops were yet beaten. The general was still untouched, though every officer of his staff had been shot down; and he now ordered the men to throw off their packs and to trust for the next assault to their bayonets only. Clinton observing two battalions on the beach in great disorder, doubtless from loss of officers, hurried across the water from Boston to rally them, while a reinforcement of the Forty-Seventh and Marines had already arrived in the course of the engagement. Howe now abandoned the attack on the American left, converting it into a mere feint, and turned all his strength upon the breastwork and redoubt.

The British advanced without firing a shot, and the Americans as before let them come close before they drew trigger, but having exhausted their ammunition they shrank from before the British bayonets. Not a few of them stood bravely to the end, but the mass gave way, and, coming under the fire of the British warships in their retreat

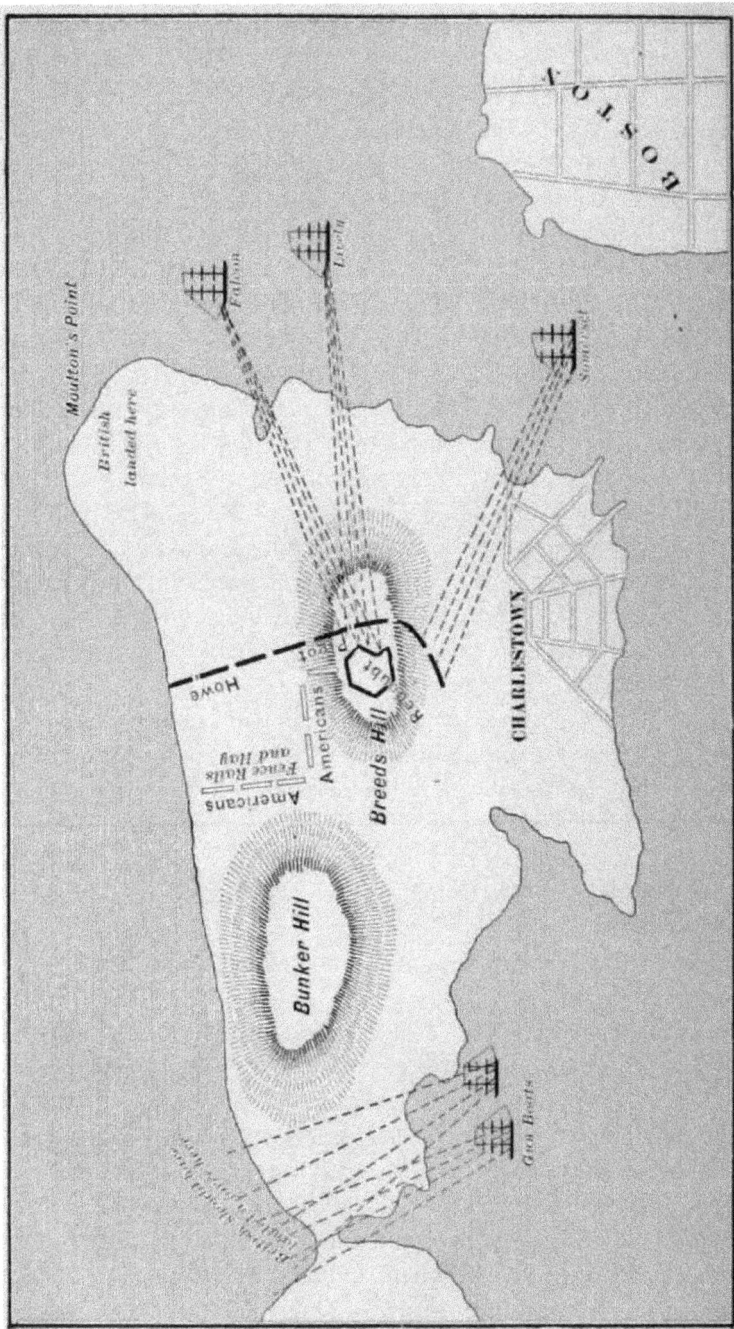

MAP OF THE BATTLE OF BUNKER HILL.

Bobbs & Co., N.Y.

across the Isthmus, suffered very heavily. Thus the redoubt and entrenchments were gained, but beyond this the British advantage was not pressed; and the day closed leaving the redcoats in possession of the fatal hill.

The losses of the British were terribly severe. Of about twenty-five hundred troops nineteen officers and two hundred and seven men were killed, and seventy officers and seven hundred and fifty-eight men wounded, making a total of one thousand and fifty-four casualties in all, or over two-fifths of the force engaged. (This does not include the wounded of the 38th, which were accidentally omitted from the official list. These probably numbered at least 100, as this regiment lost a greater number killed—25—than any other. This would raise the total casualties to 1150).

Indeed, the regiments that took part in all three of the attacks lost little if any less than half of their numbers, and it is pitiful to read of the havoc wrought among the several battalions, not one of which had brought more than four hundred men into the field. The Fifth lost one hundred and fifty-eight killed and wounded; and it is noteworthy that the grenadier-company of this regiment was led first by Captain Harris, and after his fall by Lord Rawdon, both of whom we shall know better in later days, the one as Lord Harris of Seringapatam, the other as Marquess of Hastings.

The Thirty-Eighth can have lost little fewer men than the Fifth; the Forty-Third lost one hundred and eight, the Fifty-Second one hundred and eleven. The grenadier-company of the Twenty-Third went into action with forty-nine of all ranks and returned with five; and the flank-companies of the Thirty-Fifth alone lost five officers and sixty-four men. (The troops engaged were the flank-companies only of the 4th, 10th, 18th, 22nd, 23rd, 35th, 59th, 63rd, 65th; the entire strength of the 5th, 38th, 42nd, 47th, 52nd, and two weak battalions of Marines).

In truth, the return of the British infantry to the third attack after two such bloody repulses is one of the very greatest feats ever recorded of them, and points to fine quality among the men, grand pride in their regiments, and supreme excellence of discipline. Equally does the coolness and steadfastness of the Americans, thanks to the example of a few brave and experienced officers, call for our warm admiration; though of course it is fallacious to look upon them simply as raw peasants, for a large proportion of them had been in action before. British writers for the most part estimate the American numbers as superior

BATTLE OF BUNKER HILL.

to our own, but it seems probable that not more than seventeen hundred of them were engaged at Bunker's Hill at any one time, though there may have been more on the peninsula.

Their acknowledged loss was four hundred and fifty killed and wounded, and there seems to be no reason to doubt that this figure is substantially correct. Of the action of the general officers on both sides, the less said the better. There is no need to expatiate on the folly of Gage; and it must be confessed that the apathy or indiscipline which denied reinforcements to the American detachments on the peninsula was anything but creditable to the American commanders. For the rest, the combat produced a remarkable effect on the future operations of the war. It shook the nerve of Howe, and showed the British that the subjugation of the Colonies would be no child's-play. On the other hand, it not only elated the Americans, as was but natural and just, but encouraged them to a blind and fatal confidence in undisciplined troops, which went near to bring ruin to their cause. Notwithstanding the mistakes of generals and the deplorable waste of excellent troops, Bunker's Hill was probably a greater misfortune, taken altogether, to the Americans than to the British.

The captured position on the hill was entrenched and occupied by Gage, after which there remained nothing for him but to sit still and await what might come. Meanwhile great events had been going forward in Congress. Just two days before the action, George Washington had been chosen unanimously to be Commander-in-Chief of the Continental Army—the only man, as events were to prove, who could possibly have carried the war to a successful issue. On the 2nd of July he arrived in the camp before Boston to take command; and shortly after him came a contingent of three thousand men from Pennsylvania, Maryland, and Virginia, to swell the ranks and give better justification for the title of Continental Army.

Other officers in that camp who now claim our attention were Major-General Horatio Gates, who had long held a commission in one of the king's independent companies at New York, and had recently retired on half-pay as major in the Sixtieth; and Major-General Charles Lee, who had served in the war against the French, had risen to the rank of Lieutenant-Colonel in the king's service, and was still on half-pay. Both, though English by birth, owned property in America, and both were a discredit to the country alike of their birth and of their adoption. Two more remarkable officers, Brigadier Richard Montgomery, who had also held the king's commission in the regular army, and Benedict Arnold, were absent on an expedition to which we must follow them.

The attack on Ticonderoga by Ethan Allen is said to have been viewed at first with mixed feelings by Congress, as at variance with its professions of acting solely on the defensive, (Fiske, i.). Why the members should have felt these scruples, if indeed they did feel them, is not very clear, since American emissaries had already been despatched to Bermuda and to the Bahamas to stir up sedition; which step was now followed in Bermuda by a raid of American sloops upon the forts, (August 14th), and by the abstraction of all the powder in the magazines. It may easily be guessed, therefore, that means were found to quiet uneasy consciences, as well as pretexts to justify an attempt at the conquest of Canada.

The enterprise was accordingly approved, and entrusted to Montgomery and Benedict Arnold. The former, a very capable officer, therefore started at the end of August from Ticonderoga with two thousand men for an attack on Montreal; while Arnold set out a week or two later with fifteen hundred men to advance up the Rivers Kennebec and Chaudière and through the forests of Maine upon Quebec.

On the 12th of September Montgomery laid siege to St. John's, which, however, held out stoutly, for Carleton had thrown five hundred out of his eight hundred regular troops into the fort, together with one hundred Canadian volunteers. Finding that he could make little impression and that his ammunition was running short, Montgomery detached three hundred men with two guns five miles down the river to Chambly, which post, though held by one hundred and fifty men, made a most discreditable surrender.

This was the saving of Montgomery's campaign. The fall of Chambly gave him stores sufficient to renew the siege of St. John's, which after a very gallant defence of fifty days was forced on the 3rd of November to capitulate. Carleton, who had been repulsed in an attempt to march with a handful of troops to its relief, now evacuated Montreal; and on the 12th of November Montgomery entered that town in triumph.

Just a week earlier Arnold's force had appeared before Quebec. His troops had suffered much from a terrible march of thirty-three days through a wilderness of forest. They had endured indescribable toil and hardship through lack of supplies, and had been forced to devour even their dogs. Two hundred men had died of starvation and hard work, as many more had been sent back sick, and quite three hundred more had deserted with a colonel at their head; but still Arnold with magnificent tenacity pushed on to the St. Lawrence, and encamped his exhausted force at Point Lévis.

The alarm at his coming was intense, for the fortifications of Quebec were weak and the garrison trifling. The Canadians, in whom Carleton had reposed such confidence that he had sent nearly all of his regular battalions to Boston, remained loyal indeed to the king, but would not serve him in the militia. Fortunately there was stationed at Sorel a very capable officer, Colonel Allan Maclean, with nearly four hundred recruits for a regiment which he was then raising, who no sooner heard of Arnold's arrival at Point Lévis than he made a forced march on Quebec, reaching it safely on the 13th of November.

On that same day Arnold had climbed the Heights of Abraham and challenged the garrison to come out and fight, or surrender. Since the garrison declined to oblige him, he made an attack on the same night, but was beaten off with loss. He then resigned himself to await Montgomery's arrival; but there was no sign of his coming for a full fortnight, in the course of which Carleton slipped down the river in disguise, and began vigorous preparations for the defence of Quebec.

At last, on the 3rd of December, Montgomery appeared with a small body of troops, which, joined to Arnold's, raised the American force to twelve hundred men. Carleton had about as many of one kind and another, but sixty only were British regular troops, and a large proportion of the rest were anything but trustworthy. After a feeble bombardment of field-guns which produced no effect, Montgomery came to the daring resolution to attempt a storm.

The time chosen was two o'clock on the morning of the 31st of December, when by signal of rocket four simultaneous attacks were to be delivered, two of them false, and two of them, led by Arnold and himself at opposite ends of the town, real and earnest. A blinding snowstorm favoured the adventure, but the false attacks were begun prematurely, and, their actual character being thus revealed, the garrison was concentrated to meet the real danger. Montgomery's column was met at fifty yards' range by a withering blast of grape which laid him dead among the first; and his followers, though they did not at once retreat, after half an hour abandoned the assault.

Arnold, being opposed at first only by Canadian volunteers, forced his way into the fortress, and, when he was himself wounded, found a brave successor in General Morgan to lead his men on. But the arrival of Maclean quickly turned the tide; the foremost of the Americans were surrounded and taken, and the rest easily driven back. The casualties on the British side did not exceed twenty in all, while those of the Americans were far heavier. (Carleton gives them as 750 killed, wounded, and prisoners; but this must be an exaggerated estimate). Thus Quebec was saved, and with Quebec the whole of Canada.

So ended the boldest attempt made by the Colonies to add to their territory during the war. It was a daring enterprise, conducted with remarkable ability both by Montgomery and by Arnold; yet it was a foolish one, for even if the Americans had taken Quebec they could not have held it without an adequate naval force. Nor is there the least ground for supposing that the Canadians, cold though they were in the cause of Britain, would have warmed towards the Americans. By promises and proclamations the invaders succeeded indeed in instilling a spirit of lawlessness and insubordination into the Canadian peasants; but such a spirit is as unfavourable to usurped as to displaced authority; and the priests and upper classes remained on the side of the British.

The Americans actually attempted to raise two regiments in Canada; but, in the words of an American historian, the Canadians proved themselves nowise inclined to be conquered into liberty. Montgomery had taken great pains to avoid offence to the religious scruples of the Canadians, and Washington had issued special orders with the same object; but orders are one thing and obedience is another. It would be unjust to hold the American officers responsible for the fact, but a fact on their own showing it is, that Montgomery's men were a gang of undisciplined ruffians. They would fight boldly under shelter, but they would not stand in the open ground.

They broke almost into open mutiny because they were forbidden, according to the terms of the capitulation, to strip the clothes off their prisoners at Montreal and take them for themselves; while by fraud and by robbery they did more to strengthen Canadian loyalty to England than did all the blandishments of Carleton. (Washington's *Works*, iii.). The invasion of Canada ought therefore to have been pure loss to the Americans; and so it might have been had the British Ministry taken the advice of Sir William Howe, the commander-in-chief of its own choice. Indirectly, however, as shall be seen, it lured the British Government into a false plan of operations, and to a disaster which, less for its strategic consequences than from its moral effect in Europe, virtually decided the issue of the war.

CHAPTER 3

Brooklyn and After

In the course of the summer the British Government gradually opened its eyes to the fact that a war, and a serious war, was actually staring it in the face. On the 12th of June, five days before Bunker's Hill, Gage had written that fighting was inevitable, adding that fifteen thousand men would be required on the side of Boston, ten thousand at New York, and seven thousand on the side of Canada. The statement reveals the plan which was in the mind of Gage, and indeed of many officers. Though there was not a province in which the king's authority had not been overthrown by the end of 1775, yet the heart of the rebellion lay in the New England Colonies, situated between the Hudson River and the sea.

By occupying the line of the Hudson these Colonies could be practically isolated and reduced; and this operation, if conducted by simultaneous advance of three corps from Boston, Lake Champlain, and New York, could hardly be prevented by the enemy. (Lloyd's *War in Germany*, i.). This scheme of isolation was likely to be the more effective since the New England provinces drew most of their supplies from the more fertile provinces of the south. On the other hand, it would require from thirty thousand to fifty thousand men, almost all of whom must be transported from the British Isles over three thousand miles of ocean, a distance which made America in those days practically more remote than the Antipodes at the present time.

Thus, when critically examined, the task of subduing the whole of the American Colonies by force appeared to military men an impossibility. It was reckoned that the population of the thirteen provinces numbered from two to three millions, scattered over a vast extent of territory. The principal towns were of course on the coast; but, even if one of these were captured as the base for the British, there was no stronghold inland which could command any great tract of country, and therefore no certain line of operations. The enemy had but to retire inland, if pressed, and the invader could not safely follow them, from the impossibility of maintaining his line of communications.

The one exception to the rule was the line of the Hudson above mentioned; but even there the American force that could be brought forward against the British was an extremely uncertain quantity. General Conway reckoned that the American Colonies could raise an army of one hundred and fifty thousand men; and this number, viewed merely in its proportion to the total population, was no extravagant estimate. Moreover, the reduction of New England might not necessarily mean the conquest of America. General Harvey, who as Adjutant-general was, in the absence of a commander-in-chief, the highest military official in the kingdom, wrote:

> Taking America as it at present stands, it is impossible to conquer it with our British Army. . . . To attempt to conquer it internally by our land force is as wild an idea as ever controverted common sense.—*Commander-in-Chief's Letter Books*. Harvey to General Irwin, 30th June 1775.

It was therefore the opinion of many, and among others of the Secretary at War, that the operations should be entirely naval, that the principal ports of America should be occupied as naval bases, that the external and coasting trade of the Colonies should be cut off, and that occasional predatory expeditions should be made upon the enemy's stores and depots of merchandise. This, it was thought (and probably with sound judgment), would bring the revolted Colonies speedily to reason and induce them to listen to proposals for conciliation. On the other hand, the governors of various provinces reported, not without good reason, that the loyalists were in such a majority as to be able with very little help to overcome the disloyal. Governor Martin wrote very strongly in this sense as to North Carolina, and Governor Lord Dunmore, though driven from Virginia, pledged himself to recover the province with three hundred men. (Secretary of State to Howe, 22nd October 1775).

Such a pledge was of course ridiculous, but it was not considered to be so at the time. It was therefore concluded that the mere presence of British troops in certain quarters would be sufficient to rally the entire population to the royal standard; and it was resolved in effect to base the military operations on the presumed support of a section of the inhabitants. Of all foundations whereon to build the conduct of a

49

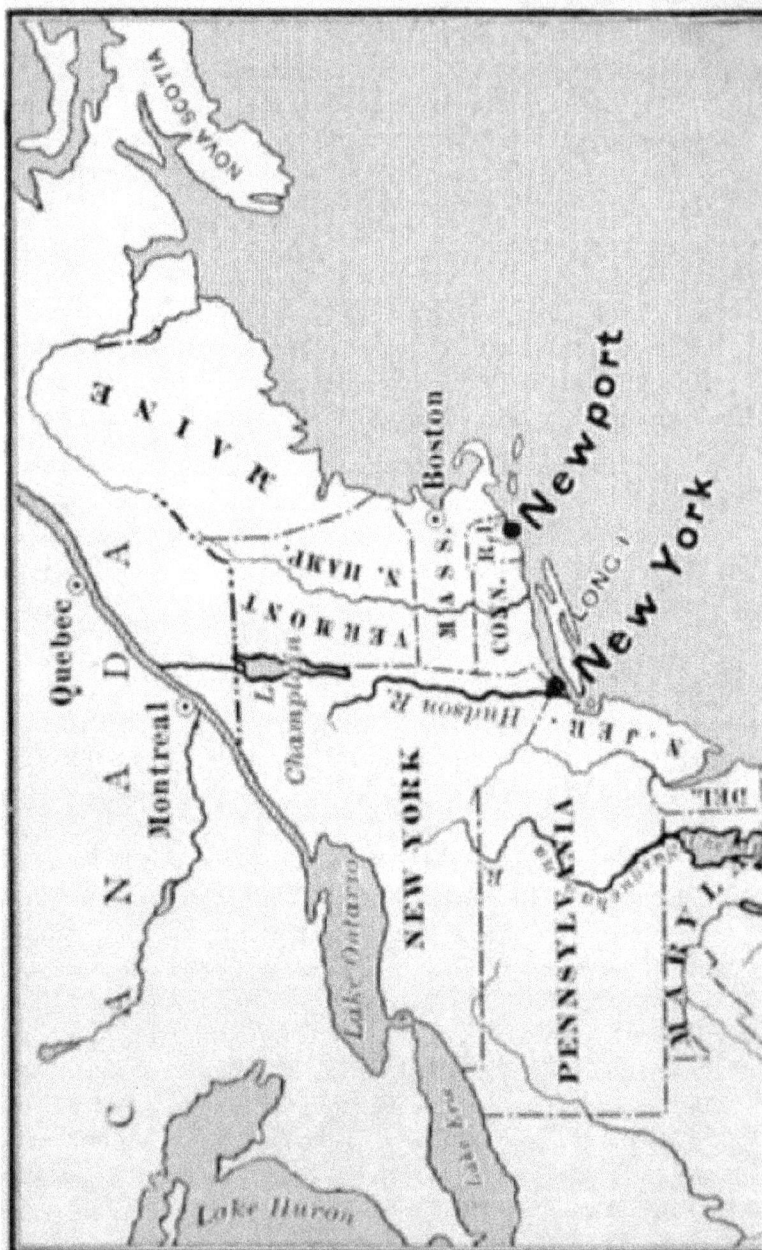

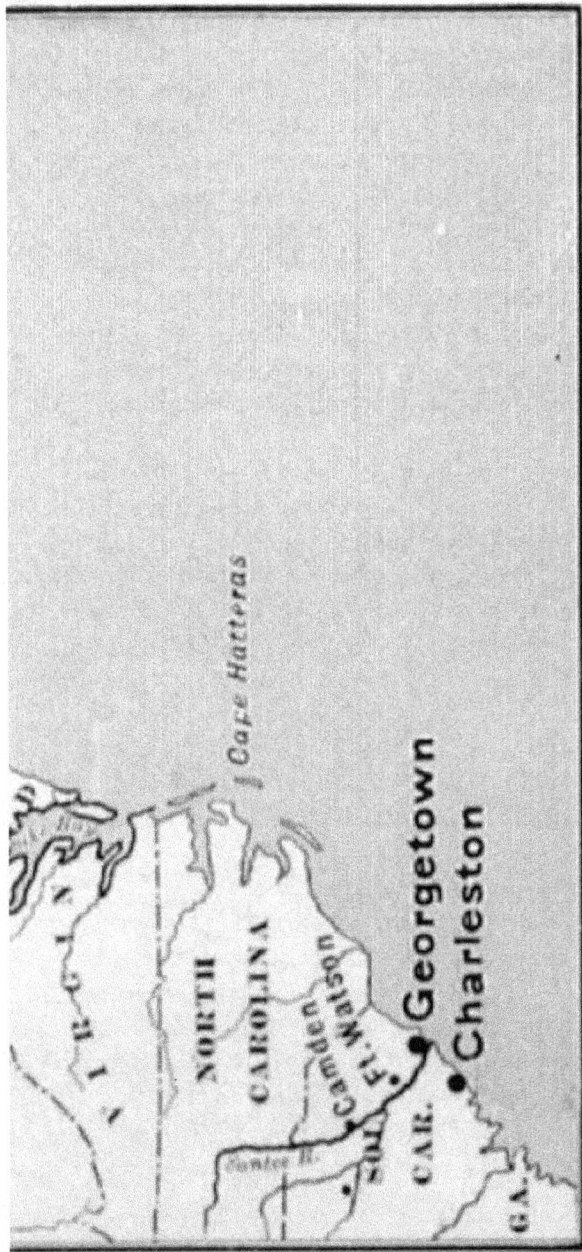

MAP SHOWING THE STRATEGICAL POINTS WHICH MIGHT BE OCCUPIED BY THE BRITISH ARMY TO OBTAIN COMPLETE MILITARY CONTROL OF THE COLONIES,—VIZ., NEWPORT, NEW YORK, WITH THE LINE OF THE HUDSON VALLEY TO CANADA, CHESAPEAKE BAY, AND CHARLESTON, WITH OUTPOSTS IN SOUTH CAROLINA

campaign this is the loosest, the most treacherous, the fullest of peril and delusion; yet, as shall be seen in the years before us, there is none that has been more in favour with British ministers, with the invariable consequence of failure and disaster.

I know of but one instance of the success of such a design, namely, the invasion of England by the Prince of Orange; and this is perhaps the reason why the English are so firmly wedded to the principle. The temptation to the British Ministry in 1775 was great, for the loyalist party was very strong in America; and it is, I think, unquestionable that the American Revolution was, as is generally the case, the work of a small but energetic and well-organised minority, (the fact was recognised eighty years ago, as at 1911 first publication, by Johnson, the American biographer of General Greene), towards which the attitude of the mass of the people, where not directly hostile, was mainly indifferent.

In truth, there was no tangible issue which should unite the Americans against England. The Mother Country had pledged herself to abjure the right of imposing taxation, in return for a very reasonable equivalent; and the Acts of Trade and Navigation, which furnished the only pretext for discontent, had been so long accepted in principle even by the revolutionary leaders that they could hardly be called a grievance. The British Government therefore counted on internal divisions, and on provincial jealousies and prejudices to weaken the spirit of revolt among the Americans; while the Americans, encouraged by the Whig Opposition, counted not less on faction in Great Britain and Ireland to paralyse the arm of the British Government. It may fairly be said that neither party reckoned in vain, and that both were brought to the verge of ruin by intestine discord.

The mere fact that the British Ministry rested its hopes on the co-operation of the American loyalists was sufficient to distract its councils and to vitiate its plans. Their purpose being vague and undefined, ministers proceeded without any idea of what an army could or could not do, or of the force that was required for any given object. General Harvey's impatience with them passed all bounds. He wrote, with all the vigour of a veteran of Flanders:

> Unless a settled plan of operations be agreed upon for next spring, our army will be destroyed by damned driblets . . . America is an ugly job . . . a damned affair indeed.—*Commander-in-Chief's Letter Books*. Harvey to Howe, 30th June; to Lieut.-

Col. Smith, 8th July 1775.

In July Gage had written that Boston was a disadvantageous base for all operations; and a month later he strongly urged that it should be evacuated. But it was not until September that Howe was authorised to remove the army before the winter, unless the situation should improve; and, when this conditional order arrived, he could not collect ships enough for transport of the troops. (Secretary of State to Howe, 5th September; Howe to Secretary of State, 26th November 1775).

Nor was it possible for the generals on the spot to broach plans of their own, for they knew not—nor indeed in the prevailing confusion were ministers in a position to inform them—what number of men would be placed at their disposal.

The weakness of the armed force of Great Britain had indeed revealed itself at last in all its naked peril. The Navy had been suffered by successive Ministries to decline; and as late as in December 1774 the establishment of seamen had been reduced from twenty thousand to sixteen thousand men. The minister now at the head of the Admiralty was Lord Sandwich, a politician of evil reputation and an inveterate jobber; but though he was the best-abused man of his time, and though everything that concerned him, from the conduct of the war to the misconduct of his mistress, was virulently assailed, he was by no means solely to blame for the state of the navy.

The army likewise had been left in December 1774 with an unchanged establishment, nor was it until the spring of 1775 that it was augmented by a paltry four thousand men, of whom one-half were invalids. The king had long since condemned the dangerous weakness of the country in time of peace, and early in the summer of 1775 had pleaded, though in vain, that recruiting should begin at once; (King to General Conway, 11th August 1775. *Correspondence of George III. and Lord North,* 1.), and when at the end of August it was at last resolved to increase the army from thirty-three thousand to fifty-five thousand men, much valuable time had already been lost.

But even this increase, supposing it to be realised, was far too small to provide for the conquest of America; and the king therefore agreed to transfer four Hanoverian battalions to Minorca and Gibraltar in order to release as many British battalions from those garrisons.

Simultaneously he entered into treaty with the rulers of Brunswick and Hesse-Cassel for the supply, in return for a liberal payment, of some eighteen thousand mercenary troops. The bargain was quickly struck; and at once there arose a storm of indignation against both parties to the contract. Natural and even commendable as this indignation now appears, it was really rather ridiculous, for there was nothing new in this hiring of German soldiers. Apart from the constant employment of mercenaries by England, (it is hardly necessary to add that mercenaries were as freely employed by other nations as by the British), particularly during the conquest of Canada in Germany, foreign troops had been called into Britain itself to suppress the Highland rebellions both of 1715 and of 1745.

The Sixtieth or Royal American Regiment, which by the last augmentation had been again increased to four battalions, was composed almost entirely of foreigners, both officers and men; yet no American province would have hesitated to employ it, if she could, against her neighbour in a quarrel over boundaries. As a matter of fact, the Sixtieth had already been used to keep order among the turbulent frontiersmen of Virginia and Pennsylvania; yet neither province had uttered a word of complaint.

Moreover, the aggressive attack of the Americans upon Canada had altered the entire complexion of the quarrel. The Colonists might or might not be justified in taking up arms against British authority within their own boundaries, but they could have no excuse for attempting to annex British territory. Now, judging by the account given by Lord Barrington to Parliament in October 1775, it was extremely doubtful whether even Canada could be recovered without the hiring of foreign troops. The existing fragment of a British Army was far below its establishment, and few recruits, even among Irish Catholics, were obtainable, in spite of bounties raised and of standard lowered, (*Parl. Hist.* xviii.).

Barrington had long ago foreseen the impossibility of raising the force in America to twenty thousand men by the spring of 1776; and he complained in private that in England there were but thirteen thousand regular troops, and in Scotland no more than a single regiment of foot and a single regiment of dragoons. Worst of all, the Militia had decayed so rapidly in efficiency since the peace, that it was hardly safe to call them out. (*Political Life of Lord Barrington.* Barrington to Dartmouth, 31st July, 26th October 1775).

In a situation of such peril the government can hardly be blamed for resorting to the hire of mercenaries. It is interesting and important in its bearing on the history of the army to observe the behaviour of the Whig Opposition at this crisis. First it must be noted that since

1772 the Opposition had gained an important recruit in the person of Charles James Fox, a young man of considerable talent, great eloquence, and singular charm. Principles, as shall be seen, he had none, but he found a substitute sufficient for his purpose in three dominant passions for women, play, and politics which he indulged with impartial recklessness at enormous cost to himself and to his country; though it is fair to add that he accepted his own losses always with good humour and his country's even with exultation. The reader must bear in mind that there were already rumours, disseminated by a vile and seditious press, of disaster to Gage's force and of the fall of Quebec, and that the question immediately before the country was not whether we should impose our will upon the Americans, but whether they should impose their rule on Canada.

The Whigs then, with almost indecent ignorance of their country's history, began by railing furiously against the despatch of Hanoverians to Minorca and Gibraltar as unconstitutional and illegal, a charge which was easily rebutted by the adduction of indisputable precedents. Next, Fox violently opposed a bill which was introduced for the embodiment of the Militia, protesting that he saw no difference between a standing Militia and a standing Army. Next, a Militia Bill for the embodiment of six thousand men in Scotland was as vehemently combated by Burke, on the ground that the number was excessive.

But the most shameful utterance was that of Barre, himself not long since a good and gallant officer, who accused the heroic troops of misbehaviour at Bunker's Hill, owing to their aversion from the service. Barre had a real grievance, since he had been unjustly deprived of his commission for political reasons; but such a speech as this makes one ashamed that he should ever have held a commission at all. Such was the Whig Opposition; such had been the Tory Opposition in Marlborough's time; such, it should seem, are all Oppositions at all times; and yet the country looks for success in war.

However, the money for the augmentation was voted, and the recruiting sergeants were set to work, in the hope that strict enforcement of the Act against Vagabonds, aided by enlistment for short terms, might further their efforts. (*Miscellaneous Orders*, 16th December 1775).

One new regiment only was raised, namely, Major-General Fraser's of two battalions of Highlanders, which, though it no longer survives, we shall see on many fields, (*Secretary's Common Letter Book*, 27th November 1775, Fraser's Highlanders while it lasted bore the number

71st).

Five battalions had already been despatched to Boston in August 1775, (17th, 27th, 28th, 46th, 55th); and by the end of November five more, (15th, 37th, 53rd, 54th, 57th), besides the Sixteenth Light Dragoons, were under orders to take ship. Eight more were directed to embark from Ireland, but in deference to the protests of the Irish executive the number was reduced to six, (9th, 20th, 24th, 34th, 53rd, 62nd), which when finally despatched in April 1776 did not muster as many as three thousand men. There was great show of activity but very little progress.

The naval preparations were much retarded by the severity of the winter; and everything was behindhand. Worst of all, Lord Dartmouth had suffered himself to be persuaded by Governor Martin to send an expedition to Cape Fear, (Dartmouth to Howe, 22nd October, 8th November 1775), in order to rally the loyalists of North Carolina and Virginia, though this was directly contrary to the opinion of the military authorities. (*Commander-in-Chief's Letter Books*. General Harvey to General Cunyngham, 13th February 1776).

Howe, who by the recall of Gage in September had been left in command at Boston, deplored this dispersion of force as likely to reduce him to a defensive campaign in 1776, and urged earnestly that all efforts should be concentrated on the side of New York. Not even the American conquest of Canada, which at one moment seemed inevitable, could turn him from this purpose. No doubt, as he wrote, the reconquest of Canada could be accomplished; but he added, with strong conviction, that the enemy could be more distressed by adherence to the original plan of seizing the line of the Hudson. (Howe to Dartmouth, 3rd December 1775, 16th January 1776).

No better proof could be produced of the soundness of his judgment.

Dartmouth had hardly initiated this most foolish scheme of operations before he was displaced to make room for the minister who, by adherence to the same false methods, was destined to end British rule in America. This was Lord George Germaine, (he had assumed the name of Germaine on inheriting property from Lady Betty Germaine), better known to us as the Lord George Sackville who had brought such disgrace upon himself and upon the army at Minden. There can be no question but that he was a man of more than ordinary ability, though, owing to the persistent English mistake of confounding a certain dexterity in Parliamentary management with genuine administrative power, his capacity has been rated more highly than it deserves.

In any case it was a disgraceful thing that one who had been publicly degraded for misconduct and struck off the list of the Privy Council should have been restored to high office; still more that he should have been appointed to a department which gave him control of the army abroad, from which he had been expelled as unworthy to hold a commission. It was asking very much from the loyalty of brave officers that they should receive their orders from one whose name they could never hear without shame; and the evil of the appointment was not diminished by the fact that Germaine nourished an old grudge against Carleton, and was not too well disposed towards Howe. (*Correspondence of George III. and Lord North*, i.).

The only excuse for the selection of such a man to direct the operations in America would have been exceptional ability as a minister of war; and this talent Germaine most assuredly did not possess.

Throughout the long, dreary winter Howe remained blockaded in Boston, his troops distressed by cold and by want of fresh provisions, and consequently suffering greatly from sickness. Washington on his side had passed through even greater difficulties than Howe. His troops were enlisted only until the 1st of January 1776, some of them indeed for still shorter terms, so that he was confronted with the prospect of a gradual dissolution of his whole army. Moreover, his ammunition was so scanty that for a time he could raise but three rounds for each musket; while the arrangements for the feeding of his soldiers were of such haphazard description as to drive the troops that remained in camp almost to mutiny.

Meantime his men came and went very much as they pleased, returning sometimes to their own farms, sometimes to those of their officers, to work there for days together. As the term of engagement drew nearer its close, desertion and malingering became more and more frequent, and the re-enlistment of troops a matter of increasing difficulty. Men would not engage themselves until they were sure of their field-officers and captains. Officers belonging to the same regiment but to different provinces declined to mix together, while some openly dissuaded their men from re-enlisting. Washington wrote on the 28th of November:

Such a dearth of public spirit, such stock-jobbing and fertility in all the low arts to obtain advantage of one kind or another

57

in the great change of military arrangement I never saw before, and pray God's mercy I may never be witness to again.

To enlist five hundred men I am obliged to furlough fifty to a regiment. Such a mercenary spirit pervades the whole that I should not be surprised at any disaster. . . . Could I have foreseen what I have experienced and am likely to experience, no consideration on earth would have induced me to accept the command.—Washington, *Works*, iii.

Such defects were so obviously to be expected from the composition of the American forces and the factitious nature of the quarrel with England, that it is difficult to imagine how Washington could have felt surprise at them. Our own English Civil War, and probably every civil war, could furnish abundance of parallels to the state of things of which he complained. But with Washington a difficulty once realised was half conquered; and he would speedily have converted the rough material before Boston into excellent troops, but for the obstruction of Congress. That Assembly, mindful of Cromwell the dictator but forgetful of the work first done by the New Model Army, was insanely jealous of all military power.

In vain Washington and Greene urged upon them that discipline was essential to success, that time was needed to make a disciplined soldier, that short enlistments placed officers at the mercy of their men; nothing would induce the lawyers and praters at Philadelphia to sanction the making of an American New Model. Nevertheless, by hook or by crook the indomitable Washington succeeded (to use his own words) in disbanding one army and raising another within distance of a reinforced enemy; so that by February 1776 he was once more in command of nearly eighteen thousand men, with the cannon captured at Ticonderoga and a sufficiency of ammunition, ready to drive the British from Boston.

Howe has been much blamed for his inactivity during these months, but, as it seems to me, without due consideration of his position. He could know nothing of Washington's lack of ammunition, whereas Washington had the best of information as to all that went forward in Boston. Howe knew that all operations undertaken from the town must be futile and indecisive; for, even if he drove the enemy from their entrenchments, he could not follow them from want of transport, which the British Government had declared itself unable to furnish, (Germaine to Howe, 5th January 1776), nor could he hold their works from want of troops. A successful attack therefore could lead to nothing, and an unsuccessful attack to worse than nothing; and in fact he awaited only the arrival of sufficient shipping to evacuate the town.

This, however, was not to be. On the 2nd of March Washington opened a heavy bombardment, which on the 4th he prolonged until far into the night, landing under cover of the fire a considerable force on Dorchester Heights, which entrenched itself with remarkable rapidity and by daylight had rendered its position impregnable. Howe prepared to attack the entrenchment on the night of the 5th, but the enterprise was prevented by a heavy storm; and probably this was fortunate, for the ascent to the position was almost perpendicular, and the Americans with great ingenuity had prepared barrels, filled with stones and chained together, to roll down upon the attacking columns.

The Americans pushed their new works rapidly forward to Nook's Hill, a promontory which flanked the British lines on Boston Neck; and Howe decided to evacuate the town while yet he might. The operation was accomplished without loss on the 17th of March. The troops, though reduced to nine thousand men, (twenty battalions of Infantry and Marines, Royal Artillery, 17th Light Dragoons, Howe to Secretary of State, 7th May 1776), were much crowded on the transports owing to the presence of several hundred loyalists with them; and, for want of shipping, large quantities of guns and stores were left behind, of which it seems that a great proportion were, despite Howe's orders, undestroyed, (Stedman, i.). Howe then sailed for Halifax, where the transports arrived on the 2nd of April; and the Americans marched triumphant into Boston.

Meanwhile, in England disappointments and delays were multiplied. There had been some improvement in recruiting, but in spite of remorseless drafting it was necessary to contract for recruits from Germany to raise several regiments to even a decent strength. (*Secretary's Common Letter Book*, 27th February 1776).

The expedition to Cape Fear, though ordered in October, did not sail till the middle of February. It was the end of April before the reinforcements for Canada were embarked; and only the beginning of May saw the first division of Hessians and a composite battalion of Guards start on their voyage across the Atlantic. And all this time Howe lay helpless at Halifax, waiting for provision-ships, which were so long belated that he trembled for the subsistence of his army, to enable him to proceed to New York. June was actually come before he received his orders for the campaign.

It was therefore in Canada, where the first British transports began to arrive in the St. Lawrence at the end of April, that the operations of 1776 were opened. Since his repulse of the 31st of December, Benedict Arnold had received reinforcements sufficient to maintain the blockade of Quebec. His troops, however, had been so much reduced by smallpox and desertion that he was on the point of retiring, when three small British vessels made their way unexpectedly through the ice, severing all communication between the two divisions of his force which lay on the opposite banks of the river.

Carleton waited only to disembark two hundred men, and at once sallied out against the Americans on the Plains of Abraham, who fled almost without resistance, abandoning the whole of their artillery and stores. No immediate pursuit was undertaken, for Carleton wished first to receive his reinforcements, which would raise his numbers to thirteen thousand men, (9th, 20th, 21st, 24th, 34th, 47th, 53rd, 62nd. 4300 Brunswickers, the 47th was sent by Howe from Halifax); but as soon as these had been landed he pushed up the river to Trois Rivières, only to find that the Americans had fallen back to Sorel, where reinforcements under General Tomson had joined them.

Tomson, hoping perhaps to stem the adverse tide, attacked General Fraser's division at Trois Rivières with two thousand troops, but was repulsed with heavy loss and was himself captured together with two hundred of his men. Carleton pursued the enemy up the river as far as Sorel, the junction of the routes to Lakes Ontario and Champlain; but there he halted, although the wind was favourable, and only later despatched columns along both routes. The western column was entrusted to General Burgoyne, but with strict orders not to fight without the support of the eastern column; and it was thought that, except for this caution, Burgoyne might have reached Chambly before the retreating Americans and compelled the whole of them to surrender. As things were, the enemy was not pressed beyond Crown Point. Still, the American troops employed on this service lost no fewer than five thousand men from sickness and other causes during June, (Washington, *Works*, iv.), and were driven absolutely out of Canada.

None the less, Benedict Arnold, having gained for the present a short respite, worked with indefatigable activity to build and equip a flotilla for the protection of the lakes, and by the end of September had actually completed sixteen vessels mounting seventy guns. Carleton likewise had been dragging up to Lake Champlain gunboats, which had been sent out in sections from England; and by the beginning of October he was ready to meet Arnold with a flotilla of far superior strength and a force of twelve thousand men. On the 11th of October the British attacked Arnold, who had skilfully taken up a very strong position, and handled his ships so roughly that Carleton doubted not to capture his entire force on the following day.

Arnold, however, slipped away in the night, and the British did not overtake him until the 13th, when he very gallantly turned with a fraction of his force to cover the retreat of the rest; and though he was finally overpowered and seven of his ships were taken, he contrived to land the survivors near Crown Point and retire with them to Ticonderoga. Carleton also landed at Crown Point on the 3rd of November, but, contrary to the advice of his officers, declined to advance over the fifteen miles to Ticonderoga, which he could certainly have captured in three or four days. This was a grave mistake, for it delayed the operations of the ensuing year and disheartened the loyalists, of whom there was a respectable number about Albany. Very different would it have been if the British had been commanded by such a man as Arnold, whose amazing skill, gallantry, and resource make him undoubtedly the hero of this short campaign.

From Canada I return to the operations in the south. The belated expedition to Cape Fear, under command of Lord Cornwallis, reached its destination almost simultaneously with the reinforcements for Canada, having consumed three months in crossing the Atlantic. For its particular purpose it arrived just five months too late, for, since it had been expected in January, and General Clinton had actually left Boston in December to take command of it, the loyalists in the district had made all their preparations for that month. Unable to defer their outbreak, they began operations in January accordingly, but, being unsupported and divided among themselves, were very easily dispersed. Clinton had strict orders not to linger in the south beyond a certain day, after which he was to join Howe at New York; but since his time was still unexpired and his force amounted to two thousand men, with a squadron of eight frigates under Sir Peter Parker, he thought that at least he might attempt something.

★★★★★★

The 15th, 28th, 37th, seven companies of the 46th, the 54th, and 57th. Mr. Fiske and Sir George Trevelyan, misled by the fact that Clinton came from Boston to command, say that this force was brought from Boston, add to it six imaginary battal-

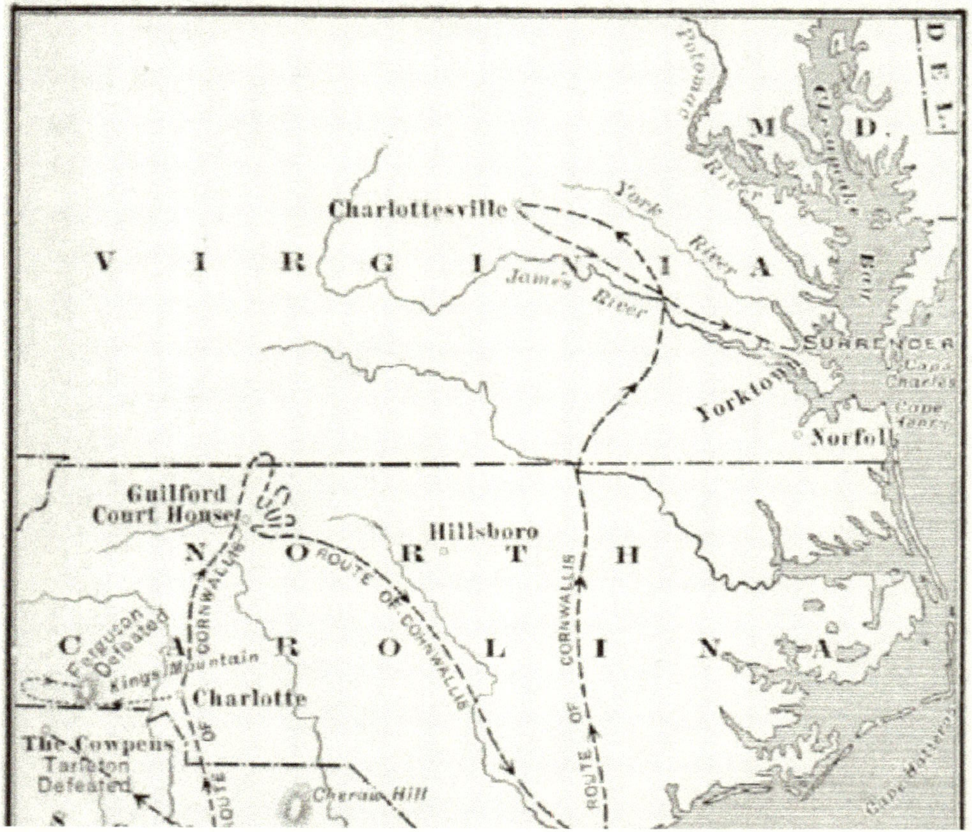

DEL.

M D.

Chesapeake Bay

Cape Charles

Potomac River

York River

James River

SURRENDER

Yorktown

Norfolk

Charlottesville

V I R G I N I A

N O R T H   C A R O L I N A

Hillsboro

ROUTE OF CORNWALLIS

Guilford Court House

ROUTE OF CORNWALLIS

Charlotte

Kings Mountain

Ferguson Defeated

The Cowpens
Tarleton Defeated

30

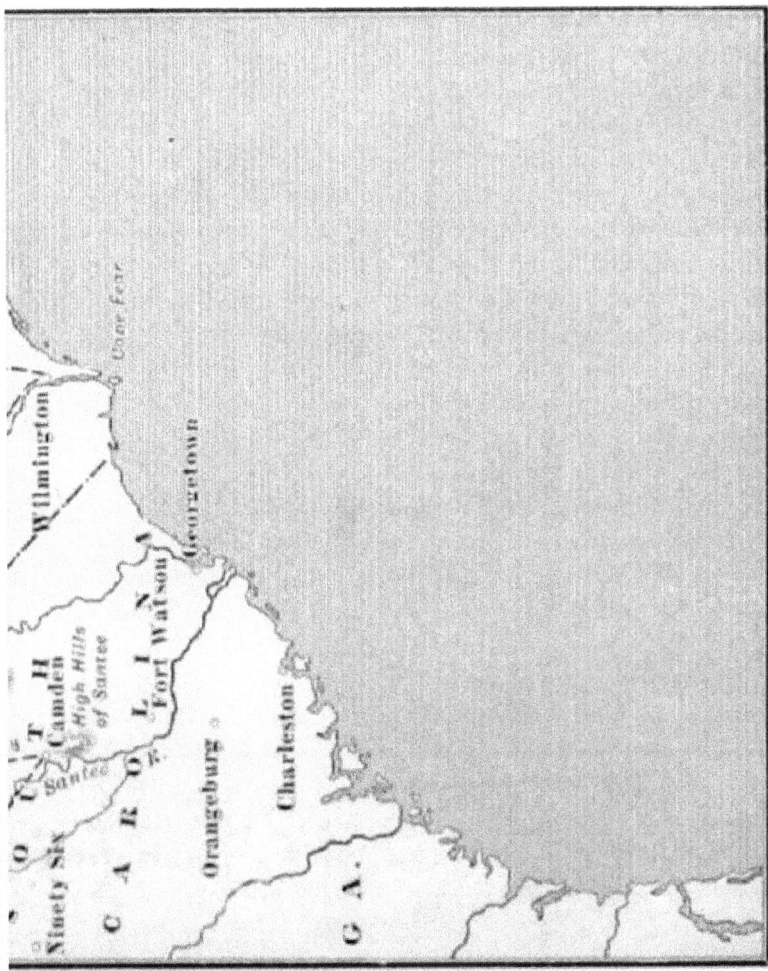

MAP SHOWING THE WANDERING CAMPAIGN OF CORNWALLIS FROM CAMDEN TO YORKTOWN

ions from England, and, having thus doubled Clinton's strength, found on this fictitious basis a necessarily unstable superstructure of criticism.

★★★★★★

Misled by false information, he selected the object recommended by his instructions, namely, the capture of Fort Moultrie on Sullivan's Island, which dominated the harbour of Charleston. Accordingly, after long waiting for missing transports he sailed to Charleston; and on the 28th of June the squadron engaged the American batteries at long range, the intention being that the troops should wade ashore through the shoals and carry the fort by storm. The result was a serious reverse. The shoals were found to be unfordable, and the squadron after ten hours' firing withdrew, heavily punished by the great guns of the fort, with the loss of one ship burned and over two hundred men killed and wounded. The loss of the Americans was trifling, and they might justly plume themselves on their success. After lingering three weeks longer in the hope of finding means to achieve the impossible, Clinton sailed for New York, (July 21st).

There, or rather at Staten Island, Howe was already awaiting him. After long and vexatious delay, due to the tardy arrival of his stores and the need for repairing his transports, he had at last embarked his troops at Halifax on the 7th of June, on which very day he seems to have received his instructions from Germaine. On the 11th a fair wind enabled the transports to sail, and on the 29th they reached Sandy Hook at the mouth of the Hudson River, leading to Howe's first objective, New York. The approach to the river, as is well known, lies between Staten Island on the west and Long Island on the east, the straitest point of the passage betwixt them being known as the Narrows, six miles above which stands New York. The city at that time covered only the south-western extremity of the slender slip of land which, enclosed between the Hudson or North River on the west, and a strait called the East River to south and east, bears the name of New York or Manhattan Island.

Having information that the Americans were endeavouring to block both the North and East Rivers by strong batteries on Long Island and Manhattan Island, as well as by lines of sunken vessels, Howe decided to land at once on Staten Island, from which he could watch their motions. He did so accordingly on the 3rd of July, just one day before the American declaration of independence. So far he had parted with one battalion to Carleton, and had received no reinforcement except half a battalion of Fraser's Highlanders, of which the other half had been captured at sea by an American privateer; but on the 1st of July the transports from England, convoyed by a squadron under his brother Lord Howe, began to arrive at Sandy Hook, and kept dropping in day after day. On the 1st of August Clinton arrived from Cape Fear, and Howe proceeded to organise his force into seven brigades and a Reserve, the Grenadier and Light Infantry companies being as usual massed into distinct battalions. (See list following).

Reserve.—Four battalions of Grenadiers, 33rd, 42nd.

First Brigade.—4th, 15th, 27th, 45th.

Second Brigade.—5th, 28th, 35th, 49th.

Third Brigade.—10th, 37th, 38th, 52nd, 55th.

Fourth Brigade.—17th, 40th, 46th, 55th.

Fifth Brigade.—22nd, 43rd, 44th, 63rd.

Sixth Brigade.—23rd, 44th, 57th, 64th.

Seventh Brigade.—Fraser's Highlanders. New York Companies. Hessian troops.

Light troops.—Three battalions of Light Infantry. 16th and 17th Light Dragoons.

Late, however, though the reinforcements had arrived, action was still delayed by the want of camp-equipage, which had not been sent out with the troops; and though Howe could now muster in British and Hessians a force of some five-and-twenty thousand men, the best part of the year was past, through no fault of his own, before he could open the campaign.

Washington on his side had about eighteen thousand men, five thousand of them distributed among the defences of New York and in the forts commanding the North River, and from nine to ten thousand concentrated in an entrenched position on Brooklyn Heights and in some very strong lines outside them. This latter force, under the command of General Putnam, was designed to cover the approach to New York from the side of Long Island.

On the 22nd of August a first division of the British landed at Gravesend Bay on Long Island, close to the Narrows, whereupon the American advanced parties retired, burning all houses and barns as they went, to a ring of wooded heights which barred the approach to their lines at Brooklyn. The greater part of Howe's army was then

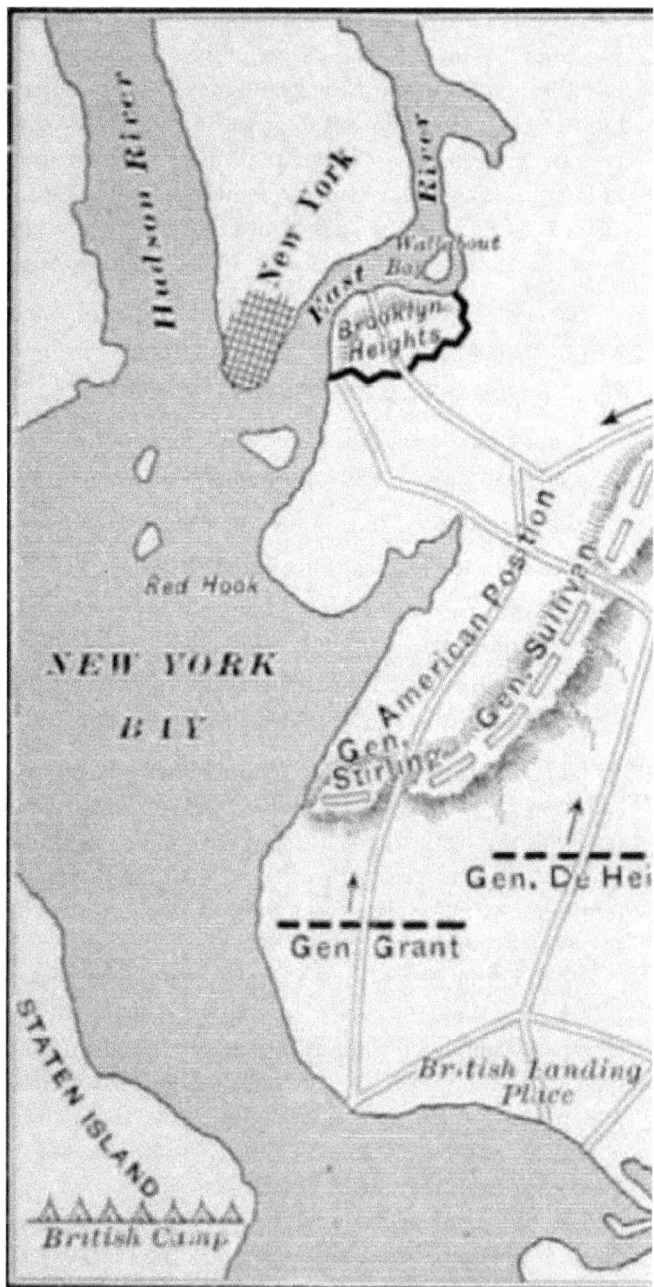

Hudson River

New York

East River

Wallabout Bay

Brooklyn Heights

Red Hook

NEW YORK BAY

American Position

Gen. Stirling

Gen. Sullivan

Gen. De Hei

Gen. Grant

British Landing Place

STATEN ISLAND

British Camp

MAP OF THE BATTLE

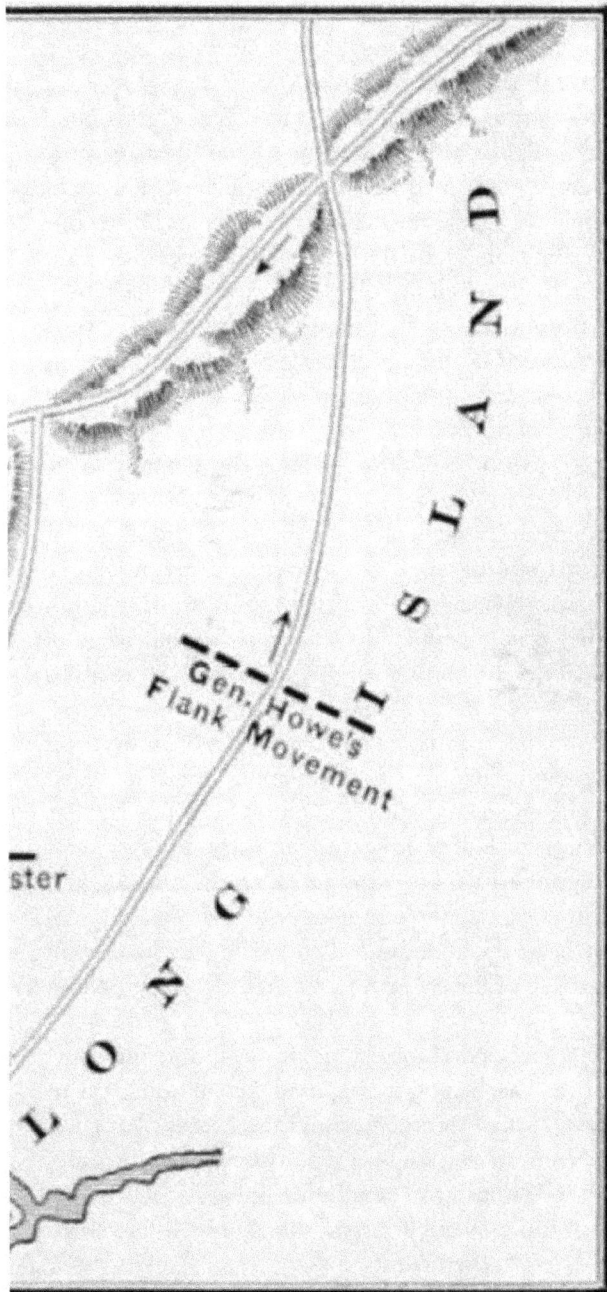

ISLAND

LONG

Gen. Howe's
Flank Movement

ster

landed at the same point, and Lord Cornwallis was at once pushed three miles forward, with the Grenadiers, Light Infantry, Thirty-Third and Forty-Second, to the village of Flatbush.

Since it was clear that the enemy intended to defend the wooded heights before mentioned, Flatbush was occupied as an advanced post, and the rest of the army encamped between the villages of Utrecht and Flatlands, two miles in rear. Four days were then spent in reconnoitring, and on the 26th of August Howe's plan had been thought out. There were three roads whereby to pass the wooded hills which blocked the way to Brooklyn, of which the westernmost, or Gowan's Road, skirted the western base of the hills close to the coast, and was defended by an American detachment under a New Jersey man, who claimed the title of Earl of Stirling.

Nearly three miles to north-east of this was the Flatbush road, leading over the very centre of the hills, astride of which was the main body of the Americans under General Sullivan. But Sullivan's camp, though extending for some distance to eastward, did not reach the easternmost, or Jamaica road, which traversed the hills a mile from their eastern extremity and descended from them on to the village of Bedford. Howe judged that he could turn the whole of these roads to good account.

At nine o'clock on the evening of the 26th Clinton moved off with the Seventeenth Light Dragoons, Light Infantry, Grenadiers, First Brigade, Fraser's Highlanders, and fourteen guns along the Jamaica road to turn the American left. Halting two hours before daybreak, he learned from a captured patrol that the pass over the hills was not guarded, and at once sent a battalion to occupy it. The Guards, Second, Third, and Fifth, brigades, under Lord Percy, following hard upon Clinton, with the baggage of the army in rear, halted close behind him an hour before dawn.

Both Clinton's and Percy's divisions, with Howe in supreme command, then passed over the heights unopposed, and pushing on to Bedford pursued the turning movement round the enemy's left flank and rear. Meanwhile General von Heister with two German brigades had advanced along the Flatbush road, confining himself to a cannonade only until the turning movement began to make itself felt, when he threw his infantry against the heights.

Sullivan's division had already begun to retire from the hill; but his retreating troops were checked by the Light Dragoons and Light Infantry until the Grenadiers and Thirty-Third had actually pushed

BATTLE OF LONG ISLAND.

RETREAT OF THE AMERICANS UNDER GEN. STIRLING ACROSS GOWANUS CREEK

on to within musket-shot of the fortified lines in rear of the hills; and the British were only with difficulty restrained from storming them on the spot. Nearer to the hills another battalion of Light Infantry engaged a force of Americans who were retiring before Heister's attack, and being outnumbered was for a time hard pressed; but being joined by the Guards this battalion continued the struggle, even capturing three guns, until at last the arrival of the Hessians put the Americans to utter rout.

Thus Sullivan's division was beaten and dispersed; and meanwhile at daybreak General Grant with nine battalions and ten guns had opened his attack upon Stirling's division. The Americans at this point were strongly posted and held their own stoutly for four hours, until Cornwallis came up with troops in their rear, when they gave way; but the greater part of them seem to have made their escape to their lines, though with considerable loss, while Stirling himself was taken prisoner. With the rout of Stirling's men the action of Brooklyn came to an end.

The loss of Howe's force in the engagement was slight, the casualties numbering fewer than four hundred in all. (British—5 officers, 56 men killed; 13 officers, 275 men wounded and missing. Hessians—2 men killed; 3 officers and 23 men wounded).

That of the Americans seems never to have been ascertained; but close upon eleven hundred officers and men were taken prisoners, so that, with the addition of those killed and wounded in the action and drowned in a swamp which obstructed the retreat, the total of American casualties can have been little less than two thousand men. Six field-guns and twenty-six heavy guns were also taken. Yet it should seem that the victory should have been far more crushing; for when once Howe and the turning columns were fairly astride of the Flatbush road on the reverse side of the heights, the only retreat to the American entrenchments lay across a morass, traversed by a single causeway, at the western end of the lines.

Grant bears the blame of having neglected to push forward to this causeway, though with what justice it is impossible to decide. Howe, too, was much criticised for checking his men when, by his own admission, they could have stormed the American lines. But against this he urged with some force that the said lines were strongly constructed and strongly held, the troops on the hills being but an advanced detachment, and that, even if these works had been carried, the enemy's retreat was still secured by the entrenchments on Brooklyn Heights and by floating batteries on the water. It is less easy to defend the American general who, for no possible advantage, deliberately exposed an advanced detachment to the certainty of destruction by a superior force.

Complete or incomplete, the victory was at any rate telling. Washington on the next day reinforced the troops left on the side of Brooklyn to a strength of ten thousand men; whereupon Howe broke ground for the siege of the entrenchments in form. This was not what was desired by Washington, who had hoped for a repetition of Bunker's Hill. British ships could not lie off Brooklyn Ferry without exposure to his batteries, but they had only been prevented by foul winds from entering the channel and cutting off his retreat. He resolved therefore to retire while yet he might.

Accordingly, having collected every vessel that he could lay hands on from the North and the East Rivers, he embarked his whole force after nightfall of the 29th, so quietly and swiftly that, by seven o'clock on the morning of the 30th, he had transferred every man and every scrap of his stores safely across a mile of water to New York. Howe was early apprised of the retreat, but took no measures to interfere with it until too late, the British picquets arriving in time only to fire a few shots at the rearguard. Washington was so far fortunate that his movements were for some hours concealed by a fog; but there seems to be little doubt but that Howe might have cut off a part, if not the whole, of the American Army.

Indeed, so obvious was the opportunity that Howe's neglect of it was ascribed less to incapacity than to desire to promote certain negotiations for peace, which had been recently opened by Lord Howe, under special powers, with Congress. Lord Howe's overtures were of course rejected. The capture of Washington's army might have made them welcome: not so its escape. No mistake is more common nor more fatal in British statesmen than the attempt to wage war on the principles of peace.

The Americans, however, were much dispirited by the reverse at Brooklyn. The Militia at once became eager to return to their homes, and deserted in whole companies. Washington by his own confession had no confidence in the generality of his troops, (Washington, *Works*, iv.), and there was considerable distraction of counsel among his officers. Washington and Greene were very rightly for evacuating New York, burning the city, and retreating without delay; for the creek which divides Manhattan Island from the mainland on the north had but two bridges, not a mile apart, and if Howe should succeed in seizing Kingsbridge, the more northerly of these, he would accomplish the work which he had failed to complete at Brooklyn.

The American Council of War, however, decided to keep five thousand men in New York and nine thousand at Kingsbridge, disposing the remainder of their force in the intermediate space; and meanwhile their troops were employed in throwing up entrenchments in every direction. Such a disposition was of course fatuous. On the 15th of September British men-of-war sailed up the North River as far as Bloomingdale, and up the East River as far as Turtle Bay, and opened a heavy fire which sent the Americans flying out of their entrenchments. (Washington, *Works*, iv.).

Under cover of this fire the British troops landed at Kip's Bay, about three miles above New York, and took post across the island, little more than a mile broad at that point, from Horen's Hook to Bloomingdale. Washington succeeded in drawing off a number of his fugitive troops to Haarlem Heights, some two miles away, with little loss but that of their baggage; but there were still from three to four thousand men in New York, who ought to have been cut off and taken by Howe.

Nevertheless, these troops retired with little loss; and it seems that they owed their escape chiefly to an astute American lady, who invited Howe at the critical moment to luncheon. But whatever the reason, it is certain that little more than three hundred of them were captured. New York was thus recovered by the British; sixty-seven guns, mounted and unmounted, were taken with it; and the demoralisation of the Americans was considerably increased.

Still, the problem set to Howe remained unsolved. The Americans were entrenched just above Haarlem so strongly as to prohibit a frontal attack, while their flanks were protected against the fleet by batteries commanding Haarlem Creek on the east and by Fort Washington and Fort Lee, on opposite banks of the Hudson, to the west. So unpromising seemed the outlook that Howe was disposed to close the campaign on the side of New York there and then. On the 16th there was sharp skirmishing between detached parties of the two armies, but with no result; and from that day for fully four weeks Howe remained motionless, throwing up strong entrenchments across his position at Macgowan's Hill so as to cover New York from the north.

★★★★★★

It is instructive that Howe gives the British casualties (in detail) at 92, and estimates the American at 300; while Mr. Fiske quotes the American casualties at 60, and the British at 300. It is safe to assume that the smaller number in each case is the correct one.

★★★★★★

A great fire, beyond all doubt the work of American incendiaries, which destroyed one-third of the town of New York, certainly caused delay and difficulty to the British General for several days; but the only acceptable excuse for his inactivity was that the American Army was likely to break up more rapidly if left to itself than if attacked. To judge from Washington's letters at this period, such a dissolution was by no means improbable. (Washington, *Works*, iv.).

There was, however, a vulnerable point in Washington's armour of which Howe might well have taken earlier advantage, namely, by operating against his communications to eastward with Connecticut, from which most of the American supplies were drawn, and using the same route to threaten his rear at Kingsbridge. This was the plan which, after long delay, he at last adopted. Accordingly, on the 12th of October, leaving Percy with one Hessian and two British brigades to hold the lines at Macgowan's Hill, he embarked the rest of his army in boats, and passing through the dangerous and intricate channel of Hell Gate landed at Throg's Neck, a Peninsula jutting out into the East River from the mainland and connected with it by a bridge. This operation was not concluded until the 17th; and meanwhile Washington had detached a force to break down the bridge and to take up a strong position commanding the morass beyond it. Howe therefore re-embarked his troops on the 18th, and landed them again a mile to eastward at Pell's Point. (He explained that there would have been unnecessary risk in landing first at Pell's Point.—Howe's *Narrative*).

An American party which guarded a pass on the road was dislodged after a sharp skirmish; and on the 21st Howe's army advanced six miles to New Rochelle, where it was joined by a division of Hessians which had just arrived from Europe. But the delay of the double disembarkation had given Washington ample time to shift his position. Leaving two thousand men in Fort Washington, he changed front from south to east, extending his army in detached camps, each of them strongly entrenched, for some eighteen miles along a line of hills that runs northward from Kingsbridge to White Plains; his front being everywhere covered by a deep river called the Bronx, of which every ford was defended by powerful works. At the same time he prepared another entrenched camp at White Plains, fronting to the south, so as to check the march of the British to northward.

Meanwhile, Howe advanced slowly with his thirteen thousand men in two columns, and on the 25th encamped on the Bronx, about four miles from White Plains. Washington therefore on the 26th shifted into his new camp on that spot, leaving, however, a division of four thousand men under Colonel Spencer in a bend of the Bronx to his right front, and separated by that river from his main body. On the 28th Howe continued his advance; and Colonel Rahl of the Hessians, perceiving that this isolated corps had omitted to occupy a hill which commanded its flank, at once sent a battalion across the river to seize it.

Howe then directed the Second Brigade with two Hessian battalions against the front of Spencer's division, while Rahl moved upon its flank; but, the frontal attack being prematurely delivered, the losses of the British were unduly heavy, (British loss—214 killed and wounded, 99 Hessians killed and wounded. American loss, *Fiske*—140 killed), and though the Americans were driven gallantly from this very strong post, no solid advantage was gained. Howe had ordered a simultaneous attack on the American main position; but this movement, for some unexplained reason, was never executed; and indeed it seems that Washington's left was so strongly posted as to ensure his retreat to Connecticut with, at any rate, the greater part of his army. (Howe, "for political reasons," declined to account for this in his examination before the House of Commons).

Meanwhile, Washington exerted himself strenuously to strengthen his entrenchments, and on the 29th Howe sent to Percy for a reinforcement of six battalions; but a general attack, which he had ordained for the 31st, was rendered impossible by a heavy storm of rain, and on the 1st of November Washington retreated across the River Crotton to a position from which it was impracticable to dislodge him.

But the driving of Washington behind the Crotton was no barren nor purposeless operation. On the day of the combat at White Plains the German General Knyphausen had marched with six Hessian battalions, which had been left at New Rochelle, upon Kingsbridge, to secure the passage from Manhattan Island; and Howe himself now fell back to Dobbs's Ferry, on the eastern bank of the Hudson, ready either to attack Fort Washington or to cross the river into New Jersey. This movement was extremely embarrassing to Washington. His operations had been dictated by the effort to secure three principal objects,

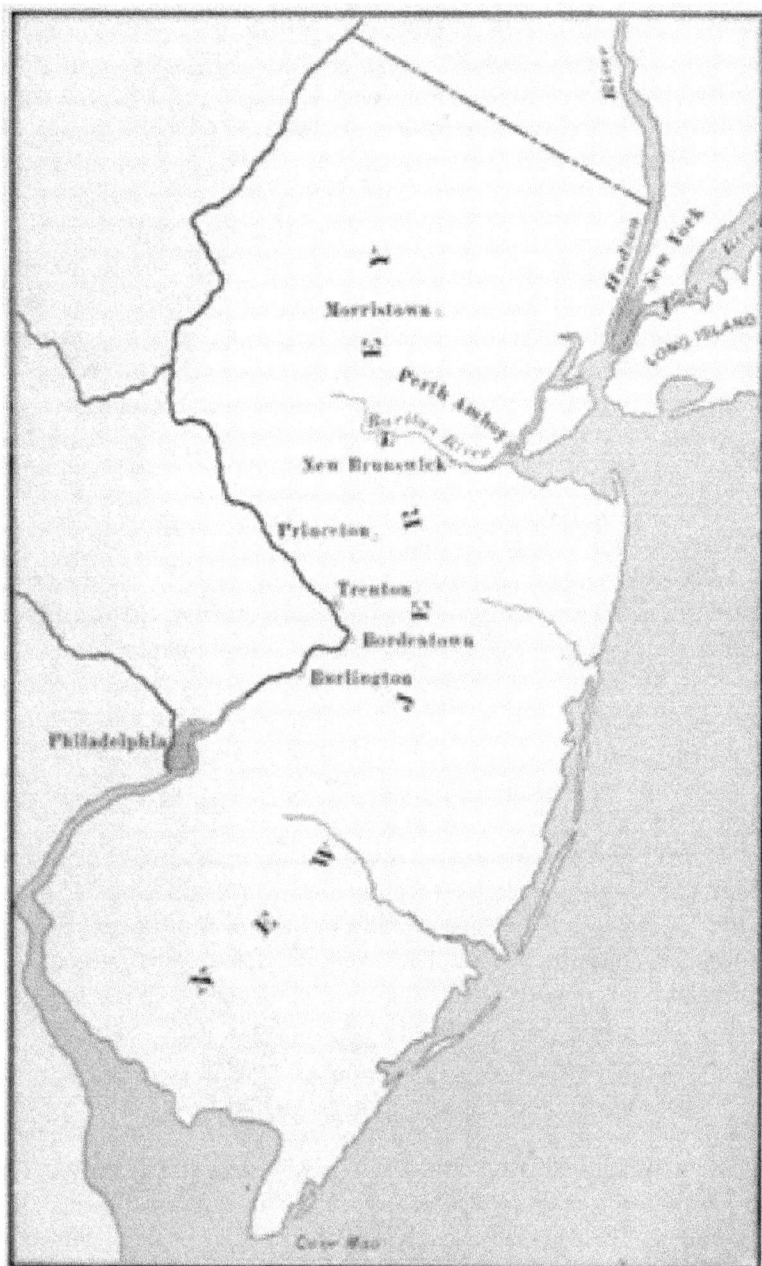

MAP SHOWING THE POSITION OF THE BRITISH ARMY IN NEW YORK IN DECEMBER, 1776, WITH ITS CANTONMENTS FOR HOLDING NEW JERSEY

namely, his safe retreat northward into the highlands on the east bank of the Hudson, his communications with the north-east, from which he obtained his supplies, and his communications with the country on the west of the Hudson.

This last had already been seriously imperilled by the passage of British frigates beyond Forts Lee and Washington, and was now still more seriously threatened by the menace to those forts themselves. Howe's position was such that the slightest false step on the American side might give him an opportunity to strike a telling blow in any one of three or four quarters; in a word, it was very well and skilfully chosen. Washington now left General Lee with seven thousand men on the Crotton, detached three thousand to Peekskill to guard the passes into the highlands, and sent General Putnam with another detachment across the Hudson to take post at Hackinsaw, about seven miles south-west of Fort Lee, in New Jersey.

His perfectly correct instinct was to evacuate both Fort Lee and Fort Washington, but in deference to his generals he hesitated to do so; and finally he gave General Greene, who lay close to Fort Lee, the option of evacuating or of reinforcing Fort Washington, as he might think best. Greene was of opinion that the post should be held, and, receiving an order from Congress that it must on no account be abandoned, decided to reinforce it. Washington, who joined Greene on the 14th of November, did not alter these dispositions; and Howe was not slow to use his opportunity against the forces thus dangerously dispersed.

Fort Washington with its outworks occupied an area of oblong shape about three miles long by one and a half miles broad, consisting of two parallel ridges running north and south between the Hudson and Haarlem Creek. The ascent of these ridges, both on the north side and from Haarlem Creek, was extremely steep and rugged, and much of the ground was also covered with dense forest, while every point of vantage was strengthened by batteries and entrenchments. On the south side the approach was obstructed by three lines of entrenchments with strong abatis, which had been thrown up on Haarlem Heights to check Howe's original advance from New York. The innermost of these lines lay about a mile and a half from Fort Washington itself, which was a work of five bastions, crowning the highest point of the western ridge. The position was in fact exceedingly strong, so much so that the American generals seem one and all to have regarded it as impregnable.

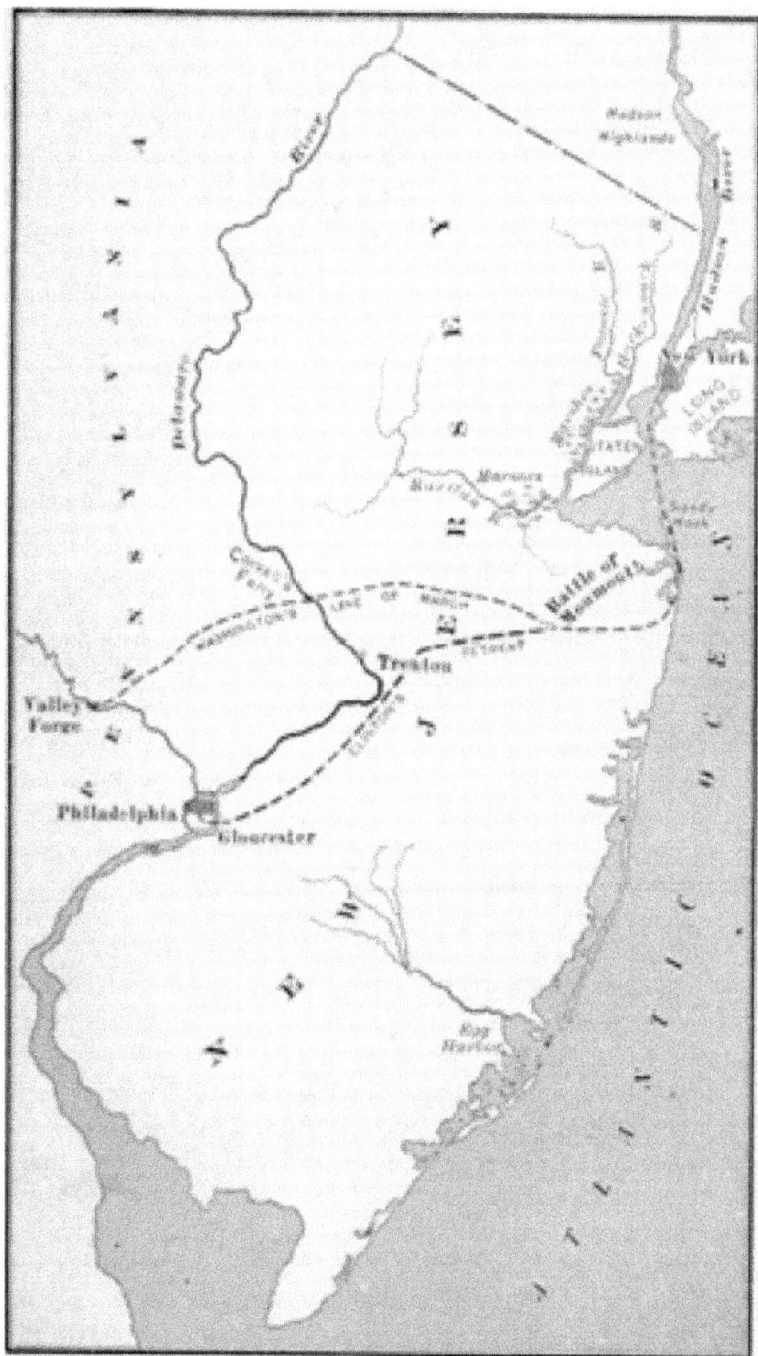

MAP SHOWING CLINTON'S RETREAT FROM PHILADELPHIA TO NEW YORK.

Howe had already constructed redoubts and batteries on the eastern bank of Haarlem Creek, to cover an attack from that side; and on the 15th of November he summoned Fort Washington, threatening to put the whole garrison to the sword unless it were surrendered. The answer was of course defiant; and accordingly, at daybreak of the 16th, the guns of the redoubts on Haarlem Creek and of H.M.S. *Pearl* on the North River opened a heavy fire.

Meanwhile, the attacking columns made ready to advance; the first, of five thousand Hessians under Knyphausen, against the north front from Kingsbridge; the second, of the Guards, Grenadiers, Light Infantry, and Thirty-Third, under Generals Matthews and Lord Cornwallis, against the eastern side from Haarlem Creek; and a third, of the Forty-Second Highlanders, which was directed to make a feint attack only, against the same side but a little further to the south. The fourth column, which had been sent down Haarlem Creek in the night to the south of the American position, consisted apparently of nine battalions (4th, 10th, 15th, 23rd, 27th, 28th, 38th, 52nd, Fraser's Highlanders. of British and one brigade of Hessians under Lord Percy).

One and all of the columns made their way forward with incredible difficulty owing to the rugged character of the ground and the obstacles, especially abatis, opposed by art and by nature to their advance.

The Americans made a very stubborn resistance, particularly on the northern side, where the Hessians suffered heavily in the task of forcing their way through the forest against skilled riflemen. Indeed, the turning-point of the action appears to have been the reinforcement of the Forty-Second by two more battalions, and the conversion of their feint into a real attack. Colonel Stirling, who was in command at this point, made his way doggedly under a very heavy fire to the shore, and thence over a wooded promontory, at the summit of which he stormed the redoubt opposed to him after very hard fighting, and captured two hundred prisoners.

The British having thus broken into the lines, the Americans gave way at all points and crowded into Fort Washington, which presently surrendered. The American loss amounted to about three thousand three hundred killed, wounded, and prisoners; for Howe had no thought of executing his threat, and at once checked the Hessians who, maddened by the resistance of the American riflemen, had begun to ply their bayonets. The total loss of Howe's army was four hundred and fifty-eight killed and wounded, (Hessians, 330 killed and wounded; British, 128 killed and wounded), two-thirds of the casual-

BATTLE OF MONMOUTH

ties falling upon the Hessians, while half of the fallen British belonged to the Forty-Second Highlanders. Altogether it was a pretty little action, neatly designed and very neatly executed; for Howe at his best was no contemptible commander.

He lost no time in following up this blow by a second. On the 18th Lord Cornwallis landed about eight miles above Fort Lee on the Jersey shore, with a flying column of some forty-five hundred men, (2 batts. Grenadiers, 2 batts. Light Infantry, Guards, 42nd, 33rd, detachment 16th Light Dragoons, 4 cos Hessians), and marched down with great swiftness and secrecy to surprise the fort. The movement was unfortunately betrayed by a deserter, or the entire garrison would certainly have been captured.

Even as things were, Greene had only just time to withdraw his two thousand men across the Hackinsack, leaving his tents standing and abandoning the whole of his provisions and stores, together with one hundred and forty cannon. Cornwallis followed hard on his track, untroubled by further resistance than an occasional bullet from some skulking patriot concealed behind a bush; and meanwhile matters elsewhere were going ill with Washington. Lee, whom he had summoned from the Crotton on the 17th and again on the 21st, refused for the present to move, having his own treacherous objects in view; the militia of New Jersey declined to come forward, and that of Pennsylvania openly exulted over the success of the British. (Washington, *Works*, iv.).

On the 24th Cornwallis was reinforced by nine battalions of the Second and Fourth Brigades and Fraser's Highlanders; and Washington, who had joined Greene, could only retreat before far superior numbers. Howe, naturally not counting on Lee's inactivity, had, in view of the lateness of the season, instructed Cornwallis to pursue no further than Brunswick. Washington broke down the bridge over the River Rariton after passing it, and Cornwallis, whose troops were half starved, and quite worn out with fatigue, was fain to halt. (Cornwallis's evidence before the House of Commons).

Meanwhile Lee's division had at last started on its march towards Washington, and required watching; but Howe, alive to the advantage of pushing on to the Delaware, joined Cornwallis on the 6th of December at Brunswick and continued the advance. Washington's army was fast dwindling through desertion, and when he reached Princeton he had with him but three thousand men; nor had he left that place an hour before Howe's advanced guard entered it, close upon his track. But, instead of hurrying on, Howe for some reason halted for seventeen hours, and reached Trenton, on the Delaware, just as Washington's last boatful of troops touched the opposite bank, 8th. Cornwallis started very early on the following morning and marched for thirteen miles up the river in the hope of finding boats, but in vain, for Washington had taken good care that every one should have been removed. The pursuit was therefore abandoned, and Washington was left to recover himself in Pennsylvania.

Even thus the British successes were not wholly ended. Lee, after doing his best to ruin his commanding officer, had taken up comfortable quarters at some distance from his army, where he was surprised and taken prisoner by a patrol of the Sixteenth Light Dragoons. This was considered a great misfortune by the revolutionary party, and in itself could not but be a discouragement. Moreover, on the 1st of December, General Clinton had sailed for Rhode Island with six thousand men, (10th, 22nd, 37th, 38th, 43rd, 52nd, 54th, 63rd, Light Infantry, Grenadiers, detachment of 17th Light Dragoons, six battalions of Hessians), under convoy of Sir Peter Parker's squadron, and had occupied it without resistance.

Nearly all, therefore, had been prepared for carrying out the original plan of campaign. New York had been taken as a base for the advance up the Hudson from the south, and Rhode Island for the movement from the east. Canada also had been cleared—though by grievous error Ticonderoga had not been captured—for advance upon the Hudson from the north. Further, the British arms had been carried not only into New Jersey, which had been the furthest limit of Howe's expectation, but even to the Delaware. But for the tardiness of the preparations in England, which kept both Howe and Carleton so long inactive, the campaign of 1776 might almost in itself have sufficed to end the war.

It remained for Howe to settle his cantonments for the winter. His original intention (and it had been well if he had adhered to it) was to have made Brunswick the left and Newark the right extremities of his line; but, at the suggestion of Cornwallis, Trenton and Bordenton were included, although the chain of posts was thereby unduly prolonged, for the sake of giving protection to the loyal inhabitants. Attachment to the king had increased amazingly in New Jersey during the victorious advance of the British, and the inhabitants had come in by hundreds together, in response to a proclamation by Howe, to take the oath of allegiance.

In a very short time numbers of these people were to be captured in arms against the British, with General Howe's protections and certificates of loyalty in their pockets. (Howe's *Observations on a Pamphlet*). It is not by oaths but by arms that men should wage war.

CHAPTER 4

Brandywine

The general results of the campaign of 1776, so far, could not but be satisfactory to the British Government and correspondingly depressing to the Opposition. Fox wrote in anguish of the "terrible news" of Howe's success at Brooklyn, (*Fox Correspondence*, i.); and, when Parliament met, Burke could find nothing cheerful in the course of the operations except the burning of New York, which, for reasons best known to himself, he thought fit to celebrate as an heroic achievement in sounding periods of incomparable nonsense. Unfortunately for Burke, an emissary of Silas Deane, the American agent in Paris, was shortly afterwards caught in the act of emulating this particular form of heroism in Portsmouth Dockyard, with the result that the whole of the rope-walk was destroyed, and that the culprit was hung in chains. The session, in such circumstances, passed off favourably enough for the Ministry; and the only cause for alarm to its supporters was the inadequacy of the military preparations for the next campaign.

The military establishment voted for 1777, including twenty-four thousand foreign troops, was just short of eighty-nine thousand men, which, after deducting a very insufficient force for the protection of the British Isles and for the Mediterranean stations, left but fifty-seven thousand men for the service of colonial garrisons and for the prosecution of the war. It must be remembered too that these figures, small enough in themselves, existed on paper only and were very far from realised in fact.

It was above all things necessary to end the war as early as possible; and this could only be accomplished by a great effort and by the employment of an overwhelming force.

Recent events had shown the urgency of the need. Spain supplied the revolted Colonies freely with money and with gunpowder. Holland sold them endless stores, which were sent, with great show of innocence, to the Dutch island of St. Eustatius. Frederick the Great threw every possible obstacle in the way of enlisting Germans for the British service. Above all, France, outwardly friendly, was full of enmity and malice. The Declaration of Independence had altered the footing upon which the American Congress could approach her to seek her alliance; but long before the arrival of the American emissaries in Paris in 1776 the French had sent a million *livres* to the Colonies, while Silas Deane in the course of the year obtained for them gifts of thirty thousand stand of arms, as many suits of clothing, two hundred and fifty cannon, and vast quantities of military stores.

Further, American privateers were sheltered, equipped, and allowed to sell their prizes in French ports, while the Caribbean Sea swarmed with ships flying American colours, but manned, fitted out and owned by Frenchmen, and in truth little else but pirates. Beyond this point the French Court for the present hesitated to go; but there could be no doubt that the first favourable opportunity would be seized for a war of revenge against England.

Moreover, yielding to the bitter complaints of Washington, Congress had actually bestirred itself a little to create an American army. Discipline, so Washington had urged, was impossible while men treated their officers as equals and regarded them "no more than a broomstick"; and when we read that many American corps would elect no officers who did not consent to throw their pay into the common stock, that officers were often leaders in plunder, that one captain was also barber to his company, and that another had been tried and cashiered for stealing his soldiers' blankets, it is easy to understand why he should have begged for the preference of "gentlemen and men of character" in the allotment of commissions.

Even the officers nominated by the different provinces were "not fit to be shoeblacks," being chosen according to the favour and interest of members of the Assemblies. Above all, the system of enlistment for very short terms must dissolve his army regularly every Christmas with much greater certainty than any operations of the British. (Washington, *Works*, iv.).

Such was the burden of Washington's representations. The simple truth was, that so long as the quarrel with England meant no more for the Americans than town-meetings, demolition of houses, tarring and feathering of defenceless individuals, assaults on soldiers who were forbidden to defend themselves, and even shooting at convoys from behind walls—so long every man was a patriot; but when it came to taking as well as dealing blows, the number of patriots was woefully diminished. (See letter of Robert Morris, Member of Congress, 21st December 1776).

It is no reflection on the Colonists that this should have been so, for it means only that they were neither better nor worse than other people; but our admiration is increased for such men as Washington and Greene, who had not only the unselfishness to devote their whole strength without reward to the cause which they had embraced, but the ability to perceive the remedy for these dangerous evils and the tenacity to force them upon such an assembly as Congress.

The outcome of Washington's repeated remonstrances was that in September 1776 Congress agreed to vote an army of sixty-six thousand men, enlisted for three years or for the war; authorising Washington also to raise fifteen thousand more, if he thought fit, and at the same time greatly extending his powers as commander-in-chief. This army, of course, like the British establishment existed on paper only, and, since its pay was also likely to consist of paper only, there was no saying how far it could be realised in the field; but the step was at any rate full of significance for the future of the war.

At the end of November, Howe, still intent on the original plan for the isolation of New England, had written to England proposing that his force should be made up to thirty-five thousand men, eight thousand of them to cover New Jersey, twenty thousand to advance in two armies upon Albany from Rhode Island and New York, and the remainder to garrison the bases of operations. For this design he requested reinforcements of fifteen thousand men and ten ships of the line. (Howe to Germaine, 30th November 1776).

But after reaching the Delaware he became more anxious to gain possession of Philadelphia, and proposed to hold Rhode Island, New York, and the lower Hudson defensively only, employing ten thousand men for the invasion of Pennsylvania. (*Ibid.* 20th December 1776).

He had, in fact, every intention of advancing on Philadelphia as soon as the Delaware should be frozen, and had returned with Cornwallis to New York to mature his plans, when his security was disturbed by a rude shock.

Washington's force had lately been raised to six thousand men by the remnants of Lee's division and by reinforcements from the north, but was about to suffer its annual dissolution on the expiry of its term of service. The state of the revolutionary cause was so desperate that,

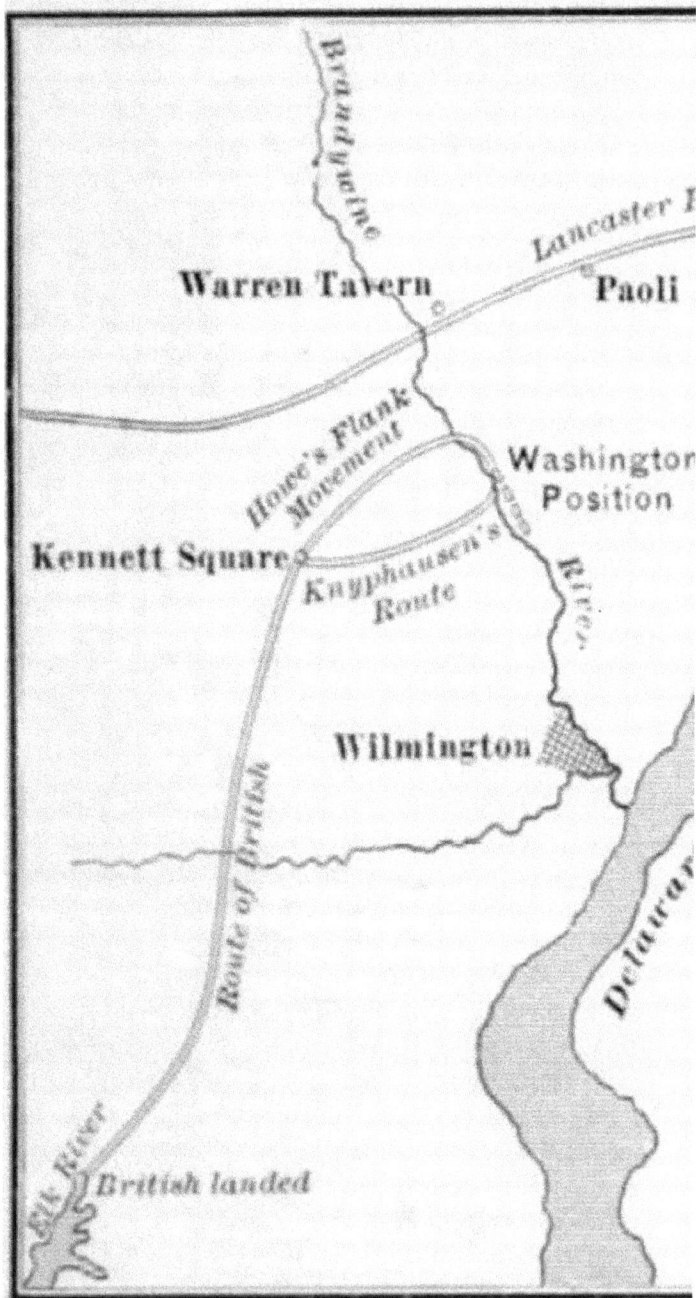

Brandywine

Lancaster R

Warren Tavern

Paoli

Howe's Flank Movement

Washington Position

Kennett Square

Knyphausen's Route

River

Wilmington

Route of British

Delawar

Elk River

British landed

MAP OF THE BATTLE

Valley Forge

White Marsh

Swedes Ford

Schuylkill

Germantown

Road

River

Philadelphia

Fort Mifflin

's

Chester

Red Bank

River

Billings Port

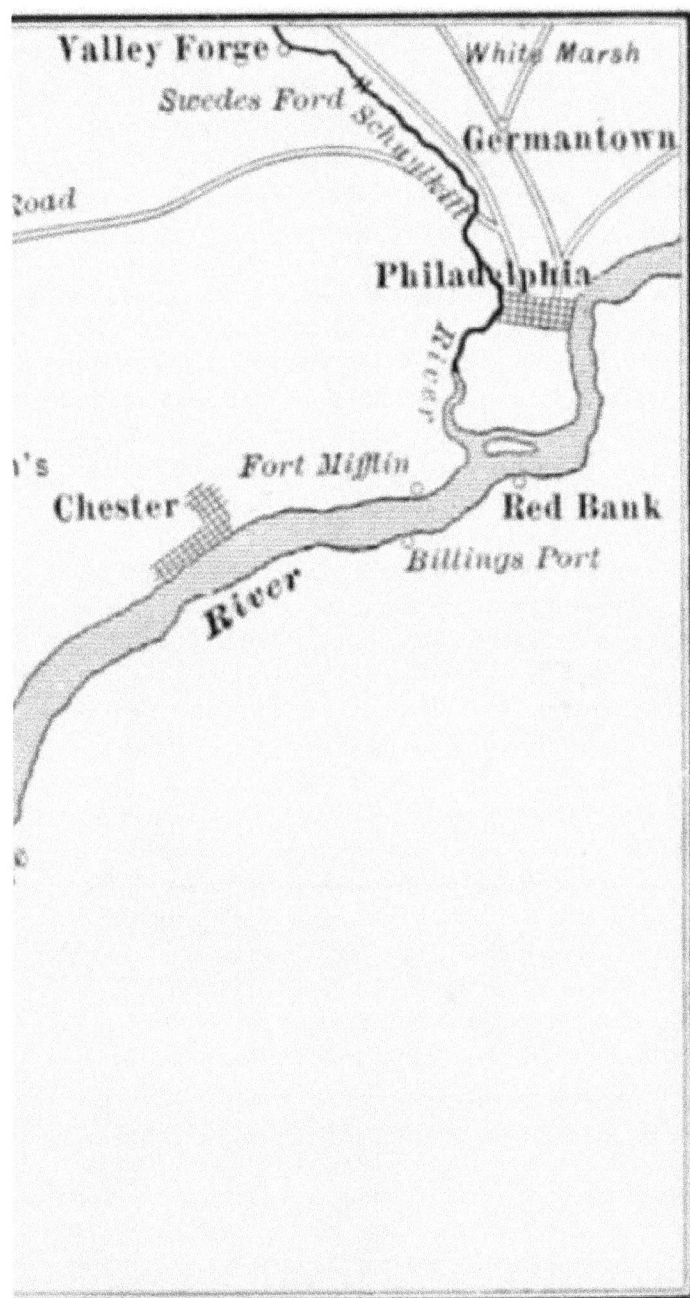

OF THE BRANDYWINE

in order to hearten his despondent followers, he resolved to hazard a sudden blow at Howe's frontier-posts. These posts, as Howe himself had confessed, were too much extended; and Trenton and Bordenton, which formed the extreme left of the line, were, pursuant to etiquette, garrisoned entirely by Hessians, Trenton by thirteen hundred men under Colonel Rahl, and Bordenton by two thousand men under Count Von Donop.

Moreover, despite Howe's express orders, Rahl had neglected to throw up redoubts for the defence of Trenton. Fully alive to this omission, Washington selected Rahl's post as the object of his attack. Having drawn Von Donop southward to Burlington by a clever feint movement, he divided his own force into three corps and arranged that all three should cross the Delaware upon Christmas Day, the first near Bordenton to attack Von Donop, the second at Trenton Ferry, and the third, under his own command, nine miles above Trenton, in order to converge with the second corps against that post.

So severe was the weather, (December 25th), that Washington's own column alone succeeded in passing the river, after which it marched through a storm of sleet upon Trenton. Rahl had full warning of the coming attack, but he had allowed his men to lose discipline and to go plundering, with the result that he could not assemble them. Having no entrenchments, he could make little resistance against odds of two to one, for Washington had brought artillery with him. Hence, Rahl himself being mortally wounded early in the attack, his troops laid down their arms, though they had suffered but trifling loss. Von Donop, on learning what had happened, at once fell back to Princeton, abandoning his sick and his heavy baggage. Washington judged shrewdly, when he fell upon the Hessians on Christmas Day.

Cornwallis had been on the point of embarking for England, but the news of the mishap brought him hastily back from New York to Princeton. On the morning of the 2nd of January he advanced against Trenton, which Washington, after safely depositing his thousand prisoners at Philadelphia, had reoccupied on the 29th of December. The march of the British was much harassed by small parties lurking in the woods and by a force of six hundred men under Greene; and it was not until late in the afternoon that Cornwallis reached Trenton, to find Washington drawn up a little beyond the town, in a good position behind a stream called the Assunpink. After a sharp cannonade from both sides, Cornwallis decided to send for reinforcements and to renew the attack on the following morning; but Washington was not so easily to be caught.

Leaving his camp-fires burning and a few small parties to make a sound of work in throwing up entrenchments, he stole away with the rest of his force at two o'clock in the morning, fetched a wide compass to south-eastward in order to clear Cornwallis's left wing, and marched upon Princeton to capture by surprise the stores which he guessed to be there. At sunrise his leading column met a British detachment, consisting of the Seventeenth and Fifty-Fifth regiments, under Colonel Mawhood, which by Cornwallis's orders were on march towards Trenton.

The morning was foggy, and Mawhood at first mistook the Americans for Hessians, (the same mistake was made at the action of Brooklyn, and thirty British became prisoners in consequence); but discovering his error, and being unable to discern their numbers, he conjectured that Washington was retreating before Cornwallis, and resolved at all hazards to check him. Summoning, therefore, the Fortieth Regiment from Princeton to reinforce him, he took up a position; and after some sharp play with the artillery, which did considerable execution among the Americans, the Seventeenth charged with the bayonet, killing the American General Mercer and driving back his column in confusion. But Washington now came galloping up to rally Mercer's men, with the rest of his troops close after him, and the British were quickly driven back by superior numbers.

Yet even so the Seventeenth fought their way through the enemy to Cornwallis, escaping with the loss of sixty-six killed and wounded and five-and-thirty prisoners. Since the battalion could not have taken more than two to three hundred men into action, this feat was rightly judged to be one of the most gallant exploits of the war. The two other regiments lost several prisoners, the casualties of the whole force amounting to two hundred and seventy of all ranks, while Mawhood lost also all of his guns.

★★★★★★

So say Howe's official figures. Stedman says that the 40th and 55th lost half of their numbers, but the battalions were so weak that probably the three together on this occasion did not muster 700 bayonets.

★★★★★★

It is said that he might well have made good his retreat, but in the circumstances he can hardly be blamed for risking an action; for it was difficult for a man to divine that Washington, who was credited with

BATTLE OF PRINCETON.

the glaring blunders of the past campaign, could be capable of movements so brilliant and so audacious.

Cornwallis, on discovering how he had been duped, hastened back with all speed to save the stores at Princeton; but Washington reckoned it prudent to abandon his design against that place and to retire to Morristown, where he could be sure of obtaining supplies, while Cornwallis pursued his retreat to New Brunswick. Washington then extended his chain of cantonments from Peekskill southward to Morristown, and thence eastward to Newark, leaving Howe with no more of New Jersey than the slip of land enclosed within a line drawn from Paulus Hook southward to New Brunswick and thence to Amboy.

Washington, (Jan. 25th), now issued a proclamation in counterblast to Howe's, calling on the people to swear allegiance to the United States. To this there was naturally a willing response. The people flocked in and took the oath cheerfully, not however omitting, as has been told, to keep their certificates of loyalty to King George in their pockets. Herein doubtless they displayed strong common sense, for they cared very little about the quarrel though a great deal about their farms, and were quite ready to swear allegiance to any one for the sake of peace. It is said that the people of New Jersey were alienated from the British by the misconduct of the troops, who gave themselves up without restraint to violence, plunder, rape; and there seems to be no doubt that the Hessians were guilty of great excesses while in cantonments. But Howe strenuously denied the charges of misbehaviour against the army in general, and proved conclusively that he and Cornwallis took every precaution, and with success, to maintain order.

★★★★★★

Howe's *Narrative*, Stedman presses the charges against the troops, but his strong bias against Howe and his favourable contrast of the behaviour of the Americans, which was condemned by Washington himself, seem to me to render his statements valueless. The whole of his criticism is based on the allegations of Joseph Galloway, who, as a renegade member of Congress, had every motive to try to ingratiate himself with the public and the government at the expense of Howe. The statements of such a character are *prima facie* open to suspicion.

★★★★★★

Of course endless accusations, accompanied by endless affidavits, were circulated for the purpose of rousing animosity against the British; but affidavits, never a very costly article, are remarkably cheap in times of revolution, (I speak not without experience of American affidavits in particular, having examined and abstracted many hundreds of the troublous period 1678-1694).

While the denigration of adversaries, political or belligerent, by wholesale lying is so common a matter that I see no reason why Howe's statement should be doubted. On the other hand, Washington, who never told a lie, complained bitterly that his own militia plundered all inhabitants indiscriminately, on the specious pretext that they were loyalists, or, to use their own expression, Tories, (Washington, *Works*, iv.).

The truth seems to be that the people of New Jersey were for the most part heartily sorry to see either army among them, which is neither more nor less than might have been expected from ordinary human nature.

It is probable, therefore, that Howe was wise in making no immediate attempt to recover the lost ground. Had Rahl obeyed his orders there would have been no mishap; had Von Donop, on the first news of his defeat, marched at once to recover Trenton, the mischief might have been repaired; but, as things fell out, the whole cause of the rebellion in America was saved by Washington's very bold and skilful action. The spirits of the revolutionary party revived; and an advance of five thousand militia upon Kingsbridge showed Howe that enemies were ready to swarm upon him from every side at the first sign of a British reverse. In a word, the moral effect of the past campaign was in great measure cancelled, and the whole of the work, excepting the capture of New York, required to be done again. (Cornwallis to Germaine, 20th January 1777).

The situation was extremely embarrassing. The operations had been based on the assistance of the loyalists; but the loyalists, as might have been anticipated, had not fulfilled the requirements expected of them. In New York, during the winter of 1776, certain gentlemen, notably Mr. Delancy and Mr. Skinner, offered to raise troops to the number of more than six thousand men; but only eleven hundred of them were ready for the campaign of 1777, while even of these but a small proportion were Americans. (Howe's *Observations on a Pamphlet*).

There were, however, great promises of solid help from Pennsylvania; and in that direction Howe had accordingly turned his thoughts. Any advance towards that quarter, however, necessarily implied the abandonment of the scheme for isolating New England; so Howe recalled three thousand of the six thousand troops in Rhode Island, though, for the advantage of the fleet, he still held Newport instead of evacuating the island altogether. Meanwhile he was absolutely in the dark as to the prospect of obtaining the reinforcements for which he had asked, and as to the general scheme of operations which might be favoured in Downing Street.

Very strange designs, from a military point of view, were under consideration in London during those first weeks of 1777; and, intricate though they may appear, they demand the reader's close attention. In the first place, Germaine's dislike towards Carleton had ripened into rancour, (*Correspondence of George III. and Lord North*, ii.), and the minister was urgent for the general's recall. On military grounds Carleton's failure to advance to Ticonderoga might have justified this step; but since Germaine's hatred arose less from military than from political and personal sources, the king was for retaining Carleton at Quebec, though he was disposed, with Germaine, to entrust any expedition from Canada to Burgoyne, as being an officer of greater enterprise.

★★★★★★

Chatham had sent young Lord Pitt, who had joined the 47th Foot, to Carleton in Canada. Carleton sent him home with despatches in September 1775, and on his arrival Chatham withdrew him from the service. As we shall see, the young man re-entered the army at a later period and rose, through no great merit of his own, to high command.

★★★★★★

For as yet nothing was known of Howe's misfortunes on the Delaware; and the latest letter from him before the Ministry was of the 30th of November, in which, as will be remembered, he had asked for thirty-five thousand men to cover his conquests and to pursue the plan of campaign against New England. This letter reached England on the 30th of December; and a few days earlier Burgoyne himself, as was the custom for officers who were also members of Parliament, had arrived to take up his winter quarters in England, bringing with him full details of the situation on the side of Canada.

Howe's request for fifteen thousand additional troops staggered Germaine, who declared it impossible to send more than at most eight thousand; but he answered Howe by calmly assuming that this reinforcement would raise his numbers to thirty-five thousand, or in other words that one is equal to two, and left the general to draw his own conclusions. (Germaine to Howe, 14th January 1777).

He then proceeded to compose a scheme for the invasion of New York from Canada, which Howe had never suggested and had formerly disapproved. On the 28th of February Burgoyne submitted a memorandum on this subject, working out in full and careful detail the advance from Crown Point to the Hudson, either by way of Lake George, or by South Bay and overland to Skenesborough. He pointed out clearly the difficulties of the latter route and the danger to any force that might adopt it, through the necessity of leaving a chain of posts to guard the line of communication with Canada. Concurrently he suggested that a diversion by a small body of British and Indians should be made from Oswego upon the Mohawk River, putting forward Colonel St. Leger for the command of this force; but he was careful to add that he doubted whether the strength of the army would justify even so small a detachment.

Finally, he pleaded the expediency of allowing to the general who should command the expedition to Canada the option of moving eastward from Ticonderoga to the Connecticut River, in order to co-operate with the force at Rhode Island; and above all, he urged that the general should have the latitude to embark his force and join Howe by sea, if he should think it prudent. None the less he decidedly advocated an advance from Ticonderoga as the most effectual measure for ending the war; and this was the true flaw in the scheme. Burgoyne indicated the purely military difficulties and risks of an advance to Albany from Canada by land so clearly, that a wise man might well have hesitated to incur them; but he omitted to take into account the supreme peril of a march in a very wild country through the midst of a hostile population, of which every man was a rifleman trained by sport in the forest.

Indeed, at the bottom of the whole design lay the fundamental error of reliance on the help of the loyalists; while no notice was taken of the fact that the New England militia, though unwilling to sacrifice themselves for other provinces, had shown themselves ready enough to fight in defence of their own homes. Again, viewed from a purely military standpoint, the convergence of three distinct columns upon Albany from three points, each over one hundred miles distant from it to north, south, and east, must necessarily give the Americans the advantage of operating on interior lines—of massing their forces, so to speak, at the centre of a circle, ready to overwhelm in detail the columns directed upon that centre, before they could effect their junction with one another. The virtual impossibility of communication between the convergent armies in those days made such movements the more hazardous; while the situation in America was widely different from that which had enabled Amherst and Wolfe to close in from Lake Ontario, Lake Champlain, and Quebec upon Montreal. Moreover, as has already been seen, it was more than doubtful whether any advance would be made from Rhode Island at all. Finally, it was quite certain that to attempt to direct the operations from London was simply to court disaster.

Either just before or simultaneously with the delivery of this memorandum, Howe's letters of the 20th of December 1776 and of the 20th of January 1777 reached Germaine, the former of them favouring offensive operations on the side of Pennsylvania, the latter reporting the complete change wrought in the situation by the disaster at Trenton. A letter from Lord Cornwallis of the same date in January pressed urgently for a reinforcement of at least fifteen thousand men. Germaine answered, (Germaine to Howe, 3rd March 1777), by approving an attack on Philadelphia; but simultaneously he reduced the promised reinforcement from eight thousand to three thousand men, and yet at the same time recommended a "warm diversion" on the coasts of Massachusetts and New Hampshire.

The obvious inference was that he had abandoned all idea of an expedition to the Hudson from Canada; but it was not so. On the 26th of March he sent instructions, insulting in their minuteness, to Carleton, bidding him furnish Burgoyne with seven thousand regular troops for the advance on Albany, and St. Leger with seven hundred men for the diversion on the Mohawk, according to the plan of Burgoyne's memorandum. But Germaine made an important divergence from Burgoyne's recommendations, in that he allowed no latitude to him to strike eastward to Connecticut, nor to Carleton to send the expeditionary force to New York by sea; and this although the ostensible purpose of the whole movement was the junction of Burgoyne's army with that of Howe.

This done, Germaine sent a copy of these instructions to Howe, but without a word to modify his former directions to that General. Meanwhile Howe had received Germaine's letter of the 14th of January, when, perceiving that he would obtain few or no reinforcements, he wrote at once to Carleton, April 5, warning him that he could do little to help the advance of the army from Canada, since he would probably be in Pennsylvania. He then enclosed a copy of this letter to Germaine, adding that all offensive operations from the side of Rhode

Island must now be abandoned, and that even those against Philadelphia must be conducted by sea.

This letter reached Germaine some weeks after the departure of Burgoyne for Quebec, so that it was too late to alter plans except by sending a messenger across the Atlantic; but Germaine, far from altering them, only repeated his assent to Howe's embarkation against Philadelphia, adding vaguely that he hoped that Howe's projects might be accomplished in time for him to cooperate with the army moving southward from Canada. (Germaine to Howe, 18th May 1777).

A few days later it seems that a despatch was drafted giving Howe positive orders to march up the Hudson, but that Germaine, finding it unready for signature when he called at the office on his way to the country, left it to take care of itself. (Fitzmaurice's *Life of Shelburne*). The natural result was that this despatch was never sent at all; so that Howe was left with directions to attack Philadelphia, and Burgoyne with positive and unconditional commands to advance to Albany and there to place himself under Howe's orders. The reader will, I fear, have grown impatient over this confusion of dates, orders, and letters; if so, he will the more readily understand the distraction of the generals. Never was there a finer example of the art of organising disaster.

The necessity for this preliminary explanation having led me in some measure to anticipate events, I shall for the present forsake Burgoyne, merely premising that he embarked on Lake Champlain on the 17th of June; and I shall return to follow the fortunes of Howe. Since he had first conceived the design of an attack on Philadelphia, Howe had been strengthened therein by the advice of the American General Lee who, while a prisoner at New York, had turned traitor, and had represented that both Maryland and Pennsylvania were full of loyalists, waiting only for the arrival of the king's army to rise against the party of revolution.

Meanwhile the preparations of the Americans to northward of New York demanded his immediate attention; for Washington, fully aware of the British plan to master the line of the Hudson, was amassing large quantities of stores at Peekskill and at Danbury, on the eastern and western confines of the Eastern Highlands. On the 22nd of March a small British detachment was sent to Peekskill, which, meeting with no resistance, destroyed such few stores as were found in that post. A month later, (April 25), a far stronger force of two thousand men was sent up to Danbury, which met with better success so far as regarded the destruction of supplies, but was intercepted on its return and subjected to much the same treatment as the expedition to Concord in 1775.

It was, in fact, compelled to fight for every yard of its retreat, and escaped only with the loss of two hundred men killed and wounded, (men of 4th, 15th, 23rd, 27th, 44th, and 64th were the troops engaged). Throughout the spring also petty warfare never ceased before the cantonments in New Jersey, with varying fortune, but never without loss, which, though fairly even on both sides, could not from the nature of the case but be more injurious to the British than to the Americans.

Yet Washington's difficulties were seldom greater than at this time; for his old army had as usual disappeared, and his new army was yet in the making. In the middle of March he had but three thousand men, two-thirds of them militia; for the various provinces seemed, as he said, to think it a matter of moonshine whether they furnished their contingents today, tomorrow, or a month later. He wrote on the 12th of April:

If Howe does not take advantage of our weak state, he is very unfit for his trust.

But Howe's only effort at an offensive movement had been foiled by a heavy fall of snow, while his information, doubtless carefully inspired by Washington himself, reported the strength of the Americans to be not less than eight thousand men. (Washington, *Works*, iv.).

On the 8th of May, Howe received Germaine's letter of the 3rd of March, approving of his project for invasion of Pennsylvania; and on the 24th there arrived drafts from England which raised his total strength to about twenty-seven thousand men. At about the same time Washington, having at length increased his numbers to eight thousand men, moved southward from Morristown and took up a strongly entrenched position at Middlebrook, about ten miles west of New Brunswick.

Then, to embarrass Howe still further, there arrived on the 5th of June the copy of Carleton's instructions for the Canadian campaign, without a word of direction to himself. However, he decided to follow his own plans, and having concentrated his force at New Brunswick, advanced on the 12th of June along the southern bank of the Rariton, in the hope of tempting Washington to forsake his stronghold at Middlebrook.

Failing in this he withdrew to Amboy, (June 19), and had completed his preparations for crossing to Staten Island for the embarkation of his troops, when he was made aware that two American divisions, numbering in all some four thousand men, had come down from the hills in pursuit of him, and that Washington with the main body had also moved eastward to Quibbletown so as to remain in touch with these detachments. Observing the success of his retrograde movement in luring Washington from the hills, Howe very warily laid his plans to force him to a general engagement.

After lying inactive for a while so as to lull his enemy into false confidence, he marched early on the morning of the 26th with eleven thousand men in two columns, to fall upon Washington's flank at Quibbletown. But the American General made haste to retreat with the main body on the first sound of firing, though Cornwallis engaged one of the detachments with considerable success, killing and wounding two hundred and fifty Americans and capturing three guns with trifling loss to himself.

★★★★★★

Mr. Fiske (*American Revolution*, i) puts forward Washington's movements of 12th-28th June as one of the most remarkable examples of his skill; assuming that Howe's object was to march to Philadelphia by land, and that Washington's manoeuvres prevented him. Howe's letters, however, prove conclusively that as far back as in April he had decided that he must sail to Philadelphia; and the little action of the 26th (of which Mr. Fiske says nothing) seems to me to show that Washington for once was off his guard. Moreover, Washington had as far back as the 9th of May convinced himself that Howe had no designs on the Delaware.—*Works*, iv.

★★★★★★

But so slight an advantage was not worth the loss of precious time. On the 28th Howe withdrew again to Amboy, and in the first days of July he embarked some fifteen thousand men, (Howe's *Narrative*, his exact numbers were 13, 799 rank and file, adding one-eighth for officers, sergeants, and drummers, total about 15,500 of all ranks), for the expedition to Philadelphia. He did not, however, at once set sail, waiting first to see Clinton, whom he intended to leave in command at New York with about nine thousand men, and desiring also to hear something of the army in Canada.

Clinton duly arrived on the 5th, and a letter from Burgoyne, reporting all to be well, reached him on the 15th; but foul winds delayed the fleet until the 23rd, when at last it got under way. Meanwhile

Washington remained in painful doubt and embarrassment. He had information of the plans of Burgoyne, which indeed had been long the talk of Montreal, but could not believe that they could be seriously entertained; and he came to the conclusion that Burgoyne's advance must be a mere feint, or that Howe would move up the Hudson to meet him.

★★★★★★

I had the surprise and mortification to find a paper handed about at Montreal, publishing the whole design of the campaign almost as accurately as if it had been copied from the Secretary of State's letter.—Burgoyne to Harvey, 19th May 1777

★★★★★★

For a full fortnight he marched and counter-marched, until on the 31st of July he learned that Howe's transports were off Delaware Bay. Still the idea of Howe's deserting Burgoyne remained inexplicable; and further news that Howe had again put to sea from the Delaware Capes made Washington tremble for Charleston. At last, on the 22nd of August, came definite intelligence that Howe was in Chesapeake Bay. Washington, (*Works*, iv.), wrote exultingly:

Now, let all New England turn out and crush Burgoyne.

The mystery of Howe's movements is very easily explained. He had made up his mind originally to land in the Delaware, (Howe to Germaine, 16th July 1777), so as to be nearer to New York and to Burgoyne, but gave up the attempt on the remonstrances of the naval officers, and sailed on to the Chesapeake. Whether the naval officers may have exaggerated the risks of disembarkation in the Delaware I cannot pretend to decide; but the fact remains that the voyage to the Chesapeake was disastrous, since contrary winds prolonged a passage of three hundred and fifty miles over no fewer than twenty-four days.

★★★★★★

Mr. Fiske regards Howe's defence of his action as "trumped up and worthless." It may be so; but he certainly intended to land in the Delaware when he started, and threw himself on the naval officers for his defence. The evidence of the naval officers is so highly technical that I am quite incompetent to weigh it; and I greatly doubt whether Mr. Fiske ever cast eye over it, or he might have been more cautious in giving his opinion.

★★★★★★

Then the army was disembarked at the head of Elk River, Aug. 25, unopposed indeed, but actually only thirteen miles west of Delaware Bay. By a strange irony it was not until he reached the Chesapeake that Howe received Germaine's letter, wherein was expressed the hope that his work in Pennsylvania would be finished in time to allow him to co-operate with Burgoyne's army.

Immediately on learning of Howe's true destination, (Aug. 22), Washington had marched southward to Wilmington; while Howe, having landed on the 25th of August, moved slowly and cautiously north-eastward till, on the 3rd of September, the advanced parties of both armies came into collision. Manoeuvring always to turn the right or northern flank of the Americans, Howe continued his march in two columns, driving Washington's scouts before him.

On the 9th the American army was concentrated in its selected position in rear of Brandywine Creek, barring the road to Philadelphia where it crossed that stream by Chad's Ford; and on the 10th the British encamped within four miles of it at Kennett Square. Washington, who had with him a force nominally of fifteen thousand men, but probably not exceeding twelve thousand effective soldiers, had as usual prepared his ground with skill. The passage of the Brandywine at Chad's Ford was commanded by batteries and entrenchments, while just below the ford the stream became a torrent, pent in between high, steep cliffs, which effectually forbade any attempt upon his left.

Behind these cliffs therefore he stationed his militia, taking command himself of the centre at Chad's Ford, while his right, under General Sullivan, was extended for some two miles up the stream in broken, wooded, and difficult country. A frontal attack was out of the question, for Howe's numbers were probably inferior to Washington's; and the only hope of success lay in the turning of the American right flank.

Howe's manoeuvres for this end prove how great was his ability when he chose to exert himself. Hitherto in all marches and movements since the disembarkation Cornwallis had commanded the right column and the German General Knyphausen the left, (see list following).

★★★★★★

Knyphausen's Column—

1st Brigade, 4th, 5th, 23rd, 49th, Major-General Vaughan.

2nd Brigade, 10th, 27th, 28th, 40th, Major-General Grant.

Four Hessian battalions. Three battalions Fraser's Highlanders.

Queen's Rangers (Irregulars). One squadron 16th Light Dragoons. Six 12-pounders, 4 howitzers, and battalion-guns.

Cornwallis's Column—
3rd Brigade, 15th, 33rd, 44th, 55th, Major-General Grey.

4th Brigade, 17th, 37th, 46th, 64th, Major-General Agnew.

Two battalions Guards, 2 battalions Light Infantry, 2 battalions Grenadiers, 2 squadrons 16th Light Dragoons.
Three battalions Hessians, mounted and dismounted *chasseurs*, four 12-pounders, and battalion-guns.

Note.—The English brigades are given as organised in May 1777, with corrections from Howe's subsequent returns, but they may have been changed.

★★★★★★

At daybreak of the 11th of September the whole army advanced from Kennett Square; but, while Knyphausen took the direct road eastward upon Chad's Ford, Cornwallis's column filed off in rear of it to the left, making for the upper forks of the Brandywine, some twelve miles to the north-east. After a march of seven miles, prolonged by continual skirmishes with Washington's light troops, Knyphausen reached the creek at ten o'clock, when he unlimbered his guns, deployed his columns, and opened a vigorous cannonade, as if about to force the passage of the ford.

Washington appears to have taken steps to ascertain the safety of his right flank; but his parties either failed to discover Cornwallis's turning movement or were checked in the attempt by Knyphausen's light troops. It was not until noon by Howe's report, not until two o'clock by American accounts, that he realised what was going forward; and by two o'clock Cornwallis had forded both branches of the upper Brandywine, and was marching upon Dilworth, to the right rear of the Americans. Washington's first impulse was to make a counter-attack with his whole force upon Knyphausen; and he actually sent two thousand troops across the creek for that purpose, which were driven back without difficulty.

★★★★★★

Most narratives give the impression that the counter-attack was only contemplated, but Major Andrè's *Journal* states that it was actually made and defeated. I take this opportunity of acknowledging my obligations to Lord Grey for kindly giving me access to this *Journal*, which is still in MS.

★★★★★★

Then contradictory reports from his right induced him to withdraw them, and fortunate it was for him that he did so. For Knyphausen was an able commander, his troops were far superior to Washington's in training and discipline, and by Howe's forethought he had been supplied with plenty of guns, so that he could certainly have held his own until Cornwallis came up in the enemy's rear and destroyed the Americans utterly. So unobservant were Washington's officers that he only by mere chance gained accurate information that Cornwallis's turning movement was not merely in progress but actually accomplished.

Washington then detached Sullivan's division farther to his right, where it took up a position on some heights above Birmingham Church, at right angles to the original line of battle. There, with his left close to the Brandywine, both flanks protected by dense forest, and his artillery advantageously posted, Sullivan hoped to check the British, at any rate for a time. At four o'clock, after a march of eighteen miles, Cornwallis appeared, and deployed with a front of eight battalions in first line, seven more in support, and four in reserve. (2 batts. each of Guards, Grenadiers, Light Infantry, and Hessians).

After a sharp struggle the Americans were driven back in confusion, and retired two miles to Dilworth before they rallied; but unfortunately two battalions of Guards, besides two others of the first line, became entangled in the woods during the pursuit and to all intent passed for a time out of action. In fact, as is usual in woodland fighting, the troops seem to have become much scattered, though the Light Infantry and Hessian Chasseurs were able by themselves to disperse Sullivan's rallied battalions; but meanwhile Washington with excellent judgment had ordered the two brigades of his reserve, under General Greene, to a strong position about a mile in rear of Dilworth, so as to cover Sullivan's retreat to Chester. Greene was here attacked by two battalions of Cornwallis's first line, and by a brigade of the second, but held his own skilfully and gallantly until nightfall, when he made his retreat in safety.

Meanwhile, as soon as Cornwallis's movements began to make themselves felt, Knyphausen attacked the position at Chad's Ford in earnest, and the Fourth and Fifth regiments crossing the ford quickly stormed the first entrenchment and captured four guns. The Guards then came blundering through the woods—accidentally but most opportunely—upon the uncovered flank of the American centre, and the retreat of the enemy became general; but darkness came on before Knyphausen and Cornwallis could join hands, and thus saved the Americans from absolute destruction. Sullivan's division had been utterly routed; and though the rest of Washington's army seems to have retired for a time in tolerable order, the road to Chester soon became a scene of the greatest confusion. (Chastellux, i.).

But Cornwallis's troops after such a bout of hard marching and hard fighting were in no condition to pursue, and the ground was not such as to give any opportunity for cavalry; so Washington escaped with an army shaken indeed but not demoralised. Howe's losses did not exceed five hundred and seventy-seven killed and wounded, nearly all of whom were British; the loss of the Americans exceeded one thousand, four hundred prisoners having been taken, besides eleven guns.

★★★★★★

British 8 officers and 73 men killed; 45 officers and 411 men wounded. Hessians 8 men killed; 4 officers and 28 men wounded. Mr. Fiske (*American Revolution*, i.) says that, according to British rolls captured at Germantown, the British loss far exceeded the American. What these rolls may have been I do not know, nor how they fell into American hands; but I prefer the evidence of Howe's casualty-list to that of these apocryphal rolls.

★★★★★★

Though far from decisive, Brandywine was a skilful action, very creditable to Howe considering that he had little or no superiority of numbers. There has always been a conspiracy to belittle Howe, but, whatever his failings, he could fight a battle and handle his troops on occasion with uncommon ability.

The British bivouacked on the battlefield; and on the two following days detachments were pushed forward to Ashtown on the road to Chester, to Concord and to Wilmington, in which last, on its evacuation by the Americans, Howe on the 14th established his hospital. On the 16th, since the Schuylkill was impassable by the direct route, the whole army moved north-eastward towards Goshen, whither Washington was himself on march by way of Derby, with intent to offer battle. But a general action was prevented by a deluge of rain, and the British pursued their advance eastward by the Lancaster road, the Americans retiring rapidly before them.

Washington now passed the Schuylkill, distributing his troops about the fords so as to delay Howe's passage for as long as possible, and at the same time detaching a force under General Wayne to harass Howe's left flank and rear. Howe promptly sent Major-general Grey with three battalions, (2nd battalion Light Infantry, 42nd and 44th regiments), to deal with Wayne, which that officer very effectually did. Removing the flints from every musket in his force so that by no possibility could a shot be fired, Grey fell upon Wayne's camp at night by surprise, killing and wounding three hundred of his men and capturing one hundred more, with the loss of no more than eight British killed and wounded. From that day forward Grey was known by the name of "No-flint."

On the 21st Howe's whole force encamped on the Schuylkill from Flatland Ford to French Creek, and on the next day Howe, having by a variety of perplexing manoeuvres, (Washington's own expression, *Works*, v.), lured Washington higher up the river, crossed it unopposed at Flatland Ford, and captured six guns in one of the American redoubts. There was nothing now to bar the entry of the British into Philadelphia, which was accordingly occupied on the 25th. In one respect the invasion of Pennsylvania seemed to justify itself, for the people were sufficiently well affected to the British to give intelligence to Howe and to withhold it from Washington, (*ibid*).

It remained now to remove three lines of heavy *chevaux de frise*, which had been sunk by the Americans to obstruct the navigation of the Delaware, and to open the river to the British fleet. For this purpose it was necessary first to capture a fort on Mud Island, near the Pennsylvanian shore, and a redoubt and entrenchment called Red Bank, together with a smaller stronghold at Billingsport, on the opposite shore; these works having been constructed to cover the sunken obstacles with their cannon. Accordingly, on the 29th three battalions were sent across to Billingsport, which being abandoned by the Americans was at once dismantled; but, as the navigation of the river was still blocked, Howe was obliged further to detach three thousand men to escort his supplies overland from the Chesapeake, thus reducing his main body to fewer than nine thousand men.

Of these the greater part were encamped at Germantown, then a long, straggling village of widely detached houses extending for some two miles along the road from Philadelphia northward to Skippack Creek, where Washington was encamped. At about the middle of the village was a four-cross-way, formed by the junction of the Limekiln Road from the north-east and the Old School Lane from the west with

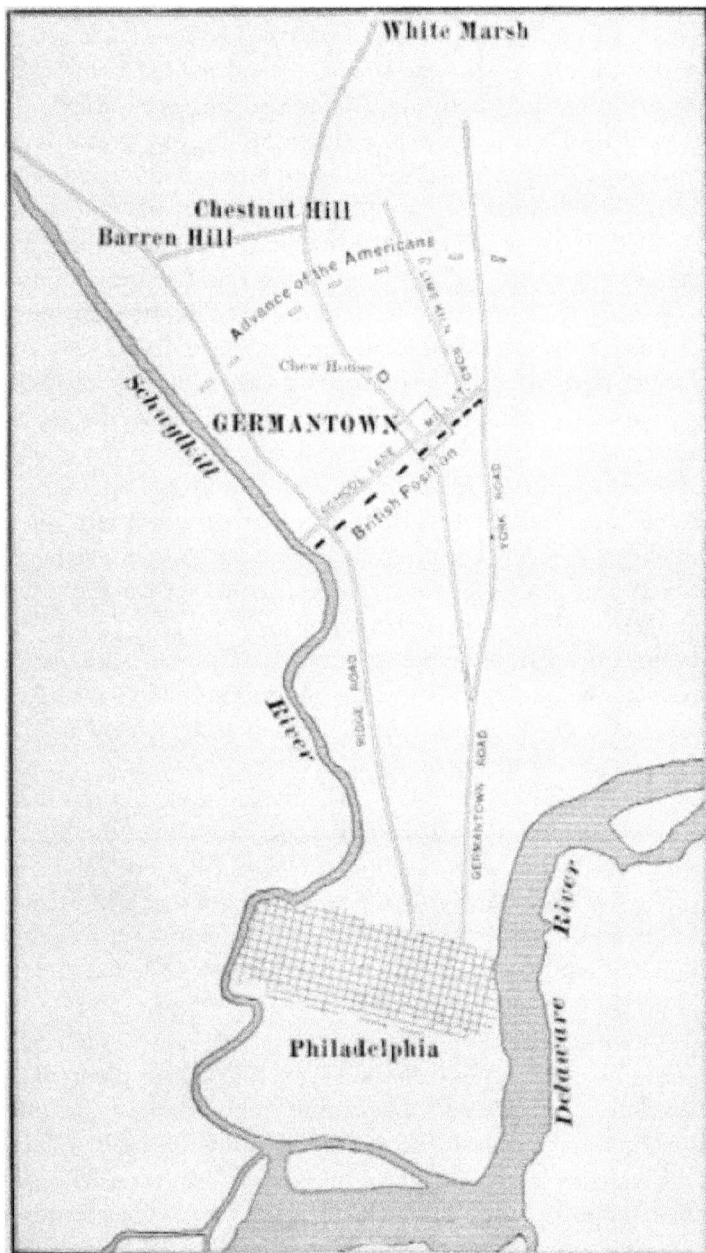

White Marsh

Chestnut Hill

Barren Hill

Advance of the Americans

Schuylkill

Chew House

GERMANTOWN

SCHOOL LANE

British Position

YORK ROAD

RIDGE ROAD

River

GERMANTOWN ROAD

Delaware River

Philadelphia

MAP OF THE BATTLE OF GERMANTOWN

the main road; and it was astride of this main road, in rear of the four-cross-way, that the British troops were encamped, with detached posts in front and flanks. Yet another road, called the Old York Road, ran from the north-east, parallel with the Limekiln Road and to southward of it, falling into the main road two miles in rear of the encampment.

Observing the detachments made by Howe, and having himself reinforcements which raised his strength to eight thousand regular troops and four thousand militia, Washington determined to attempt the surprise of the camp at Germantown. To this end he marched on the evening of the 3rd of October, directing five brigades, (these brigades were of course very weak, not exceeding 1000 bayonets at most), under General Sullivan down the main road upon Howe's centre and left, two brigades of militia along the Old School Lane to make a feint attack on his left flank, three brigades down the Limekiln Road to fall upon his right flank, and two more down the Old York Road to sweep round upon his right rear; these last five brigades being under command of General Greene. Howe had full information of the intended attack, but resolved to await it without entrenching his position, only pushing his advanced posts rather farther forward and enjoining special vigilance on his patrols.

At three o'clock in the morning the American advance was duly reported by the outposts, and the British troops stood to arms. About sunrise, however, there came on a dense fog, which involved the whole engagement in perplexity and confusion. At four o'clock Sullivan's division opened the attack on the main road, and was met by a vigorous resistance from a battalion of Light Infantry and from the Fortieth Foot, which were in advance. Fighting at every step the two battalions withdrew slowly to a house belonging to a Mr. Chew, a little to northward of the village, when Colonel Musgrave occupied the building with six companies of the Fortieth, while the Light Infantry fell back on the main body.

Musgrave at once opened so sharp a fire that Sullivan's whole line was for some minutes stopped; and Howe, looking for the most serious attack to fall on his left flank, reinforced his troops in that quarter so as to hold the militia at bay. But it was really on the British right that the danger was greatest. There the picquets had been driven back on their supports, though these had retired very steadily, contesting every yard of ground; and Greene was pushing his advance gradually forward, when the sound of tremendous firing about Chew's house led him to believe that a general action had begun. In truth, Washing-

BATTLE OF GERMANTOWN

ton's attack on the centre had been abruptly checked by the little band of the Fortieth in the house, who held on stoutly to their stronghold in utter contempt of the American artillery. Washington therefore decided to mask the house and to continue his advance; but, the ground being strongly enclosed, this was a matter of some difficulty.

The result was that Sullivan's division deployed prematurely on both sides of the road, and not, as had been prearranged, on the west side only. Greene, knowing nothing of this and unable to see anything in the fog, also deployed, as his orders bade him, with his right resting on the main road. Wholly unconscious that he was thus overlapping Sullivan's left, he then opened his attack with vigour, guided only by the flashes of the musketry through the mist; and thus it came about that while Sullivan's left brigade was hotly engaged with the British in front, it found itself harried by bullets from Greene's brigade in rear.

Very pardonably the unlucky battalions were smitten with panic, and the disorder quickly spread to the whole of the American right, where it was increased by the action of General Grey, who, always calm and cool-headed, had wheeled up a brigade from the extreme British left upon Sullivan's right flank. Almost simultaneously General Grant brought up the Fifth and Fifty-Fifth from the British right centre upon Sullivan's left flank, and completed his discomfiture.

This movement was the more important since the American brigades on the Old York Road had forced back the Guards, Twenty-Fifth, and Twenty-Seventh from their camp to the village, where they held them hard pressed, capturing even several prisoners. By Grant's advance these brigades of the extreme American left were isolated, in spite of their success; and Grey, withdrawing to the assistance of the Guards the bulk of the force which had been opposed to the militia on Howe's left flank, speedily restored the balance of the scale in that quarter. Cornwallis too now hurried to the sound of the cannon with two more battalions from Philadelphia, and the Americans were soon in full retreat, though their left wing was recalled too late to save one regiment from being cut off. Thereby not only were the whole of the British prisoners recaptured, but four hundred Americans were taken in their stead.

The action lasted for two hours and a half, and was sharply fought throughout. The loss of Howe's army was five hundred and seventeen killed and wounded, and fourteen prisoners; that of the Americans was six hundred and seventy-three killed and wounded, and four hundred prisoners.

★★★★★★

British—4 officers and 66 men killed; 27 officers, 396 men wounded; 14 missing. Hessians—1 officer and 23 men wounded. Mr. Fiske (*American Revolution,* i.) says that the Americans captured several guns. It may be so; but Howe says nothing of it, nor Washington, nor Stedman in his *History of the American War,* nor Johnson in his *Life of Greene.* Washington says, indeed, that he is uncertain as to the fate of one of his own guns, which though dismounted was saved; but this is not quite the same as several British guns captured.

★★★★★★

The result was a great mortification to Washington, who declared that the Americans retreated in the moment of victory; but the truth is that the plan of attack was too intricate for inexperienced officers and imperfectly disciplined troops, while the fog was an accident wholly to the advantage of the better disciplined army. In effect the resolute defence of a single well-built house was sufficient to upset the whole of Washington's combinations; while, even though Sullivan's advance was thus delayed by Musgrave's handful of men, Greene's right brigade arrived so late in the field that Sullivan's division was already deployed in front of it. Moreover, the feint attack of the militia was so feeble that Grey was able to use the battalions of the left wing as if they had been the reserve rather than part of the fighting line.

Lastly, Washington's plans were not furthered by the fact that many of his officers and men had been stimulating their valour at the expense of their understanding and were exceedingly drunk. (Andrè's *Journal,* which is corroborated by Mr. Fiske's account). Howe was not unreasonably blamed for not entrenching himself, but, as he frankly confessed, he did not look for so vigorous an onslaught after such a success as Brandywine. He therefore made his dispositions to invite attack, relying on the superiority of his troops; and it is fair to add that the result fully justified his confidence.

On the 8th of October Lord Howe's fleet anchored in the Delaware below Newcastle, and General Howe withdrew his army to Philadelphia to cover the operations for opening the navigation of the river. A fortnight later an assault was delivered, (Oct. 22nd), upon the fort at Red Bank by a party of Hessians under Von Donop, but was beaten off, in spite of the gallantry of the assailants, with very heavy loss to them, (127 killed, 105 wounded and prisoners), and at trifling cost to the defenders. Howe had already sent to Clinton for five additional battalions from New York; but it was not until the 15th of November, and after immense labour, that the Americans were driven by the British batteries from Mud Island and Red Bank, and that the navigation of the Delaware was opened for the supply of the army.

Howe then marched out, (Dec. 4th), towards Washington who was entrenched in a strong position at Whitemarsh, fourteen miles from Philadelphia, but the American general was too wary to be drawn into an engagement; and after a skirmish or two Howe withdrew to winter quarters, (Oct. 22nd), in Philadelphia. Already he had written to Germaine, (Howe to Germaine, 22nd October 1777), that without ten thousand additional troops it was hopeless to think of ending the war in the next campaign, and that, since his former requests for reinforcements had been disregarded, he begged to resign his command. Not yet did he know what had happened just five days before at Saratoga.

CHAPTER 5

Saratoga

On the 6th of May, as has already been told, Burgoyne arrived at Quebec with Germaine's instructions to Carleton, prescribing the exact numbers and the precise units which were to be employed in the projected expedition. Deeply hurt that the command of this enterprise should be taken out of his hands, Carleton at once sent his resignation to England, but meanwhile exerted himself loyally to give all possible assistance to Burgoyne. The number of regular troops allotted to the service was seven thousand two hundred and thirteen, to which it was designed to add two thousand Canadian levies and a large body of Indians. As a vast deal of false sentiment and a still larger allowance of false statement has been lavished over this employment of Indians by the British, it is as well to mention that the British hesitated to use them until the Americans set the example in 1775, (Gage to the Secretary of State, 12th June 1775. And see Adolphus, *History of England*, ii.).

Nor are the Americans the least blameworthy in this respect, since any attempt to exclude the Indians from a share in the war was, in the words of an excellent judge, (Mr. Pownall, ex-Governor of Massachusetts), dangerous, delusive nonsense. The Indians were ready enough to join the British, but the Canadians hung back. Only one hundred and fifty would serve as soldiers, while even for employment in the matter of transport they were backward and unwilling. Nevertheless, by sheer energy and perseverance Carleton and Burgoyne pushed the preparations forward; and at length, despite bad weather, foul winds, and sundry other impediments, the army assembled on the 20th of June at Cumberland Point on Lake Champlain. A short time before this Colonel St. Leger had also been despatched with a small force of light troops and of Indians to make a diversion on the Mohawk.

Halting for three days at Crown Point to establish magazines, Burgoyne marched from thence by land, and on the 1st of July came before Ticonderoga. The American garrison of the place numbered three thousand men under General St. Clair, and occupied not only Ticonderoga on the western shore but a hill called Mount Independence on the eastern shore, of which the sides had been strengthened by entrenchments and batteries, and the summit crowned by a star-fort. The two fortresses were connected by a bridge, constructed with infinite labour and protected on the northern side by a boom. Advancing with great caution, Burgoyne wound his troops round the whole position and began to throw up trenches so as to invest it completely; but an eminence called Sugar Hill had caught the eye of an old artilleryman, Major-General Phillips, who, finding that it commanded the whole of the enemy's works, lost no time in erecting a battery on the summit. The Americans, seeing the hopelessness of the position, embarked such stores as they could in their *bateaux*, and, since communication with Lake George was cut off, sent them up the South River to Skenesborough, while the army retired by way of Castleton upon the same point.

Brigadier Fraser, anticipating Burgoyne's orders, at once started in pursuit with his own brigade of Light Infantry and Grenadiers by land, while Burgoyne set about forcing the boom so as to carry on the chase by water. By nine o'clock on the morning of the 6th July a passage had been broken through the boom, when the British gunboats hurried forward with such speed that they overtook the enemy's rear and destroyed a number of galleys and *bateaux*. Fraser, meanwhile, had pushed on with all possible haste from four in the morning until one in the afternoon, when he halted to await General Riedesel, who was advancing to his support. He then started again, bivouacked for the night within three miles of the enemy, renewed his march at July 7. three o'clock next morning, and in two hours came upon the American picquets, which fired on him and instantly retired.

Anxious above all things to delay the American retreat, Fraser at once attacked, though with no more than eight hundred and fifty men against nearly, if not quite, twice that number. The Americans made a very fine fight, being picked troops and skilled marksmen under a most gallant leader, Colonel Francis. They had further every advantage of position, the forest being so thick that the British could not advance to the attack in regular order; but none the less the redcoats, for all their rigid training, faced the new conditions with perfect readiness and resource. For two hours the unequal contest went on, until Riedesel's division at last came up and decided the action in Fraser's favour.

The Americans left Colonel Francis and over two hundred men dead upon the field, and about the same number prisoners in Fraser's hands. The British loss did not exceed one hundred and forty killed and wounded, nor would the figure have been so high but for an unfortunate occurrence. In the course of the action about sixty Americans approached two companies of grenadiers with rifles clubbed in token of surrender, and were allowed to come within ten yards unharmed; when they suddenly stopped, fired a volley, disabling many of the grenadiers, and ran away to the shelter of the forest. (Anbury, *Travels in America*, i.).

Such methods of warfare, though not unusual among half-disciplined men who have lost touch with civilisation during long life in a wild country, never fail to rouse bitter indignation among regular troops. Burgoyne now detached the Ninth Foot to Fort Anna, some fifteen miles south of Skenesborough, to intercept any fugitives that might be making their way, by water up Wood Creek.

The regiment was heavily attacked on its way, July 9th, but held its own against very superior numbers until reinforced; and the Americans in Fort Anna then set fire to it and retreated. Their main body also retired southward to Fort Edward on the Hudson, using their axes skilfully as they went, so as to drop a tree at every few yards along the road.

Meanwhile, on the 10th, Burgoyne's whole force assembled at Skenesborough, where the men were employed for many days in clearing the track southward, and in opening up the communications by Lake George and Wood Creek for transport of artillery and stores. Some hundreds of loyalists joined Burgoyne at this time, both armed and unarmed, with offers of service; but to southward the revolutionary committees threatened death to all who would not remove their cattle and stores and take up arms against the British.

Considering the immense difficulties of the road through the forest, and the fact that no fewer than forty bridges, some of them of great length, needed to be constructed, it was no small feat that Burgoyne should have reached Fort Edward on the 30th of July, having accomplished the twenty miles from Skenesborough in exactly twenty days. Slow though his progress was, he only narrowly missed intercepting the American garrison of Fort George, which, finding its

INDIAN MASSACRE

rear threatened, had fallen back from the head of Lake George to join the main body under General Schuyler.

Meanwhile Schuyler with the soundest judgment withdrew his army still farther southward to Stillwater, some thirty miles above Albany; Burgoyne being again detained at Fort Edward by the extreme difficulty of transporting his supplies and *bateaux* overland to the Hudson. The number of his baggage-animals was inadequate to his needs, the Canadian contractors having failed to fulfil their engagements; and he dared not advance without plenty of artillery against an enemy who in a few hours could throw up wooden forts and abatis that defied any but heavy metal.

Had any latitude of enterprise been permitted to him he would probably have turned eastward into New England; but as matters stood he was committed by positive orders to operations in which rapidity of movement, though essential to success, was impossible. St. Leger he knew to be moving on the Mohawk, and, if any good was to come of the diversion, it was of the greatest importance that his own advance should correspond with St. Leger's. Then trouble sprang up with the Indians, owing to Burgoyne's stringent regulations against pillage and murder, and several of them left the camp in a rage. Every cause conspired to increase the general's anxiety, for nothing was more certain than that the enemy's numbers were augmenting in his front and flank.

The New Englanders had been roused to madness by an outrage of the Indians, and every day's delay meant accession of strength to the Americans. His army, it is true, was in grand condition and spirits, his operations so far had been brilliantly successful, and he had captured considerably over one hundred guns; but advance without provisions he could not. The problem of supply seemed indeed insoluble. Every day showed him more clearly the hopelessness of attempting with the transport at his command to form magazines; while his weakness in numbers forbade him to establish posts or to furnish escorts for convoys between the line of his advance and Lake George.

The only alternative was to endeavour to supply himself at the enemy's expense. A magazine had been established by the New England militia at Bennington, about thirty miles south-east of Fort Edward, where many hundred horses had been collected, besides ample stores of food and ammunition. Accordingly, on the 13th of August, a motley detachment of about five hundred men was placed under the orders of Colonel Baum, a very competent German officer, for the surprise of

Bennington, (150 Brunswick dismounted dragoons, 50 picked British marksmen, 150 Provincial soldiers, 56 Provincial and Canadian Volunteers, 80 Indians. Mr. Fiske (i. 283) describes Baum's force as consisting entirely of German veterans; but the above is Burgoyne's list, and I conceive that Burgoyne was in a position to know).

The force had been made thus small because Major Skene, a loyalist who acted as its guide, had assured Burgoyne that the country swarmed with men who wished to take up arms for the King. At the same time, to make a diversion, the army moved down the east bank of the Hudson, an advanced corps crossing the river to Saratoga, and a detachment taking post at Battenkill, five miles above Saratoga, on the direct road to Bennington. Baum was soon aware that his march had been discovered and that the surprise of Bennington was impracticable; but he pushed on to within four miles of it, at which point he was met by a party of professed loyalists, who cheerfully took the oath of allegiance and invited him to proceed farther. Presently, however, he found himself opposed by a strong force of militia, and was obliged to take up a strong defensive position as his bivouac for the night.

On the next morning, (August 16th), about five hundred militia attacked him in front, while five hundred men in rustic attire, many of whom had sworn allegiance on the previous day, came round upon his rear. The disparity of numbers added to the treachery was too much for Baum's party, with its nucleus of only three hundred regular troops. The Indians fled at the first fire, but the little handful of soldiers fought gallantly until, their ammunition failing, they were overpowered, when all who were not killed or captured ran away into the forest.

The American militia had just dispersed to the plunder of Baum's camp when a party of five hundred Germans with two guns, under Colonel Breyman, appeared on the scene. These had been despatched to the assistance of Baum, but for some reason had consumed sixteen hours in marching twenty-four miles. Most fortunately, however, for the Americans, a reinforcement of five hundred additional militia had just come up, which checked Breyman's advance. The same tactics were then repeated against him as against Baum, with the same result. The Germans fought bravely and held their own until their ammunition was expended, when all but sixty or seventy men were captured. Thus disastrously ended the attempt upon Bennington, with a loss to Burgoyne of about five hundred men and four guns.

★★★★★★

Mr. Fiske gives the British loss in the two engagements at 207 killed and wounded and 700 prisoners, making a total in excess of the entire force engaged. He admits also the escape of 60 men. Burgoyne's official list of casualties is undiscoverable. He reckoned his losses in the two actions at about 430 men, but added that missing men were dropping in daily.

★★★★★★

The blow was a heavy one to the general, for, had the enterprise been successful, he had hoped to push an advanced corps forward to Stillwater, and thus to ensure his junction on the Mohawk with St. Leger's column. Meanwhile his news of that force was not reassuring, and was soon to be disquieting. St. Leger, in obedience to his instructions, had landed about the middle of July at Oswego, where he had been joined by two small parties of loyalists and by some Indians, which raised his total strength to seventeen hundred men. But of these not six hundred were regular troops, and of the six hundred not one-half were British. His first task was to capture Fort Stanwix and so to open to himself the navigation of the Mohawk; and accordingly, after a cautious march through the forest, he on the 3rd of August invested the fort, which was garrisoned by six hundred men.

On the 5th, hearing that eight hundred American militia had arrived within twelve miles of him for the relief of the fort, St. Leger determined to sally out and attack them, and, since he could spare no more than his Indians and eighty white men for the service, to try the success of an ambuscade in a ravine on the line of the enemy's march. It had been arranged that the Indians should not show themselves on the flanks and rear until the white men should have engaged the Americans in front; but the savages were hurried by their impatience into a premature attack, with the result that the enemy's rearguard was not entrapped, but was able to retreat. The main body of the Americans though surrounded made a most gallant fight, and succeeded at length in driving off the Indians, but with such heavy loss to themselves that they were obliged to abandon all hope of raising the siege.

During the engagement the garrison of the fort seized the moment to make a sortie, and succeeded in pillaging part of the camp, including that of the Indians.

★★★★★★

Mr. Fiske mentions that five British standards were captured. I know not what they can have been, since but 200 men of the 8th and 34th were with St. Leger, and such detachments were

117

not likely to have taken the colours with them.

★★★★★★

This misfortune, added to the loss of many of their bravest warriors, roused deep discontent among the savages. The siege also went forward but slowly, for St. Leger's guns were too light to make any impression upon the fort, so that he was compelled to proceed by regular approaches.

Meanwhile Benedict Arnold had collected twelve hundred volunteers from Massachusetts and was advancing up the Mohawk from Albany. Finding that he made little progress, he very artfully contrived to convey reports to St. Leger's camp that Burgoyne's army had been cut to pieces, and that an overwhelming force was on its way to relieve Fort Stanwix. St. Leger was not to be deceived, but the Indians were greatly discouraged, and presently broke into open mutiny.

Finally a large party of them deserted, and the rest threatened to do the like unless St. Leger should retreat; and with practically no other force at his disposal, St. Leger was obliged to comply. But now the savages laid violent hands on the liquor, and turned the camp into a pandemonium. It was only with immense difficulty that St. Leger was able to protect his boats and withdraw his regular troops, abandoning his camp and the whole of his artillery. No blame can be attached to him for his failure, which was due entirely to the insufficiency of the force and of the guns allotted to him.

Thus the diversion on the Mohawk had gone to wreck; and even apart from this Burgoyne was already in a very critical situation, he wrote:

> Wherever the king's forces point, militia to the number of three or four thousand assemble in a few hours. . . . Had I a latitude in my orders, I should think it my duty to wait in this position near Saratoga, or perhaps as far back as Fort Edward, where my communication with Lake George could be perfectly secure until some event happened to assist my movement forward.

His force too was so seriously reduced by casualties and by the detachment of a garrison for Ticonderoga, that his regular troops amounted to little more than five thousand men; but, since his instructions were imperative, he decided to continue his advance after collecting thirty days' provisions, a task which, with his limited resources of transport, occupied him until the 13th of September.

On that and the following days he threw his whole army across to the western bank of the Hudson by a bridge of rafts, and encamped on the heights and plain of Saratoga. There heavy rain delayed him until the 19th, when he resumed his march by the road along the river upon the American encampment near Stillwater.

The enemy had taken up a strong position on Bemis Heights, which had been skilfully entrenched and fortified by a Polish engineer, later to become famous, named Kosciusko. Burgoyne, however, was a better soldier than the Pole. He remarked very quickly that there was a hill on the American left which commanded the whole of their position, but which was still unoccupied. Could he but seize this hill by a vigorous attack, he could haul his heavy guns to the summit and rake the American trenches from end to end. For this object accordingly he laid his plans.

The army was to advance in three columns; the left column under General Riedesel, with General Phillips in charge of the artillery, being appointed to follow the road by the river and engage the American right; the centre column, under Burgoyne himself, to advance parallel with Riedesel's upon the enemy's left centre; and the right column under General Fraser, to make a wide detour and, on regaining touch with Burgoyne's, to fall upon their left flank. Since the whole of the ground was clothed with dense forest, the discharge of three heavy guns was to be the signal to Riedesel that Fraser and Burgoyne had joined hands and that the attack should begin.

The officer in command of the Americans at this time was Horatio Gates, who had recently been appointed in place of the far more capable General Schuyler; but he had with him a force of fourteen thousand men, and at least one very able subordinate in the person of Benedict Arnold. Burgoyne's march was quickly perceived by the American scouts, and Arnold, who had at once divined the British general's intentions, was anxious to move forward with the whole army and attack him on the march; but it was long before Gates, a thoroughly incompetent officer, could be induced to give Arnold even a detachment.

The idea of Gates was to await attack within his entrenchments, he being too slow-witted to perceive that Burgoyne could turn them. Meanwhile the British columns steadily pursued their advance, Burgoyne reaching his station first and deploying his four battalions, the Ninth, Twenty-First, Sixty-Second, and Twentieth, in due order of precedence from right to left. The whole four of them mustered fewer than eleven hundred men, (Burgoyne's *Narrative*), but they were no

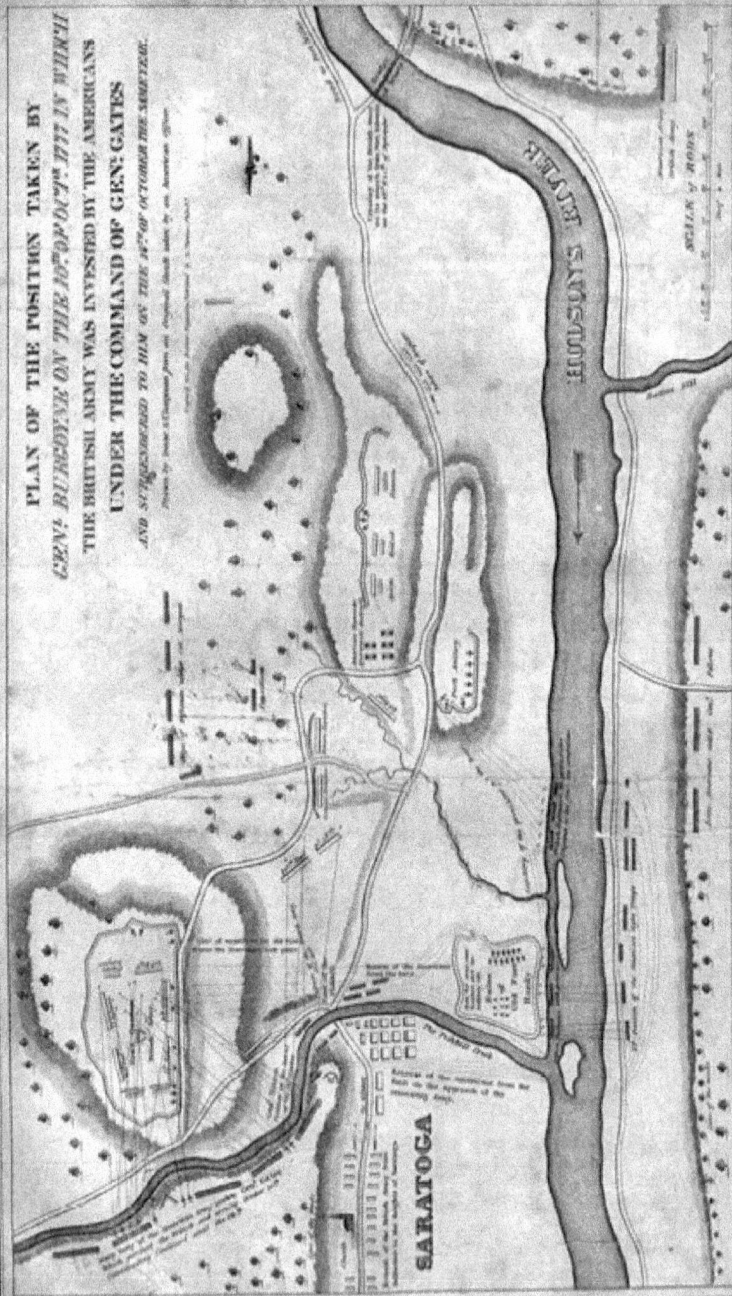

PLAN OF THE POSITION TAKEN BY
GENL. BURGOYNE ON THE 10TH SEP/OCTR. 1777 IN WHICH
THE BRITISH ARMY WAS INVESTED BY THE AMERICANS
UNDER THE COMMAND OF GENL. GATES

AND SURRENDERED TO HIM ON THE 17TH OF OCTOBER THE SAME YEAR.

HUDSON RIVER

SARATOGA

SCALE OF MILES

ordinary soldiers.

Then Fraser appeared punctually with the Grenadiers, Light Infantry, and Twenty-Fourth Foot, and took up a good position on some heights to Burgoyne's right. Between one and two o'clock the signal-guns roared out their message to Riedesel; and after another hour of march through the forest the attack began.

The action opened with the driving of an American picquet from a house, known as Freeman's Farm, in a cleared space immediately before Burgoyne's front. About three o'clock Arnold, who had at last succeeded in obtaining from Gates three thousand men, including a famous corps of marksmen, came upon the scene and attempted first to turn Burgoyne's right, but was beaten back with heavy loss by Fraser's brigade, whose position he had not yet discovered.

Then quickly marking the weak point of the British line, Arnold turned all his strength upon Burgoyne's brigade in the centre, now reduced to the Twentieth, Sixty-Second, and Twenty-First only, for the Ninth were held back in reserve. Never were troops more hardly tried, nor met their trial more grandly than these three noble battalions, with the forty-eight artillerymen who worked their four guns by their side. Attack after attack of far superior numbers was launched upon them without intermission for four hours; and it was only occasionally that Fraser's brigade could leave its station on the heights to relieve them, lest so valuable a position on the way to the coveted hill should be lost.

Again and again the three battalions charged with the bayonet, but Arnold could always bring forward fresh troops to replace those who had fallen, while the American sharpshooters, perched aloft in the trees, picked off officer after officer with their rifles. At length support came to them from the left. General Phillips arrived first with four guns and took personal command of the Twentieth, as befitted a veteran of Minden; while a little later Riedesel came up on Arnold's flank and forced him to abandon his attack. Darkness closed the action, which was most gallantly fought on both sides. Had Gates sent to Arnold the reinforcements for which he asked, Arnold must certainly have broken the British centre, which, even as things were, could barely hold its own.

The three devoted battalions suffered terribly, losing three hundred and fifty killed and wounded out of a strength of little more than eight hundred. The Sixty-Second had scarcely sixty men standing at the close of the combat, while the gallant little detachment of artillery, which had served its guns to the very end, lost all its officers and thirty-six out of forty-eight men. The total loss of the British troops was over five hundred, or little less than one-third of the whole force engaged; that of the Germans seems to have been about fifty men.

******

It is extremely difficult to ascertain the number of men engaged. On the 3rd of September the British fit for duty were 2935; the Germans on the 1st of September numbered 1741; the artillery cannot be reckoned at more than 400. The Provincials, Volunteers, etc., numbered 830 on the 1st of July, but had been since greatly reduced by desertion. It seems therefore that when he crossed the Hudson, Burgoyne's force cannot have exceeded 5000 regular troops and 700 irregulars fit for duty; and there had been many casualties from skirmishes and "sniping" before the action. Until Riedesel came up, I think it unlikely that Burgoyne had above 1800 troops engaged or above 2200 on the field. With Riedesel's troops added, the numbers would hardly have exceeded 3000. See Evidence, etc., in Burgoyne's *Narrative*.

******

That night the British bivouacked on the ground, only a few hundred yards in extent, which they had won, and on the next day they moved up almost to within cannon-shot of the enemy, fortifying their right and extending their left so as to cover their stores and *bateaux*. Gates likewise threw up new entrenchments to guard his left. But the Americans had already bethought them of sending a force in rear of Burgoyne to cut off his supplies, and on the 18th of September these troops surprised and took the British flotilla at the head of Lake George, together with three companies of the Fifty-Third. Emboldened by this success, the Americans pushed on to the siege of Ticonderoga, which, however, they quickly abandoned.

A further attack which they essayed upon an island on the lake was brilliantly repulsed by two companies of the Forty-Seventh, who, following up their victory, retook the whole of their cannon and some of the shipping previously captured by the enemy. The news of the mishap to the flotilla might well have prompted Burgoyne to retreat, had not intelligence reached him on the very same day that General Clinton was about to undertake a diversion in his favour. He waited therefore behind his entrenchments in hope of the promised relief.

Nor was Clinton worse than his word. Towards the end of September he had received a body of about three thousand recruits, which enabled him at last to take the offensive on a small scale without endangering the safety of New York. The great object of the British was to open the navigation of the Hudson to the north, which was still barred about three miles above Peekskill by a boom, covered by two strong fortifications named Forts Clinton and Montgomery, on the western bank of the river.

At Verplanks Point, some four miles below Fort Clinton and on the eastern bank, stood a weak breastwork with two guns, which had been erected by the Americans to cover the landing-place of the stores for their troops at Peekskill. Upon this work at Verplanks Clinton suddenly descended with three thousand men, drove out the garrison and captured the guns. He then bivouacked on the Point for the night; whereupon the American General Putnam, who commanded at Peekskill, at once concluded that Clinton designed to attack the passes of the Eastern Highlands, and collecting two thousand men from the posts on the river hurried off to occupy them.

This was precisely what Clinton wanted. At dawn of the following day he passed two thousand men over the river to Stony Point, where they separated into two columns for simultaneous attack on Forts Clinton and Montgomery. The only road in that steep and rugged country was so narrow as to admit but three men abreast, and so circuitous and difficult that the march of twelve miles from Stony Point was not accomplished until near sunset. Then both attacks were delivered simultaneously with great precision. Fort Montgomery being of no great strength was carried, (the attacking force consisted of. the 52nd, 57th, and detachments of Provincial corps, in all 900 men), with little difficulty or loss, though most of the garrison made their escape.

Fort Clinton was a more serious matter, the only possible approach to it lying over a space, about four hundred yards square, between a lake and the cliffs overhanging the river. The whole of this patch of ground was blocked by abatis and swept by the fire of ten guns from a central battery and two flanking redoubts. Clinton had brought no cannon with him, knowing that his only chance of success lay in a swift advance with the bayonet. The attack, was led by the flank-companies of the Twenty-Sixth and of Fraser's Highlanders, together with one company of German *Chasseurs*, while the Sixty-Third endeavoured to break in on the opposite or northern side. (The attacking force consisted of the flank-companies of the New York garrison, the 26th, 63rd, one troop of the 17th Light Dragoons—dismounted—

STORMING OF STONY POINT.

Hessian *Chasseurs.* The 7th Fusiliers and a German battalion formed the rearguard. Total, 1200 men).

In perfect silence the men of the storming party pushed on through the abatis under a terrible fire, and on arriving at the foot of the fort itself very coolly hoisted each other into the embrasures. The American garrison, four hundred strong, made a brave defence, but being at length driven from the ramparts fired a final volley and surrendered. The Americans in the two attacks lost about one hundred killed and three hundred prisoners, while the British lost eighteen officers and one hundred and sixty-nine men killed and wounded. Sixty-seven cannon, a sloop of ten guns, and a large quantity of stores were captured; while the American flotilla behind the boom, being unable to escape up the river owing to foul winds, was burned to prevent it from falling into Clinton's hands. On its own scale the enterprise was as well and skilfully conducted as any operation of the war. Clinton wrote to Burgoyne from Fort Montgomery on the 8th:

> *Nous y void*, and nothing between us and Gates. I sincerely hope
> this little success of ours will facilitate your operations.

This short message, written on the thinnest of paper, was enclosed in a tiny silver bullet and entrusted to a single messenger for delivery. The British squadron then sailed up the river as far as Kingston, destroying stores and capturing petty batteries; but meanwhile Burgoyne's situation was growing desperate. He knew the difficulty, if not the impossibility, of a retreat to Canada before the daily increasing numbers of Gates's army, but on the other hand he hesitated to set free even a portion of that army to join Washington against Howe.

At length, on the 7th of October, he resolved to make a last attempt to turn the enemy's left. The overwhelming numbers opposed to him forbade him to withdraw more than fifteen hundred men from the protection of his camp; but with these and with ten guns, under the direction of Riedesel, Phillips, and himself, he moved out between eleven and twelve o'clock in the forenoon, so as to ensure the advantage of darkness for his retreat in case of need. Posting the Germans in the centre, and the British on either flank of them, he formed his line within three-quarters of a mile of the American left, while the very few Indians and Provincials that remained with his army defiled by secret paths through the forest, to make a demonstration upon the American rear.

All hopes of success were instantly and rudely dispelled by a sudden attack of the American General Morgan upon Burgoyne's left. The British Grenadiers, wheeling back at right angles to cover the left flank, met this onset with great firmness; but the Americans, bringing some four thousand men into action, speedily extended their offensive movement to the Germans on Burgoyne's left centre, where one battalion of Brunswickers gave way immediately. At the same time a separate column came down in force to turn Burgoyne's right flank, whereupon General Fraser withdrew the Light Infantry and Twenty Fourth from Burgoyne's right to cover the retreat.

But meanwhile the grenadiers on the left gave way before overpowering numbers, and Fraser was obliged to move his detachment hastily to their support, during which movement he was mortally wounded by a bullet from some hidden rifleman in a tree. Burgoyne had early perceived that it had become a question of saving not only his tiny attacking force but also his fortified lines, and had ordered the artillery to retire; but the *aide-de-camp* who carried the message was mortally wounded before he could deliver it, and thus much valuable time was lost.

He therefore directed Phillips and Riedesel to cover the retreat as best they could, and withdrew his troops, hard pressed indeed but in good order, within his entrenchments, though at the sacrifice of six guns, which were perforce abandoned after every man and horse belonging to them had been shot down. Had Gates only been in command of the Americans, the combat might have ended at that moment; but Benedict Arnold, with true military instinct, seized the opportunity to order a general attack upon the British entrenchments. The first assault was delivered against the British right centre, and was beaten back with heavy loss by Lord Balcarres and the Light Infantry; but the post next to the right of Balcarres, being defended only by Canadian irregulars, was easily carried, admitting the Americans to the flank of the extreme right of Burgoyne's line.

This station was held by the German Grenadiers and Light Infantry under Colonel Breyman, tried and gallant soldiers who fought hard until their commander was killed, and prolonged their resistance so late that Burgoyne only learned of their defeat after night had fallen. Realising then that the enemy had established themselves on his right flank, he withdrew his army during the night to some heights immediately above the river, where he showed a new front. That this change of position should have been accomplished in good order and without loss speaks highly for the general and for his troops, after so much gallantry expended in vain.

On the following day, October 8, Burgoyne offered battle in his new position; but learning that the enemy were on march to turn his right, he found himself compelled to retire up the river to Saratoga, abandoning some five hundred sick and wounded men to the enemy. The retreat itself was accomplished without hindrance; but so heavy was the rain and so severe the weather, that the men on coming into camp had not strength to cut wood or make fires, but threw themselves down, old soldiers though they were, on the sodden ground to sleep. When the light came on the morning of the 9th, it revealed the Americans in the act of entrenching the heights on the opposite side of the river, so as to prevent the British from crossing.

Burgoyne therefore decided on the following day to abandon his artillery and baggage and to withdraw by a forced march to Fort Edward. Scouts, however, came in to report that the whole of the fords on the road were beset, and that the Americans were strongly entrenched, with cannon, between Fort George and Fort Edward. The British were in fact surrounded. Gates had by this time from eighteen to twenty thousand men; and there was no escape. For yet a few days Burgoyne waited in the vain hope of news from Clinton; but the message in the silver bullet had been intercepted and the messenger hanged.

The army was not only surrounded but starving, and on the 14th Burgoyne made overtures for a capitulation, which was finally concluded on the 17th. It was agreed that the British troops should march out with the honours of war, pile their arms, and be conducted at once to Boston for shipment to England, on the understanding that they should serve no more in America during the continuance of hostilities.

The army marched out accordingly, a bare thirty-five hundred men fit for duty, nineteen hundred of them British and the remainder of them Germans, all that were left of the seven thousand who had started from Canada four months before in all the confidence of perfect discipline and of reputation won on a score of fields. (The full total of men surrendered, including the sick and wounded abandoned on the 9th, Provincials, Canadians, *bateaux* men, etc., was 4880).

Gates, with a chivalrous feeling which did him honour, kept his troops in camp while the British piled their arms; and all ranks of the victors vied with each other in showing to the vanquished that courtesy and consideration which is never denied by brave men to brave men. Not such was the behaviour of the Assembly of civilians, which was called Congress. With shameless ill faith they evaded the agreement to return the prisoners to England, under a series of pretexts, each flimsier than the last.

In vain Washington and other of the American generals remonstrated, with all the indignation of gallant officers and honourable men. Burgoyne was indeed allowed to go home on parole, but the rest were retained, and every effort was strained to drive the British rank and file to enter the American service. As the American provinces had formerly thrust the burden of their own defence upon sick and disabled Highlanders, so Congress now hoped to commit the battle of American independence to British deserters.

Transported first to New England, all ranks of the captured British were treated with the greatest indignity and even cruelty by the civil authorities. One individual, who bore the rank of Colonel of Militia, actually bayoneted a defenceless British corporal because of some trifling matter; and this example of brutality was speedily copied by his men. Burgoyne endeavoured to obtain redress before an American court-martial, but despite much eloquence was unsuccessful. A few weeks later a British officer was wantonly shot dead by a boy of fourteen who was standing sentry. The boy was tried and commended; and when the officer was buried in the Anglican Church at Cambridge, the mob entered the building during the funeral and plundered or destroyed every article on which they could lay hands, (Anbury, ii.), Finally, after every kind of insult and ill-treatment suffered in New England, the troops were ordered by Congress to march down in the depth of winter to Virginia, partly to relieve New England of the burden of supporting them, partly in the hope of hastening the process of desertion.

On arriving at their destination in Virginia, the troops found neither food nor shelter ready for them, although the snow lay thick upon the ground. The officers indeed received much consideration and generous hospitality from the gentlemen of the upper class, while the foreigners of all ranks were persistently favoured; but the British soldiers were still abominably fed and otherwise neglected.

It is noteworthy that by this contemptible conduct Congress defeated its own object; for although there were a few men who purchased comfort at the price of desertion, the majority stuck faithfully to their officers, or escaped and made their way to the British Army at New York. Finally, in 1781, the men, by direct infringement of the capitulation, were separated from their officers, and vanished no man knows whither. So ends this sordid story of meanness, cowardice and ill faith, an indelible blot on the reputation of Congress.

As to Burgoyne's campaign at large, it seems to me that no more honourable attempt of British officers and men to achieve the impossible is on record.

Burgoyne was denied the satisfaction of a court-martial, and was treated both by the king and by Germaine with great harshness and injustice; but he was allowed to defend himself before a Committee of the House of Commons, where, in my judgment, he vindicated himself completely. A stronger man might indeed have retreated, whatever his instructions, after the reverse at Bennington; but Burgoyne's instructions were undoubtedly positive, nor could he tell how far other operations might be dependent upon his advance.

His movements were extremely skilful, and the quickness with which he hit the vulnerable point of Gates's position shows that he was a capable commander. Even more to his honour is the unfailing loyalty and confidence of his troops towards him, while their behaviour in the field was beyond all praise. In the whole history of the army I have encountered no grander display of steadfastness and fortitude than the heroic stand of the Twentieth, Twenty-First, and Sixty-Second, with their little handful of gunners, on the 19th of September; and it is surely a marvellous instance of gallantry and discipline that fifteen hundred men should have moved out cheerfully and confidently as they did on the 7th of October, in spite of much hardship and heavy losses, to attack an enemy of five times their number; that when forced back they should have retired with perfect order and coherence; and that though fighting all day and marching or entrenching all night, they should never have lost heart.

Assuredly, too, it is not every commander who can command such unwavering devotion. In fact, what men could do, Burgoyne and his army did. Burgoyne's one stroke of good fortune was the substitution by Congress of Gates for the far more competent Schuyler as commander of the American Army; but this was neutralised by Washington's foresight in appointing Benedict Arnold to a subordinate command. But for Arnold, Burgoyne might have made his way to Albany; as things fell out, he failed; and the only pertinent comment on the capitulation of Saratoga is that of General Carleton:

This unfortunate event, it is to be hoped, will in future prevent ministers from pretending to direct operations of war in a country at three thousand miles' distance, of which they have so little knowledge as not to be able to distinguish between good, bad, or interested advices, or to give positive orders upon matters which from their nature are ever on the change.—Carleton to Burgoyne, 17th November 1777.

Carleton was too sanguine. It was not until Germaine had received another such fatal lesson that he was to relinquish the direction of operations in America from his desk in Downing Street.

CHAPTER 6

The French Join the Fray

Few events in our history have been more momentous in their results than the disaster of Saratoga. In itself it might have seemed to be nothing past repair. The loss of four thousand troops for service in America only (for such were the terms of capitulation) was not so great as to be irremediable, and the operations of the campaign had not been entirely thrown away. Ticonderoga had been recovered, and, though much material of war had been lost, infinitely more had been captured and destroyed both by Burgoyne himself and by Clinton.

Nevertheless the fact remained that a British army, or the remnant of one, had been beaten and captured. Thereby a great blow had been dealt at the reputation of England, and great encouragement given not only to the revolutionary party in America, but to that far more dangerous and unscrupulous enemy, the Opposition in the British Parliament.

The Houses met early in November, when the country was still exulting over the capture of Ticonderoga and the victory of Brandywine; but the news of Bennington was also come, and newspapers and politicians were already croaking prophecies of disaster to Burgoyne. They spoke not from any military knowledge, for they had uttered the same sinister predictions as to every movement of British troops during the war, but from that heedless malignity of faction which would cheerfully wreck an Empire to pull down a Ministry.

★★★★★★

On this ground I must very respectfully reject Mr. Lecky's tribute to Chatham's military prescience when that statesman in debate predicted disaster to Burgoyne. Chatham could inspire men to great deeds, but he was a very poor designer of a campaign; and he was simply repeating the commonplaces that had been current in the mouths of the Opposition for several weeks.

★★★★★★

The estimates for the army allowed for but trifling increase on the establishment of the previous year, an omission which, in the face of Howe's repeated remonstrances, can be characterised only as sheer madness. Then the usual dreary round of talk began, and Chatham, now drawing very near to his end, made the usual passionate appeals for peace and for withdrawal of the army from America, always on the fatally false presumption that American dependence and submission to the Acts of Trade and Navigation were matters not yet wholly obsolete. Then, as though he of all men had had no concern with the Canadian operations of 1759, he fell to wild denunciation of the employment of Indians in civilised warfare.

The Duke of Richmond, himself once an officer, feebly echoed the thunders of Chatham, and declared that a British army associated with such allies would be a menace to liberty on its return home. Like Chatham, he ignored the fact that British troops had been associated with those identical allies for the best part of a century. A fortnight later, rumours of the surrender at Saratoga were noised abroad; and when the news of this national disaster was confirmed in the House of Commons, it was received by the Opposition with such a howl of insulting triumph as exasperated the government once more into cheerfulness. Chatham once again opened his mouth, and, while very justly defending Burgoyne, condemned his campaign as "a mad, uncombined project," which undoubtedly it was, though it was not for Chatham to make such a criticism.

Then returning in an evil moment to the question of the employment of Indians, he was remorselessly pinned to his own sanction, in 1759, of the very measure which he now condemned. In vain he wriggled and shuffled and raved: there was no escape from the facts. Never was seen a more pitiful exhibition of the wreck of a great mind.

Happily, in other quarters there was more patriotism; for, from the moment when the news of Saratoga arrived, all thinking Englishmen were filled with apprehension for its possible influence on the policy of France. Very early in December the town of Manchester volunteered to raise a battalion of eleven hundred men at its own expense. Liverpool shortly afterwards followed this example, and was immediately imitated by Glasgow, Edinburgh, and Aberdeen; and the offers of all except Aberdeen were accepted. Birmingham, Warwick, and Coventry made like proposals, which, however, were not embraced.

London, being still under the spell of the ignoble Wilkes, and Bristol, a great centre of colonial trade, held sullenly aloof; though private subscriptions of their citizens atoned in some measure for the studied apathy of their municipal councils.

Simultaneously a number of Scottish noblemen and gentlemen offered to raise regiments, though not at their own expense. Lord Macleod, son of Lord Cromartie, and late of the Swedish service, came forward first to create the corps which now bears the famous title of the Seventy-First Highland Light Infantry. Five more Scottish gentlemen likewise raised regiments, of which the last, Lord Seaforth's, still survives as the Seventy-Second Highlanders.

Nor was this patriotic spirit confined to Britain, for in Ireland also Lords Ross, Granard, Lanesborough, and Bellamont, together with a Major Blakeney, all tendered their service to raise regiments or corps, though the proposal was in every case gratefully declined. (S.P. Ireland, Lord Lieutenant to Secretary of State, 16th September 1777, 7th January, 28th February 1778).

Finally, it was resolved to raise in Wales independent companies sufficient to be incorporated into a regiment. (Picton's, numbered then the 75th; afterwards disbanded). In all, about fifteen thousand men were given by private subscription for the service of the State.

★★★★★★

The following is the full list of the regiments raised in the spring of 1778, with the numbers which they then bore:— 72nd (Manchester), 73rd (Macleod's, now the Seventy-First), 74th (John Campbell), 75th (Picton), 76th (John M'Donnell), 77th (James Murray, the Athol Highlanders), 78th (Seaforth's, now the Seventy Second), 79th (Liverpool), 80th (Edinburgh), 81st (William Gordon), 82nd (Francis M'Lean), 83rd (Glasgow).

★★★★★★

It was indeed none too soon, for the disaster at Saratoga had decided the French Government to conclude a treaty with the revolted Colonies, whereby France agreed not only to acknowledge but to uphold their independence, on the sole condition that the States should make no peace with England that did not acknowledge that independence. The treaty was not immediately signed, and indeed the French ministers denied, with shameless mendacity, that it was even on foot; but the British ambassador at Paris knew enough to rouse his suspicions, while Fox and other members of the Opposition had early intelligence of the real state of affairs. In the face of an imminent rupture with France the behaviour of the Opposition is worthy of remark.

First they attacked the raising of troops without consent of Parliament as unconstitutional; and Fox railed at Manchester and the Scottish towns for the example which they had set, affirming that "they were so accustomed to disgrace that it was no wonder if they pocketed instances of dishonour and sat down with infamy." Then Fox in the Commons and the Duke of Richmond in the Lords moved simultaneously that no more of the old regiments should be sent out of the kingdom, which, as they had already condemned the raising of new regiments, amounted practically to a motion for the sacrifice of all external British possessions whatever. Then Burke came forward with hysterical utterances about the employment of Indian allies; to which Governor Pownall, with the weight of long experience of America, gave the decisive answer, already quoted, that the idea of Indian neutrality was dangerous, delusive nonsense.

Meanwhile Lord North, after vainly pressing his resignation upon the king, brought forward proposals for conciliation, which included the suspension of all acts relating to America which had been passed since 1763, and virtually conceded all that England had been fighting for since 1778.

This forced the hand of France; and on the 6th of February her treaty with the revolted Colonies was signed, though it was not until the 17th of March that the fact could be authentically reported to Parliament.

At such a crisis it was felt that Chatham was the one man who was fit to take the helm, and some effort was made to place him at the head of an administration. But the king would not hear of Chatham except as subordinate to North; and, however hardly his resolution may be judged, there was very much to be urged in its favour. In the first place, Chatham's body was half dead and his mind probably more than half unhinged. It was under Chatham's administration that the crowning folly of Charles Townshend had been committed; and there was no certainty that similar disloyal action might not be repeated by some mutinous subordinate.

There was no discipline among the Whigs, as was proved when Fox and Shelburne took office in 1782; and the Opposition was so much divided on the American question that all prospect of uniting it was hopeless. Chatham was still firm for British sovereignty over the Colonies and for the Acts of Trade, which Rockingham and the Duke of Richmond with truer insight were prepared to sacrifice, as indeed already lost, (*Chatham Correspondence*, iv.).

******

It was recognised by at least one shrewd observer in America, Thomas Paine, that Chatham's "plans and opinions towards the latter part of his life would have been attended with as many evil consequences and as much reprobated by America as those of Lord North." See Adolphus, iii.

******

The attitude of the Colonies also was unpromising, for even with the depression of Burgoyne's success at Ticonderoga still heavy upon them, they had named the cession of Canada, Nova Scotia, and New-foundland as essential conditions to the conclusion of a federal treaty, offensive, defensive, and commercial, with the Mother Country, (*Parl. Hist.* xix.). To such a surrender the king, though anxious to end the war with America, absolutely declined to agree; nor can his refusal be called unreasonable. (*Correspondence of George III. and Lord North,* ii.).

Meanwhile the usual factious embarrassment of the government continued. The egregious John Wilkes brought in a bill, of course aimed at the gratuitous creation of regiments by patriotic men, to forbid subscriptions for giving money to the Crown without consent of Parliament; and it is significant that Burke, who posed as the apostle of liberty, actually supported this monstrous and tyrannical proposal.

A few days later, (April 7th), Chatham delivered his last speech in Parliament, calling upon his countrymen to fight the whole of Europe rather than yield the independence of America from dread of foreign powers; but before he could end his oration he fell down in a fit, and a few weeks later, (May 11th), he was dead.

He was not a great minister of war, nor was he a great administrator; and his wild intemperance of speech, his incorrigible proclivity to faction, and his lordly contempt for all detail, impair his claim to the title even of a great practical statesman. But never has England produced one who was more emphatically a leader and a king of men. He is known as the Great Commoner; but his habits, his speeches, his writings were rather those of a king.

His orders read like royal edicts; his letters, in outward form no less than inward substance, bear the semblance almost of royal charters; and in truth his passion for the grandiose amounted nearly to a disease. His qualities, with the exception of what may be called his driving power, were, indeed, rather those of the poet than of the statesman.

His deep insight pierced into the heart of things, his wide imagination delighted to compass great designs, his imperious will brushed aside all difficulties, his fiery enthusiasm kindled all subordinates to like energy with his own, his passion for the greatness of his country carried his countrymen with him on an irresistible wave of patriotic sentiment; but he trusted overmuch and too often to sentiment.

His genius showed him the broad foundations on which to build; but he was impatient when the superstructure which his imagination had raised did not at once spring into being, obedient to sentiment; and it is not sentiment but patience which conquers all things. His reign was short, and possibly his reputation would have suffered had it been longer; but he was a king of men.

France having now joined the Americans in war, it was imperative to readjust the British plans so as to meet the entry into the situation of that new and important factor, the French fleet. The forces of England were widely dispersed. Setting aside India, there were troops in America at New York, on the Delaware, in Florida, Quebec, Halifax, and on the Lakes; in the West Indies at Jamaica, Grenada, St. Vincent, Tobago, Bermuda, and the Bahamas; in the Mediterranean at Gibraltar and Minorca. Amherst, being consulted, gave his opinion that forty thousand men would be required for offensive operations by land in America, and recommended a naval war only.

Forty thousand men, at a moment when every British garrison needed reinforcement, was quite out of the question for America; and, until Burgoyne's army could be replaced, it was obvious that New York at any rate must stand on the defensive. There was also the question of keeping the French well occupied by some offensive movement, so as to distract them from sending succour to America. Every consideration pointed to the desirability of concentrating the British forces as far as possible; and the king early made up his mind that Pennsylvania must be evacuated. But he still clung tightly to every other post which he held in America, not only to Halifax and to New York, which were essential to naval operations, but also to Rhode Island, which was superfluous, and to the stations in Florida, which were of no value, commercial or strategical, and were most unhealthy for the troops.

Most unfortunately too the governors of North Carolina and Georgia had during the past summer urged upon Germaine the fruitlessness of operations in the north, and had begged that the British arms might be turned upon the Carolinas; arguing that not only would many loyalists be heartened to come forward for the king, but that the supplies of indigo and tobacco, with which the Colonies paid for their arms and ammunition, would be cut off. Germaine was not yet cured of reliance on the loyal section of the American population, and the king was tempted by the thought of retaining the southern provinces, even if he should be forced to part with New England. Thus the old fatal principle was once more made the pivot upon which all operations were to turn.

On the 21st of March the ultimate instructions to Clinton, who was to succeed Howe in command, were finally drawn up. The first duty enjoined upon him was to embark five thousand men, with artillery and stores, to attack St. Lucia, the significance of which operation shall presently be explained. He was then to detach three thousand more men, fully equipped with artillery and stores, to St. Augustine and Pensacola, and to withdraw the troops from Philadelphia to New York, until the result of Lord North's conciliatory proposals should be known. If these proposals should fail of their effect he was to evacuate New York, leave sufficient garrisons at Rhode Island and Halifax, and send the rest of the troops to Canada. Subsequent orders directed further small parties to be sent to Bermuda and to the Bahamas.

As to reinforcements to fill the gaps created by these detachments, there were merely vague promises often or twelve thousand men to be despatched at some time in the course of the summer. The instructions indeed were throughout characteristic of Germaine. Canada, into which he was pouring fresh battalions, and bidding Clinton to pour yet more, was in little or no danger. Rhode Island could not be held if New York were evacuated, because it depended on New York for fuel; while, after the deduction of all the detachments, there were hardly men enough left to hold both. Yet he wrote casually to Clinton about six months later:

I suppose that if you evacuate anything, it will be Rhode Island.

It is hardly surprising that, before this last missive reached Clinton, the unfortunate General should have asked permission to resign. (Germaine to Clinton, 8th, 21st March, 1st July, 25th September 1778. Clinton to Germaine, 15th September, 8th October 1778).

But before proceeding farther, it is necessary to return to General Howe and to take note of what had passed in Philadelphia during the winter of 1777-1778. The successful close of his campaign had given him and the army comfortable quarters in Philadelphia; and these he determined to enjoy to the utmost. Washington meanwhile encamped his army at Valley Forge, in order to narrow as far as possible the country that lay open to the British for forage, bidding his men build huts to shelter themselves during the severe weather.

Never was he so hardly pressed by his own people as during this winter. Gates, always a jealous man, and other officers had formed a cabal to oust him from the chief command; and their intrigues had for a time been not unsuccessful with the ignorant civilians of Congress, who opined that Washington ought long ago to have ended matters by a short and violent war. Though ultimately the conspirators failed of their object, they yet caused such neglect and disorganisation of the army during the winter of 1777 that Washington was driven almost to despair.

His force rapidly melted away through desertion; and by Christmas the small remnant of less than three thousand men, which remained with him, was driven by starvation into open mutiny, (Washington, *Works*, v.) Yet no adequate measures were taken for its relief; and throughout the long winter the men, ill clad, ill fed, and ill sheltered, suffered terribly from famine, cold, and sickness. Nevertheless Howe made no effort to drive Washington from his position; and it is fair to add that Major-General Grey, an excellent officer, declared that an attack upon Valley Forge would have been wholly unjustifiable.

Howe's own plea was that no great advantage could be reaped from success at that season of the year; and if by a great he meant a decisive advantage, he was undoubtedly right. But as to indirect gain, we have Washington's own statement that he himself used, though without success, the greatest severity towards the inhabitants to prevent them from furnishing the British with horses and with every kind of supplies; (Washington, *Works*, v.), and, since the whole campaign rested on the support of the loyalists, it was certainly false policy in Howe to allow them to be oppressed.

The truth seems to be that Howe's natural indolence and unwillingness to impose unnecessary hardships upon his men were increased by the thought that the command would shortly pass out of his hands, and that his action might be misconstrued if he should transfer to his successor an army enfeebled by severe winter operations, which at best could lead to no serious result. There was also much to be said for allowing the American Army to go to pieces of itself, without risking the life of a single British soldier; and had it not been that a successful attack would have brought about the downfall of Washington, and interrupted one of his best foreign officers, Baron von Steuben, in the work of reorganising the staff and remodelling the discipline of the American Army, Howe might well have put forward this plea in justification of his conduct. But he lies under the further and more serious charge of suffering the discipline of the British to become relaxed by neglect and inaction; and it is certain that the amount of sickness among the troops during the winter was alarming.

These are accusations which are less easily rebutted, and which remain a grave reproach to Howe. It seems indeed that, weary of his whole task, realising the hopelessness of success without large reinforcements, and above all chafing against the constant interference of Germaine, he abandoned himself to simple inertness pending the appointment of his successor. It is easy to censure him; and indeed Howe has been made the scapegoat for the failure of the war; but no war could have gone well under the direction of Germaine.

After the successful execution of a few petty operations in March, Howe received in April the acceptance of his resignation; and on the 8th of May Clinton arrived to take over the command. A few days later, after a very ridiculous festival held by his officers and by the prettiest women in Philadelphia in his honour, Howe sailed for England. Whatever might be said of him, he had at least beaten the Americans in several actions, and taken some five thousand prisoners besides a large number of guns.

Clinton at once began to ship his stores for the evacuation of Philadelphia; but finding that he could not embark the troops at any point nearer than Newcastle, some forty miles away, and that his transports were insufficient to convey both the army and some three thousand refugees who claimed his protection, he decided to retreat to New York by land.

Accordingly, at three o'clock on the morning of the 18th of June, he marched with his fifteen thousand men and an immense train of baggage, and crossed the Delaware at Gloucester Point before the Americans could molest him. His position was no enviable one, for Washington speedily set fifteen thousand well-trained and well-equipped men in motion to pursue him, while small parties of the enemy in his front broke down all the bridges in order to retard his progress. Pursuing a parallel course to northward of Clinton, Washington rapidly gained on him; and on reaching Allentown after five days' march, (June 23rd), Clinton learned that Gates was moving down from the north to bar the passage of the Rariton. He thereupon struck eastward for Sandy

Hook instead of holding on his course for Amboy; and placing Kny-phausen with ten battalions and the Seventeenth Light Dragoons in charge of his baggage, he himself took personal command of fourteen battalions and the Sixteenth Light Dragoons, which formed the rear-guard. Washington meanwhile sent six thousand men under Lee, who had lately been released by exchange, with orders to attack the flank of the British rearguard and to hold it engaged until he should arrive with the main body.

At dawn of Sunday the 28th of June, Knyphausen and the bag-gage moved off from its encampment on the heights of Freehold, followed at eight o'clock by the rear division. At ten o'clock Lee's cannon opened fire on Clinton's rearguard, while parties of his men appeared on both of its flanks. A charge of the Sixteenth Light Dra-goons drove back the American cavalry; and Clinton, after sending to Knyphausen for reinforcements, made his dispositions for attack. The Americans thereupon fell back, in obedience to Lee, who, it appears, was still playing a treacherous game; and Clinton pushed the Guards and grenadiers against their front, while his light troops fetched a compass to turn upon their flank.

Lee continued to retreat before the Guards, who, however, coming upon the American main body under Washington, were obliged to retire, heavily pressed in front and flanks, until night put an end to the combat. At ten o'clock Clinton renewed his march and accomplished the remainder of his retreat without molestation. The action cost the British three hundred and fifty-eight officers and men, of whom no fewer than sixty fell dead from sunstroke owing to the overpowering heat of the day. The loss of the Americans was almost exactly the same; but Clinton's army was considerably reduced during this march by the desertion of some six hundred men, (Mr. Fiske gives the number of deserters at 2000, but this figure is irreconcilable with Clinton's returns), three-fourths of them Germans, who had contracted at-tachments of one description or another to the town of Philadelphia. Washington, after the action of Freehold, abandoned the pursuit and marched to his own encampment at White Plains; while Clinton, after waiting two days on the Navasink in the hope that Washington would attack him, embarked his troops at Sandy Hook, and on the 5th of July arrived at New York.

Three days later the French fleet from Toulon under Count d'Estaing appeared with four thousand troops at the mouth of the Delaware, marking the entry of a new element which, as Washington had long foreseen, was vital to the success of the Colonies. So far British supremacy at sea had enabled the British generals to transport their troops and to land them where they would, without anxiety for the safety of their retreat. From henceforth the loss of that supremacy even for a week might bring about disaster. D'Estaing's design had been to intercept Lord Howe's squadron in the Delaware, which was of little more than half the strength of his own; but he arrived too late, and sailed for Sandy Hook, where a council of war was held.

The British forces were now separated into two divisions at New York and Rhode Island, with no communication except by sea; and it seemed feasible with a superior naval force to overwhelm one or the other of them. New York, as the more important, was first chosen for attention, but d'Estaing, who though a brave man was a soldier and not a sailor, recoiled before the dangers of the navigation and the extremely able dispositions of Lord Howe. The allied force of French and Americans was therefore turned against Rhode Island, which was held by General Pigott with some five thousand troops.

The American general, Sullivan had been watching Pigott from Providence on the mainland since April; and to him Washington now sent fifteen hundred of his regular troops under General Greene and the Marquis de Lafayette, in the hope that this force, added to four thousand French and nine thousand New England yeomanry, would suffice to make an end of the red coats. D'Estaing duly arrived with his fleet before Rhode Island on the 29th of July; and the British were compelled to burn seven small men-of-war to prevent them from falling into his hands. But Pigott, an active and vigilant officer, had by two sudden descents upon Providence already made such destruction of the American boats and other stores as greatly to retard their preparations for attack; and it was the 8th of August before d'Estaing and Sullivan were in a position to concert their plans for joint action.

But on the 9th of August the indefatigable Lord Howe appeared on the scene with his squadron, and d'Estaing stood out to sea, where a storm of extraordinary violence separated and dispersed both fleets before they could come to a decisive engagement. A gallant battle was, however, fought between two British ships of fifty and two French ships of eighty guns, wherein the Light Company of the Twenty-Third Fusiliers on board H.M.S. *Isis* bore a distinguished part. (Lord Howe to Admiralty, 17th August 1778).

Meanwhile General Sullivan crossed over from the mainland and invested Pigott's entrenched camp, but made little progress against

141

it; and on the 20th d'Estaing, returning with his shattered ships, announced his intention of going to Boston to refit and of taking the troops with him. Thereupon the whole of the operations collapsed. The American yeomanry with their wonted indiscipline went back to their farms; and on the 28th Sullivan raised the investment and retreated.

Pigott followed him up at once, and there was sharp fighting; (the American loss was 211, and the British 260 of all ranks), but the American rearguard, skilfully handled by Greene, made so steady and stubborn a resistance that Sullivan was able to retire safely to the mainland. He was but just in time, for on the very next day Clinton sailed in from New York with five thousand men, a force which, added to Pigott's, would have sufficed to cut off and overwhelm the whole of Sullivan's army.

Thus in impotent failure, with but narrow escape from disaster, ended the first enterprise of a superior French fleet on the coast of America. It will surprise no reader, who has watched the temper of the New Englanders, to hear that the result created much ill feeling between the French and their allies. There was a dangerous riot between French and American seamen at Boston, in accordance with the traditions of that tranquil and law-abiding city, and another yet fiercer at Charlestown; while it needed all Washington's tact and patience to keep the peace between the superior officers.

In truth, Washington had been considerably embarrassed by the arrival during the past twelve months of a number of French gentlemen, full of curious revolutionary ideas, which had been minted in the coffee-houses of Paris, and still fuller of their own importance and condescension. Lafayette, who had fought with him through the Pennsylvanian campaign, was welcome to the American general as a good and energetic soldier; but the rest he would gladly have seen sail back to France by the first ship.

★★★★★★

There is a hundred times more enthusiasm for the revolution in any Paris *café* than in the whole of the United States put together.—M. de Portail to the Comte de St. Germain, 17th November 1777. And see Washington's *Works*, vi.

★★★★★★

Moreover, to increase Washington's embarrassment, Clinton, though he had missed his prey at Rhode Island, made on his return voyage a series of raids upon sundry little ports which harboured

American privateers, destroying large quantities of shipping and stores. It was during this season that the famous irregular corps of mixed cavalry and infantry known as the Queen's Rangers, commanded by Major Simcoe, the Legion under Major Tarleton, and another body of Rangers under Major Patrick Ferguson, first made their mark by sundry useful little enterprises in partisan warfare. One and all of them were recruited in America; and we shall see much of their work in the years before us.

At this point serious operations in the north came to an end. Clinton, in the perplexity caused by Germaine's foolish orders, still forbore to withdraw the garrison from Rhode Island, where the troops were kept inactive to no purpose, the station being as much of a distraction to the British Navy as to the American generals. (Lord Howe to Admiralty, 31st March 1777).

It is true that Howe should long ago have been reinforced to superior strength by Admiral Byron's squadron, but Byron had met with the luck which had earned him the nickname of "Foul-weather Jack." Though he had sailed from England on the 9th of June, his squadron had been so frequently dispersed by storms that it was not finally assembled and refitted at New York until the 18th of October. He then sailed to blockade d'Estaing's fleet at Boston, but was once more driven away by a furious gale; and on the 4th of November d'Estaing slipped out of Boston and sailed for Martinique.

On that same day a force of over five thousand British troops under Major-General Grant also sailed from New York to the West Indies; and it is now necessary to follow their fortunes in the Caribbean Archipelago.

CHAPTER 7

The West Indies

The part played by the West Indian Islands during the American War of Independence has been so little appreciated as to demand particular attention in these pages. Then as now the British West Indies depended practically upon America for their supplies of food; for, with the exception of small quantities of yams, sweet potatoes, and the like, provisions were little cultivated in a soil which could more profitably be devoted to sugar, indigo, and spices. A war with America therefore threatened the islands with scarcity, or at any rate with increased cost of victuals, while at the same time depriving them of their best market for rum and molasses, and of their share in the vast profits of smuggling on the American coast.

Colonial emissaries were early despatched to magnify the fears of the West Indian planters, and to enlist their sympathy against the tyrannical British Government which designed to bind the Americans in chains. Their task was the easier since in each island the power of the purse was entrusted to a representative assembly composed chiefly of planters, who, having little knowledge of matters outside the management of their own estates, were controlled for the most part by a small knot of busy, unscrupulous lawyers, of the same type, though of unequal ability with the eminent Samuel Adams.

Symptoms of a disloyal spirit, in the form of extremely insolent addresses from the Assembly, showed themselves in Jamaica early in 1775, and in Barbados a year later, the language employed being the same as that in favour at Boston. In Bermuda, where for a century and a half the population had been incurably restless and turbulent, the Assembly sent delegates to the Congress at Philadelphia, while the people sold to the Americans ammunition, salt, and even the fast sailing-vessels for which the islands were famous.

In fact, until troops arrived in 1779 to restore the king's authority, the Bermudians openly took sides with the revolted provinces, even passing a bill to tax prizes taken by British privateers. In the Bahamas it has already been told how the Americans successfully carried off the guns and ammunition. This was done by the deliberate connivance of the authorities, who refused to allow the ordnance to be embarked in the ships which Gage had sent for the purpose; and from that time forward the Bahamas were practically in open rebellion. In the Leeward Islands, (Antigua, Montserrat, Nevis, St. Kitts), the chance of plundering American traders proved so tempting that the inhabitants reverted eagerly to their old profession of piracy, and were only with much difficulty brought to accept commissions as privateers.

But in September 1778 a disloyal faction grew up among the people and in the Assembly of St. Kitts, and thenceforward increased continually in power. The favour shown to American privateers by the French at Martinique, even before France took open part in the war, as also by the Danes at St. Croix and the Dutch at St. Eustatius, all worked for the strengthening of this American party. The Dutch indeed drove a roaring trade during the war, and freely granted the use of their credentials to American privateers. The governor of the Leeward Islands wrote:

> If our cruisers were to spare everything with Dutch clearances and papers, there would not be a French or American vessel on the sea.

St. Eustatius was neither more nor less than a huge depot for stores of all kinds on passage from Europe to America; and the trade in these goods was so profitable as to entice large numbers of British merchants, both in the West Indies and in the United Kingdom, into providing for the wants of their country's enemies.

★★★★★★

Jamaica—Governor Keith to Secretary of State, 4th January 1775, 27th March 1776.

Barbados—Governor Hay to Secretary of State, 13th and 15th February, 25th July, 31st August 1776.

Leeward Isles—Governor Burt to Secretary of State, 30th September, 9th October, 2nd and 25th November 1776.

Bermuda—Governor Bruere to Secretary of State, 1st February, 21st July, 17th and 20th August 1775, *et passim*.

Bahamas—Governor Browne to Secretary of State, *passim*, 1775-1782.

★★★★★★

Next, a word must necessarily be said as to the strategic position of the islands. In the days of sailing ships all naval operations in the West Indies were necessarily governed by the trade-wind, which blows, roughly speaking, (more truly south-east to north-west, shifting occasionally in certain months to north-east), from east to west persistently for three parts of the year, and intermittently during the fourth part also. But from the beginning of August to the beginning of November the Archipelago is subject to hurricanes, for which reason it was customary for fleets to desert tropical latitudes during these "hurricane-months." The British West Indies were divided into two groups: first, the chain of islands to windward, that is to say to eastward, which runs, interspersed with certain French islands, from St. Kitts in the north to Tobago in the south; secondly, Jamaica, a thousand miles to leeward, to which were attached for purposes of defence the posts of Pensacola and Mobile, in the districts at that time comprehended under the name of Florida.

Practically these two divisions were distinct; for though a ship could be sure of a good passage from Barbados to Jamaica, she could be equally sure that a voyage from Jamaica to Barbados would occupy as much time as a voyage from Jamaica to England.

★★★★★★

Governor Russell wrote to the Board of Trade in 1697 that the voyage from Barbados to Jamaica was reckoned at six or seven days. A good sailer would beat back to Barbados from Jamaica in two months; a bad sailer would never reach Barbados at all.

★★★★★★

In a word, a force once despatched from windward to leeward was to all intent irrecoverable; and this fact was one with which commanders, both naval and military, had always to reckon.

The French on their side were in exactly the same case, having their two divisions of territory in St. Lucia, Martinique, and Guadeloupe to windward, and Haiti to leeward. But to leeward they had this advantage, that Haiti, being to windward of Jamaica, and within twenty-four hours' sail of it, was a perpetual menace to that island. Moreover, the harbour of St. Nicholas, which of late had been fortified to great strength, so dominated the Windward Channel between Haiti and Cuba a very important passage for homeward-bound ships that it was esteemed the Gibraltar of the West Indies. To windward, the British had somewhat of a corresponding advantage, Barbados being the most windwardly of the whole of the eastern group.

But, on the other hand, Barbados has no safe harbour, nor was there any port in Grenada, St. Vincent, or any of the British islets to northward of it, where British ships could refit, excepting the royal dockyard at English Harbour in Antigua. Barbados, it is true, was an excellent depot for troops and stores, and could be used within certain limits for repair of ships; but the true dockyard, as aforesaid, was in Antigua, some distance to leeward. The French on the contrary had three admirable harbours in St. Lucia, Martinique, and Guadeloupe, of which Martinique, the principal naval and military centre, was little further distant from France than Barbados from England.

Henceforward I shall treat all to the east of Porto Rico as the windward, and all to westward of it as the leeward sphere of operations; but it must be remembered that the law of the trade-wind is as inexorable between any two islands within each of these groups as between the two spheres taken at large. To recapitulate: Port Royal on the English side and St. Nicholas on the French were the naval stations to leeward; Barbados and Antigua on the English side, and Martinique on the French, the principal stations to windward.

Not only were the British West Indies infected by the spirit of rebellion, but their fortifications, where not in a ruinous condition, were sadly out of repair. This would have been no great matter if the troops could have been withdrawn from them; but the danger from Caribs almost compelled the retention of small parties in Grenada, St. Vincent, and Dominica, which made a grievous drain on the force, never of sufficient strength, which guarded the naval stations.

It had been laid down a century before, (by Governor Christopher Codrington, *Cal. S.P. Col.* 1689-1692), that small garrisons in the West Indies were useless, and large garrisons, except for the protection of naval bases, an unnecessary expense, since security to the British and menace to the French could be very much better assured by superiority at sea. The only difficulty in the way of putting this very sound theory into practice was the outcry invariably raised by each island for a few troops for its individual defence, a clamour which, owing to the peril of negro insurrection, was always troublesome, and in times of disaffection became unpleasantly cogent.

In 1778 the French were beforehand in taking the offensive in the West Indies. On the 6th of September the Marquis de Bouillé, embarking a couple of thousand men at Martinique, dropped down upon Dominica, which was defended only by weak detachments of the Forty-Eighth Foot and of artillery, (added to the local militia, made up a force of less than 500 men), and by the offer of very favourable terms obtained the immediate surrender of the island.

Bouillé then locked up fifteen hundred of his troops as a garrison to secure his prize, and hurried back to Martinique lest Admiral Barrington, who had arrived with a small squadron at Barbados, should reach Fort Royal before him. The loss of Dominica was of small importance, except that it was the only island where a fleet could conveniently obtain wood and water at one and the same time; and it was not long before the British counterstroke fell.

Though encumbered with the fleet of fifty-nine transports whereon Grant's troops had been embarked, Admiral Hotham arrived from New York at Barbados on the 10th of December; while d'Estaing, who had sailed from Boston without encumbrance on the same day, reached Martinique only twenty-four hours before him. Barrington was not the man to lose precious time. Without permitting the disembarkation of the troops for one minute, he sailed within twenty-four hours of their arrival for St. Lucia, and on the afternoon of the same day anchored in Cul de Sac Bay. (Grant's force consisted of the 4th, 5th, 15th, 27th, 28th, 35th, 40th, 46th, 49th, and 55th Foot, and just under 200 artillery; in all, about 5800 men).

Two brigades were immediately landed, one of which speedily forced the heights to northward, capturing a battery of four guns and opening the way to the next inlet, now known by the name of Castries Bay. On the next morning, (Dec. 13th), the remainder of the troops were disembarked, and the famous mountain called the Morne Fortuné, which commands the south side of Castries Bay, was captured almost without resistance. Before evening the British were in possession also of the peninsula of Vigie on the north side of the harbour, with all the forts, batteries, magazines, and fifty-nine guns. Thus a fortified naval base was gained, so to speak, ready made, at a trifling cost.

The last of the white flags had not been struck for one hour when d'Estaing's fleet came into sight. On his arrival at Martinique he had been joined by transports containing nine thousand troops; and with these added to a superior fleet he hoped to give short shrift to the British possessions to windward. But the fate of St. Lucia determined him to recapture that island before going any farther; the task seeming easy to him, since his fleet outnumbered Barrington's by three ships to one. Nevertheless, so skilfully had Barrington drawn his squadron across Cul de Sac Bay, that d'Estaing after two attacks failed, (Dec. 15th), to make the slightest impression on it.

Beating therefore up to windward, he landed his troops in Anse du Choc, immediately to northward of Castries Bay, designing to force the British post at Vigie, and so to open the harbour to his own fleet. On the two following days his small craft returned to Martinique to fetch more men, while the French men-of-war tried to make their way into Castries harbour and to cut off the supply of provisions from the imprisoned fleet in the Cul de Sac. But the French engineers had done their work so well when they fortified Port Castries that no ship dared approach within effective range of the Vigie; and, though the British boats were easily prevented from bringing provisions from the squadron to the army by day, they could as easily pass unharmed through the French cruisers by night.

Nevertheless the situation of the British was of the utmost anxiety and peril; for the defeat of the army would mean that Barrington's squadron would be driven by the French guns upon the land into the jaws of d'Estaing's superior fleet, while the defeat of the squadron would signify the ruin of the army from deprivation of its supplies. Moreover, the nature of the case had compelled Grant to divide his already inferior force. Four battalions under Sir Henry Calder had been left to guard the heights round Cul de Sac Bay, to prevent attack upon the transports from the land, and to maintain communication with Morne Fortuné. Five more battalions held Morne Fortuné itself, to secure the southern shore of Port Castries; while the remaining three under Medows occupied the peninsula of Vigie.

This peninsula presented a strong defensive position, inasmuch as the approach to it lay across an isthmus little more than two hundred yards wide at its narrowest point. Medows, therefore, had drawn up the bulk of his troops in rear of this neck, with a single advanced post beyond it towards the mainland.

The French meanwhile had posted themselves on ground at right angles to Medows's line and not more than two miles distant from it, pushing forward their picquets until the French sentries could, and in one case actually did, exchange pinches of snuff with the British. Such a disposition, however, gave no clue to d'Estaing's intentions. Had Medows drawn the whole of his little force to the rear of the neck, d'Estaing would doubtless have left a sufficient body to blockade him in the peninsula, and would have marched round the head of the harbour with the mass of his men to attack Morne Fortuné.

But Medows, as has been seen, had with excellent judgment secured his egress by means of an advanced post. Two alternatives therefore were left to the French commander—to leave detachments to threaten Medows and Morne Fortuné and move the bulk of his troops to overwhelm Calder, or to make an end of Medows by a single stroke. The question did not long remain in suspense. On the evening of the 17th a French deserter came into Vigie with intelligence that d'Estaing intended to attack Medows's brigade forthwith with twelve thousand men. The British commander could hardly believe the news, which, however, was not unwelcome to him. He was a veteran of the Seven Years' War, and his troops, though numbering but thirteen hundred men, had been hardened like himself by the actions of Bunker's Hill, Brooklyn, Fort Washington, and Brandywine. They consisted of the Fifth Foot, and of the flank companies of the Fourth, Fifteenth, Twenty-Seventh, Twenty-Eighth, Fortieth, Forty-Sixth, and Fifty-Fifth, massed, together with those of the Fifth, into a grenadier battalion and a light battalion. At the moment they were probably without any exception the finest troops in the world.

Throughout the night of the 17th rain fell heavily, continuing until nearly seven o'clock of the following morning, when it was observed that the French were nearer to the British advanced posts than usual, and in greater numbers. The main position of the British, in rear of the neck of the peninsula, lay on the slope of a low rugged hill, covered with scrub. Beyond the neck five light companies were stationed upon two low hills; and this was the point which appeared to be threatened by the enemy.

Medows and two of his battalion-commanders rode to it to see what might be going forward, when to their horror the officers in the main position saw two strong French battalions emerge suddenly from a belt of low brushwood and move up against the front and flank of the advanced light companies, as if to cut them off. So imminent seemed the danger lest they and the general with them should be isolated and overwhelmed that many doubted whether the main body ought not to advance to their rescue. But presently Medows came back, perfectly cool and composed. "The Light Infantry will take care of themselves," he said; "as for you, stand fast."

Then was seen the potency of the tactics learned in America. Advancing in skirmishing order and keeping themselves always under

150

cover, the light companies maintained at close range a most destructive fire upon the heavy French columns. If the enemy attempted to extend, they threatened a charge with the bayonet; when the French closed up, they were already extended and pouring in a galling fusillade; when the French advanced with solidity and determination they fell back and disappeared, but only to renew their fire, themselves invisible, from every direction. At last one of the enemy's battalions fairly gave way, and the light companies followed them to complete the rout with the bayonet. But meanwhile the main body of the French came up slowly in massive columns to the assault of Medows' s principal position, unobserved by the victorious Light Infantry, who were returning to the defence of their advanced posts.

"Come back, come back," yelled their comrades from the rear; but the five companies would not hear until, regaining their hill, they saw their danger and dashed into the scrub to join the main body. They made their escape in safety, thanks in part to the density of the brushwood, but chiefly to Captain Downing, Lieutenant Waring, and Privates Rose, Duffy, and Hargrove, who stood alone and unsupported to cover their retreat. For long they parried the bayonet-thrusts until Waring was pierced through the body, when Downing, responding to the chivalrous appeal of a French officer who had saved him from the like fate, surrendered with his three gallant companions.

The French now developed their attack upon the main position, filling the scrub at the foot of the slope with their light troops, while the battalions in solid columns continued their slow and steady advance. Medows now opened fire from four three-pounders and two twelve-pounders which had been captured at the Vigie, silencing the lighter guns of the enemy; and the British Grenadiers, who began to fall fast under the bullets of the French sharpshooters, likewise commenced their fire in perfect order and without confusion, husbanding every cartridge, for they had but thirty rounds a man.

Meanwhile the French columns never discharged a shot, though whole files of them were swept away by the British cannon. The men endured the punishment with all the bravery of their nation but made no progress, though they kept changing direction to right and left, as if looking for the easiest way to ascend the hill. One column broke twice and was twice rallied; and at last the whole came to a dead halt and stood within range, indeed, of their adversaries, but no longer tormented by the blast of their musketry.

For the British ammunition, though d'Estaing knew it not, had failed, and Medows had given the order to cease fire. Boats had long since been sent over to Morne Fortuné for the reserve of cartridges; and one officer of the grenadiers, a man of gigantic strength named Hill, had taken a box from the two men who were staggering under it and brought it up unaided to the front. The box was opened and the cartridges upon being handled fell instantly to dust from rottenness.

Medows had been wounded early in the action and was now almost disabled by the pain of the hurt, but he was still master of himself and gave his orders to Major Harris, later Lord Harris of Seringapatam, who commanded the grenadiers. All firing must cease at once; the firing line must charge the enemy with the bayonet, when they had advanced near enough, and rally upon the main body for a final charge under the general himself, "to conquer or fall." So perfect was the discipline of the British that not another shot was discharged; indeed it is recorded that some of the grenadiers, who had received the word "Present," brought their muskets down instantly upon the word "Recover."

The men quietly resigned themselves to endure the punishment of the enemy's sharpshooters. Harris hurried forward to the firing-line. The French, having recovered themselves, were advancing rapidly when they were staggered by two last shots from the captured twelve-pounders; and many of them turned about to retire. Harris, seeing that the decisive moment was come, ordered the Grenadiers to fire upon the most disordered portions of the French columns; and presently the whole body of the enemy faced about and retired, with no indecent haste, but with evident disinclination to advance once more. The fight had lasted for three hours, from eight till eleven in the morning.

The casualties of the British numbered one hundred and seventy-one, of whom only thirteen were killed; ninety of the fallen belonging to the grenadiers and sixty to the Light Infantry. Medows himself visited every injured officer and man before he would permit a surgeon to attend to him. The loss of the French was appalling; four hundred killed outright and twelve hundred grievously wounded. Yet the odds against the British had been nearly ten to one; and the defeat of the French was due, partly indeed to the two heavy guns which the British had acquired at the capture of Vigie fort, but chiefly to superiority of tactics and of discipline.

A more brilliant series of little operations by both army and navy, under the favour of fortune, it would be difficult to find. Had Barrington waited for a day longer at Barbados, his squadron and transports must have fallen a prey to d'Estaing's superior fleet. Had Grant delayed for an hour in landing and attacking the French posts, the French militia might have held their own till d'Estaing came to their relief. But for Barrington's very bold and skilful dispositions in Cul de Sac Bay, his squadron must have been dispersed, if not destroyed, and Grant's army cut off. But for Grant's equally skilful defence of his posts on Vigie, the French could have brought up guns to force Barrington's squadron from Cul de Sac Bay into the jaws of a superior fleet. As things fell out, d'Estaing was driven back with heavy loss to Martinique, and the British were left with the key of the Windward Islands in their hands. Thus installed on an excellent harbour to windward both of Martinique and Guadeloupe, "in a way looking into Fort Royal," as Grant wrote, his force was a standing menace to French power in the West Indies.

On the 6th of January 1779 Byron's fleet arrived at St. Lucia, too late, by his usual bad luck, to cut off d'Estaing's retreat to Martinique, and so much shattered as hardly to restore the British even to equality at sea. Nevertheless, his presence sufficed to keep d'Estaing locked up tightly in Fort Royal; and meanwhile Grant was still strengthening his defences, for his troops were sickening rapidly, ("850 sick in last week's state." Grant to Germaine, 5th February 1779), and Byron's crews also were so much reduced by disease that soldiers were required to make up the complement for the fleet. Grant fought with the climate as successfully as his limited supply of quinine would permit him; but his principal struggle lay, as usual, with human stupidity.

★★★★★★

"Without bark we should not have a man fit for duty in three months; but the hospital at New York would not give so much as I looked for."—Grant to Germaine, 4th April 1779. The returns for 5th April show 3300 fit for duty, 1350 sick. There were 100 deaths between 31st March and 24th April. *Ibid.* 24th April 1779.

★★★★★★

In May the disaffection at St. Kitts rose to an alarming height; the Assembly refused to pay for the provisions collected for the militia in case of need, and the governor, Mr. Burt, begged in abject terms for troops. No policy could have been more foolish, politically or strategically; for, as Burt himself admitted, the Assembly behaved properly so long as the French fleet threatened attack, and only became refractory when Byron promised protection.(Burt to Secretary of State, 3rd

153

May, 1st June 1779).

In plain words, this nest of smugglers, pirates, and receivers of stolen goods was loyal only when threatened with the loss of its ill-gotten gains. Worst of all, Byron actually sailed to St. Kitts to quiet the incessant clamour of Burt; and, as luck would have it, a French squadron under Count de Grasse was able to join d'Estaing at Fort Royal unmolested during his absence. (Grant to Germaine, 13th May 1779).

Finally, as a climax, there came an order from the incorrigible Germaine to provide garrisons for all the British islands, and to send back all the troops that could be spared, after this dispersion, to New York. (Germaine to Grant, 1st April 1779).

Fortunately, Grant was as outspoken to Germaine as to any West Indian governor, he wrote:

> Small detachments are no security against invasion, if troops are not kept together in the West Indies the best of them will soon cease to be soldiers. I shall therefore send none to the islands. Their safety must depend on the fleet.

With a just insight into the true position he declined to weaken the garrison of St. Lucia to no purpose, though he cheerfully lent Byron two additional regiments, the Fifth and Fortieth, to man the squadron. Now, however, luck turned against him. About the middle of June Admiral Byron was obliged to take his June, men-of-war to leeward in order to convoy the homeward-bound merchant-vessels beyond the islands; and in his absence d'Estaing sent a small expedition to capture St. Vincent, (June 16th). That island, though garrisoned by four hundred sickly men of the Sixtieth, who had much better have been at St. Lucia, surrendered without firing a shot; and on the 30th of June d'Estaing sailed. with his whole fleet against Grenada.

Byron on his return at once took the alarm, and on the 5th of July sailed with twenty-one ships of the line and one thousand troops under Grant's command to recapture St. Vincent; but, hearing that the French had called the Caribs to them and were entrenching themselves, he decided first to rescue Grenada. D'Estaing, however, had already mastered that island, (July 4th), though the tiny garrison of three hundred regular troops and militia made a gallant resistance; and when at daybreak of the 6th Barrington, who was Byron's second in command, arrived off St. George's Harbour, the French fleet was anchored in disorder at its mouth.

Unable to ascertain the numbers of the French owing to their confusion, Barrington made signal for a general chase, and only too late realised that he was pitting twenty-one ships against twenty-five. Readers must turn elsewhere for the story of the gallant but indecisive action that followed, and of the failure of d'Estaing to turn his advantages to account. Let it suffice that the British soldiers bore their part in the fight, losing seventy-four officers and men killed and wounded, and that Barrington, though he could not retake Grenada, brought off his fleet and transports in safety. Grant, after paying the highest compliments to the bravery of the fleet, thus pointed the moral of the operations.

> If the troops had not been kept together we could not have made the attempt to recover the islands, which would have succeeded but for our inferiority at sea. If detachments had been stationed in the islands, they could not have saved them for a day. . . . Being inferior at sea, we cannot send back the troops to New York as ordered by you.—Grant to Germaine, 8th and 17th July 1779.

He therefore made a new distribution of the troops, (see list following), since the battalions intended for America remained at his disposal, and on the 1st of August sailed for England.

(Grant to Germaine 29th July 1779):

St. Kitts, R.A., 15th, 28th, 55th	1500 men.
St. Lucia, R.A., 27th, 35th, 49th	1600 ,,
Antigua, 6 companies 40th, detachment 60th	800 ,,
Serving with the fleet, 5th, 46th	925 ,,
Total	4825 ,,

On his homeward voyage Grant crossed a letter of reproof from Germaine, containing an expression of the king's displeasure at the loss of St. Vincent, and definite orders to disperse the troops for the protection of all the islands. But Grant did not shrink from meeting the storm in London. While serving with Forbes in 1758 he had indeed on one occasion lost his wits, but he was not now disposed to submit to the like reproach, he wrote:

> I do not think that I can be blamed for the loss of St. Vincent. D'Estaing had a superior force and kept it together at Martinique, so I was obliged to do the like at St. Lucia. I knew that it was not in my instructions, but at a distance of three thousand

155

miles from the capital one must act according to circumstances.

To drive home these very shrewd thrusts, he demonstrated by a few figures to Germaine the absurdity of his orders and left him to make the best of them. I dwell on these matters with reason, for it was owing to Grant's firmness in holding on to St. Lucia at all costs, and to his boundless loyalty to the fleet, that Rodney was able in 1782 to turn the scale of arms against France in the West Indies. Otherwise all would have been lost by the folly and ignorance of Germaine, who forfeits all credit for the capture of St. Lucia by his readiness to risk the loss of it. It is refreshing to find that there was an officer who would stand up to this deplorable Secretary of State; and it is not too much to say that a few more generals of Grant's stamp in America would have altered the whole course of the war.

Here, therefore, for the present we take leave of Grant. While he was yet on his way to England, d'Estaing had sailed from the West Indies to the American coast; and it is now necessary to examine the events which led him thither.

Chapter 8

The Southern Campaign

The negotiations for conciliating the Americans having failed completely, Clinton, pursuant to his instructions, had even before Grant's departure taken steps to send an expedition to Georgia. The force selected for this purpose was two battalions of Fraser's Highlanders, (then numbered 71st), four of Provincial Infantry, and two of Hessians, in all about three thousand men, under the command of Lieutenant-Colonel Campbell of Maclean's Regiment.

It is worth remarking that among the provincial troops (of which Clinton had now some four thousand in all) there was one corps composed entirely of Irish deserters from the American army under the colonelcy of Lord Rawdon. (Clinton to Germaine, 23rd October 1778).

To co-operate with this detachment General Augustine Prevost had received orders to move up to Georgia from East Florida with such troops as could be spared, and on effecting his junction with Campbell to take command of the entire force. Campbell sailed on the 8th of November, but being blown back by a storm did not arrive in the Savannah River until the 24th of December; nor did the whole of his transports pass the bar until three days later. Having no information whatever as to the enemy's numbers or dispositions, Campbell utilised these days of inaction by seizing a few of the inhabitants, from whom he learned that the American general, Howe had just returned from a predatory excursion into East Florida and was encamped, in daily expectation of reinforcements, with from twelve to fifteen hundred men for the protection of Savannah. Accordingly, on the 28th, Campbell's transports moved up the river about twelve miles; and on the following day the disembarkation began about two miles below the town.

From the landing-place the advance lay along a causeway between rice-swamps for some six hundred yards, at the end of which the ground sloped upwards; and at the top of this ascent was stationed an American advanced-post which fired upon the Highlanders as they moved forward, but speedily dispersed before an attack with the claymore. Campbell then went ahead to reconnoitre, and found Howe's troops drawn up about half a mile from the town and astride of the main road to it; their right protected by a thickly wooded morass, with a few buildings in advance of it, their left resting on the rice-swamps that bordered the river, and their front also covered by a marshy rivulet.

Two field-guns were posted in the road before their line; and about one hundred yards in advance of the guns, at a point where the sound ground on each side of the road was no more than one hundred yards wide, a deep trench had been cut through it from swamp to swamp. The position seemed formidable; but Campbell, having learned of a practicable path through the morass on the enemy's right, determined to attack at once, though little more than half of his force had yet been disembarked. Advancing at about three o'clock in the afternoon within a thousand yards of the American line, he perceived that the enemy wished and expected his attack to be delivered against their left. Being desirous, as he said, to cherish that opinion in them, he at once pushed forward the Light Infantry against their left wing, and ordered the Highlanders to follow them in support.

Then extending the Light Infantry until they were concealed by a fold in the ground, he passed them swiftly round his rear to the other flank, with orders to turn the American right by the path through the morass. His guns also he kept concealed behind an eminence until the time should come for them to be shown with advantage.

Meanwhile the enemy opened fire with their artillery, and continued, in Campbell's quaint phrase, to amuse themselves with their cannon until the Light Infantry had fairly swept round to their right rear. Campbell then ran his four guns forward to the top of the eminence that had concealed them, and under cover of their fire ordered a general advance. The Americans quickly gave way under the double attack, suffering heavily as they passed the Light Infantry in their flight. Campbell, following in hot haste, pursued them into the town; and before nightfall he was master of Savannah, together with its artillery and stores and the whole of the shipping in the harbour.

The Americans left eighty killed and eleven wounded on the field;

whereas the British loss did not exceed twenty-six killed and wounded. On its own small scale this action, with its clever feint after the model of Ramillies, was a brilliant little affair. Numbers were equally matched, but the advantage of ground was on the enemy's side, while the British troops were in bad condition after many weeks on board ship, so that Campbell deserves as much credit for his audacity as for his skill.

Though the ships which carried his horses were not yet arrived, Campbell after only two days' halt advanced up the river, getting his guns and waggons forward as best he could, but meeting nowhere with resistance.

Many inhabitants joined him, (January 1st); some with rifles and horses, who were at once organised as rifle dragoons for duties of patrolling and scouting, and others on foot and unarmed, who were turned into militia. On the 10th of January, Campbell, having cleared the lower parts of the province of rebels with the exception of a small and unimportant body at Sunbury, returned to Savannah, where he learned that Prevost had completed his last piece of work for him. Prevost from lack of horses had been compelled to conduct all his transport by water along the creeks and water-courses of East Florida, and during his march his men had frequently been driven to live for days together on oysters.

After entering Georgia, however, he heard of the party of rebels at Sunbury, and sent his brother, Mark Prevost, forward by a forced march to surround them. After a short resistance the Americans surrendered; and forty guns, great stores of ammunition, and two hundred prisoners fell into the hands of their captors. On the 17th Prevost and Campbell united their forces at Savannah; for a new enemy had appeared on the scene in the person of General Lincoln, a brave and able officer, who on the 3rd had taken up a position with nearly three thousand men at Purysburg on the Savannah River, obstructing the navigation and watching his opportunity to do further mischief.

With four thousand men, of his own, however, (detachments of the 16th, 60th, and provincial corps, in all 989 men), Prevost thought himself strong enough to pursue the reduction of the upper province; so Campbell again advanced fifty leagues up the river to Augusta. Thus by the end of February the communications of Augusta with Savannah were secured by a strong chain of posts, and to all intent the authority of King George was re-established in Georgia. One serious mishap, however, occurred during these operations, namely, the rout and capture by some American militia of a band of loyalists who were on their way to join the British at Augusta.

Seventy of the prisoners were tried for high treason by a civil court of the Revolutionary Government, and five of them were hanged. This was but an ordinary specimen of the extremes to which the quarrel between the loyalists and revolutionists had been pushed from the first in the Southern Colonies. Everywhere the revolution had been carried forward to a great extent by intimidation, but in the Southern Colonies, and particularly in Carolina, that intimidation had been of the most violent and barbarous kind. This naturally led to retaliation not less bloodthirsty; and so came a succession of reprisals and counter-reprisals which turned the quarrel between the two factions into a strife so ruthless, savage, and indiscriminate, that it was the despair alike of British and of American generals.

That there were grave faults on both sides cannot be doubted, and that many a personal revenge was wreaked and many a blood-feud prosecuted under colour of political differences, is unquestionable; but on the whole it seems that the excesses of the revolutionary party during the period of their first ascendency were primarily responsible for the internecine struggle which followed on the appearance of the British troops in Georgia and South Carolina.

Another terrible complication in these Southern campaigns was caused by the negro-slaves, who deserted the plantations in hundreds to follow the British Army, alleging that if they returned they would be shot by their masters. (Mark Prevost to Germaine, 27th November 1779).

To pretend that, in the abstract, the Briton was a man of greater humanity than the American, would be ridiculous; but it is still possible that the British, wholly ignorant of life among a teeming black population and therefore of the meaning of what is termed colour-feeling, may have dealt with the slaves more kindly than did their owners. The negroes were certainly valuable for what are called fatigue duties; and it is extremely likely, if not absolutely demonstrable, that British officers were not indisposed on occasion to make profit out of their sale. Provincial officers would assuredly have been alive to the monetary value of slaves, and British officers would not have been slow to learn.

But in any case the desertion of the negroes must have exasperated the revolutionary party to the utmost against the British; for even if the British had no intention of raising a servile rebellion—the haunt-

160

ing dread of slave-owning communities—they at any rate attracted to themselves costly property which they had no intention of restoring. Add to these elements of faction and colour the fact that, with the exception of their very few regular troops, the Americans conducted the war on the principle that the destruction of any single man of their enemies was a solid gain to be compassed by almost any means; and it is no matter for surprise that the struggle in the Southern Colonies was carried on with the bitterness which is to be found only in a civil war.

Having established his chain of posts for the security of Georgia, Prevost found himself crippled for further offensive operations by lack of men. It was the defect of all of Germaine's plans that he left garrisons and lines of communication entirely out of account; and Prevost was in want not only of men but also of money and provisions. (See his letters enclosed in Clinton's to Germaine, 25th July 1779).

Lincoln, too, now became troublesome, detaching fifteen hundred men under General Ashe up the Savannah, with orders to cross the river and threaten Augusta. The British evacuated the town and retired southward at his approach, Ashe following them up as they retreated till they reached Briar Creek, where his pursuit was abruptly and effectually stopped.

For Colonel Mark Prevost, taking a leaf out of Washington's own book, dexterously detached nine hundred men to make a wide detour and fall upon Ashe's rear by surprise, (March 3rd), with the result that four hundred Americans were killed and wounded, two hundred prisoners, seven guns, and the whole of their baggage captured, and the rest of their force scattered to the four winds, at a cost to the British of no more than sixteen killed and wounded. But this brilliant little action, telling though it was, disabled Lincoln only for a few weeks. Reinforcements of regular troops and militia restored his army to a respectable figure; and towards the end of April he again marched up the river towards Augusta, leaving General Moultrie with a thousand men to guard the lower Savannah.

Prevost, who through the capture of a British convoy at sea was threatened with scarcity of supplies, thereupon collected two thousand men and, passing the Savannah River below the American posts, boldly invaded South Carolina. But for an extraordinary and sudden rising of the waters which delayed his movements, he would probably have cut off Moultrie's retreat; but, as things fell out, Moultrie was able to escape with little loss, and fell back with all haste upon Charleston.

Lincoln, rightly judging Prevost's march to be a mere feint to draw him to southward, continued his advance upon Augusta; but Prevost, hearing that Charleston was defenceless and finding much friendly feeling among the inhabitants, now resolved to turn his feint into a reality and to endeavour to seize the capital of South Carolina.

His march is described by American writers as having been a scene of wanton vandalism, (e.*g.* Fiske, ii.); but Colonel Mark Prevost indignantly repudiated all charges of misconduct against the troops; and, if the stories of plunder and outrage be true, the explanation may be found in the fact that Prevost's force was composed chiefly of regiments raised in the Colonies themselves. (Letter to Germaine, 27th November 1779).

★★★★★★

Augustine Prevost also wrote on 16th April, "The enemy treat loyalist prisoners very ill. Only the presence of Burgoyne's captured officers with the enemy keeps me from retaliation."

★★★★★★

Be that as it may, though every bridge over the innumerable creeks on the road had been broken down, Prevost traversed the distance between Beaufort Island and the Ashley River in five days, (May 5th–10th), crossed the river on the 11th, and on the 12th summoned Charleston to surrender. The population was so far overawed that a proposal was made for South Carolina to preserve neutrality during the remainder of the war; but this overture was of course rejected.

On examining the defences of the city, however, Prevost decided that an assault would cost him more men than he could spare, for the garrison, by the rapid collection of troops and militia from all quarters, had been raised to numbers far exceeding his own. He therefore recrossed the Ashley and occupied James Island and St. John's, where there were comfortable quarters and abundant supplies for his troops, while a flotilla of small vessels assured to him a safe retreat by sea.

Notwithstanding the ability of his operations, Prevost was greatly chagrined by his failure to seize Charleston. He wrote some weeks later;

I am in bad health and too infirm for the command had I possessed my old activity when pursuing the rebels through Carolina, I should have been at Charleston as soon as they, and have taken it without firing a shot.—Prevost to Germaine, 21st August 1779.

Meanwhile Lincoln, after reoccupying the principal posts in the upper portion of Georgia, had brought back his army in hot haste on the news of Prevost's advance; and on the 4th of June the Americans moved up in front of the British posts. They refrained, however, from attacking until a fortnight later, when Prevost began to withdraw his troops to Savannah. Lincoln then seized a favourable moment to fall with great superiority of numbers upon a remnant of five hundred men, which had been left under command of Lieutenant-Colonel Maitland on St. John's Island; and the attack was only repulsed with great difficulty by Maitland's gallantry and skill after a full fourth of the British had fallen. The island was then evacuated; and Prevost's army fell back, (June 23rd), from islet to islet upon Savannah, a detachment being left at Beaufort on Port Royal Island as a perpetual menace to South Carolina.

By this time the heat was so great as to forbid all further operations.

★★★★★★

The temperature for the last three weeks has been from 90 to 98. At Ebenezer, (twenty-five miles north of Savannah), it has been up to 103.—Prevost to Clinton, 14th July 1779).

★★★★★★

Mr. Rutledge, the revolutionary Governor of South Carolina, used the occasion to write to d'Estaing, who had arrived at St. Domingo with the French fleet, asking him to employ the hurricane season in recovering Georgia in co-operation with General Lincoln. D'Estaing willingly complied, although he had orders to return at once to Europe with certain of his ships; and indeed the time was not unpropitious, for the British had no naval force ready to meet him on the coast of Carolina.

Setting sail accordingly, his first ships arrived off the mouth of Savannah River on the 1st of September, and the remainder of the fleet on the following days; the whole force consisting of twenty-two ships of the line and eleven frigates, besides transports, with a considerable body of troops. The British were taken so completely by surprise that a fifty-gun ship, a frigate, and two store-ships fell at once, after a desperate resistance, into the enemy's hands. Prevost himself appears to have received no intelligence of d'Estaing's coming until the 4th of September, when he promptly called in all outlying troops to Savannah, and set several hundred negroes to work on the defences of the town.

On the 10th of September the lighter vessels of d'Estaing's fleet entered the river, compelling the four armed brigs, which represented the naval force of Britain, to move farther up the stream. The troops were then disembarked, and d'Estaing, without waiting for Lincoln, who was on the march to join him, moved straight upon Savannah, (Sept. 15), and summoned Prevost in extravagant language to surrender. Prevost, anxious to gain time for the arrival of Maitland's detachment from Beaufort, asked for twenty-four hours to consider the matter, within which space Maitland by extraordinary exertions contrived to bring his eight hundred men safely into the town. His coming raised the garrison to a strength of thirty-seven hundred men, of whom twenty-two hundred were fit for duty. (200 of 2/60th, 720 of Fraser's Highlanders, 350 Light Infantry, a few Marines, a few men of the 16th, 2 battalions of Hessians, Provincial troops).

Prevost thereupon returned an answer of defiance, and the siege of Savannah was begun.

The entire northern front of the city being covered by the river, and the western front by a morass, the whole circuit of the defences extended for little more than a mile, every yard of which had been made as strong as possible by abatis, entrenchments, and redoubts. Want of horses delayed the arrival of the French heavy guns for so long that d'Estaing did not break ground until the 23rd; and Prevost turned this time to the best account not only by mounting additional guns, but by making two lively and successful sorties.

At length, on the 4th of October, the besiegers opened fire from sixty-seven cannon and mortars, and continued it until the 8th, though with little effect. D'Estaing now grew impatient, for there hung over him the danger that his fleet might be driven off the coast by the autumnal gales, or attacked by a British fleet from the West Indies; and he accordingly decided upon an immediate assault. The plan agreed upon was that the American militia should make a demonstration against the southern and eastern fronts, and that two columns, numbering together four thousand regular troops, should deliver the true attack. The first column, under Lincoln and d'Estaing in person, was to storm the Springhill redoubt at the south-west angle of the lines, while the other, hugging the swamp that covered the western front, should creep from thence into the rear of the defences.

Before dawn of the 9th the attacking columns advanced; but that which was designed to take the western front in reverse went astray at once in the swamp, and was unable to extricate itself before daylight exposed it to the full fire of the British batteries. The other column under d'Estaing made its way truly through the darkness and mist, and arrived close to the Springhill redoubt before it was discovered.

The British batteries at once opened a tremendous fire, but the French and Americans came gallantly on, and reaching the redoubt closed with its little garrison—a mere hundred men of the Sixtieth and Provincial corps—in a fierce and desperate struggle. Captain Taws of the Sixtieth, who was in command of the redoubt, killed two of the assailants with his own hand, but fell dead with his sword deep in the body of a third; and for a moment the enemy's colours were planted upon the parapet.

Then Maitland with the grenadiers of the Sixtieth and a party of Marines came up in the nick of time, and charged the attacking parties with a degree of fury that sent them flying in confusion back to their camp. No attempt was made to renew the assault, nor, owing to the density of the mist, did Prevost think it prudent to pursue. So after two hours of bloody work the fight ended, the enemy leaving nine hundred killed and wounded on the ground, (637 French, 264 Americans), whereas the British loss did not exceed fifty-four of all ranks. The siege was then raised, and after a great deal of angry recrimination between the Americans and their allies Lincoln retreated to South Carolina, while d'Estaing, after despatching part of his fleet to the West Indies, sailed himself with the remainder to Europe. So far things had gone well with the British arms in the south.

Meanwhile, since the end of 1778, Clinton had remained practically impotent at New York. It is true that Washington had no more troops than himself; but if New York with all its outlying posts was to be securely held, hardly a man could be spared for service in the field. Moreover, Clinton was often in deep anxiety, from want not only of men but of money and supplies. (Clinton to Germaine, 15th December 1778).

Since he had assumed command Germaine had weakened his force by fully ten thousand men, detached to the West Indies and to the south; yet the incorrigible Secretary of State, as though Clinton's numbers were still undiminished, never ceased to plague him with suggestions for the coming campaign. Now he hoped that Washington would speedily be brought to action; now he recommended a raid of eight thousand men upon the coast of New England; now he urged the importance of recovering Carolina, and founded extravagant hopes on the successes of Prevost. (Germaine to Clinton, 23rd January, 31st March, 1st April, 5th May 1779). Clinton wrote at last:

165

For God's sake, my lord if you wish me to do anything, leave me to myself, and let me adapt my efforts to the hourly change of circumstances.—Clinton to Germaine, 22nd May 1779.

Meanwhile Germaine made great promises of newly raised regiments, (Macdonnell's—then 76th; Edinburgh—then 80th), to strengthen Clinton, as well as of three thousand recruits (which latter shrank to thirteen hundred on embarkation) to fill the gaps in his ranks; but this reinforcement did not sail until May, when the fleet that escorted them was delayed first by the alarm of a French attack on the Channel Islands and later by persistent contrary winds. The result was that these troops from England did not reach New York until the 25th of August, while those which should have been returned from the West Indies were, as we have seen, detained for want of a squadron to convoy them. In the face of these facts it is not difficult to guess that Germaine's breezy designs and lofty exhortations to action must have been more than ordinarily irritating to Clinton.

Necessarily restricted by his weakness to petty operations, Clinton did what he could. In May a small expedition to the Chesapeake took or destroyed vast quantities of warlike stores and of shipping, and in July a like descent was made for the same object upon Connecticut. American writers are loud in denunciation of these "barbarous raids," and of the brutality and wanton plundering of the British troops on these occasions; but I find no support for these charges in English narratives, even among those authors who have not hesitated to record and to condemn such misbehaviour when it actually occurred.

On the other hand, I do find that in Connecticut British sentries, who had been posted to prevent pillage, were shot down by the American inhabitants, which sufficiently accounts for any severity that may afterwards have been shown towards certain towns. But in truth the attitude of Americans in regard to certain operations of this war is to an Englishman not a little puzzling. For it seems that it was perfectly legitimate for Americans to invade Canada, for instance, to maltreat and defraud the people, and to violate capitulations towards prisoners, and not less legitimate for them to leave incendiaries to burn New York over the heads of the British Army, and to hire incendiaries to burn the British dockyards. Yet when the British in their turn destroyed American depots of stores or harried the nests of American privateers, they became by a curious transformation mere mediaeval freebooters, and their actions the diabolical deeds of a brutal soldiery.

It is perfectly clear from Washington's letters that these predatory raids were extremely embarrassing to him and that they possessed decided military value, more particularly in cutting off the resources of American privateers. But Washington was too good a soldier to take a blow without returning it, and accordingly we find him retaliating effectively from time to time. Thus he recaptured the fort at Stony Point on the Hudson, (July 15th), which had been taken by Clinton only a few weeks before, and carried off five hundred British soldiers; and August 18 he made a like descent upon Paulus Hook and took one hundred and fifty prisoners. But for the most part the operations to northward were merely desultory, Washington rightly refusing to be drawn into a general action.

Nevertheless, there was one incident which possesses for us a peculiar interest. In view of the pitiful condition of the loyalist refugees at New York, it had been determined to form a settlement of them at Penobscot, on the coast about sixty leagues north of Boston. Accordingly, in June, General Francis Maclean, who commanded in Nova Scotia, was sent to Penobscot with six hundred men of his own and of Campbell's regiments, (then numbered 82nd and 74th respectively), to build in the bay a fort which should serve as a protection at once to the settlement and to Nova Scotia.

Intelligence of this design soon reached Boston, where the prevailing hostility towards the loyal New Englanders, who had left the city with Howe, at once suggested an expedition to mar the work of Maclean. By means of large bounties and an embargo three thousand troops were quickly raised, and nineteen ships armed and fitted out; for it was expected that the service would be brief, easy, and triumphant. The building of the fort was but little advanced when on the 21st of July Maclean heard of the preparations in Boston; whereupon, abandoning the completion of the permanent works, he employed his troops night and day in raising defences to secure them against assault.

Four days later, (July 25th), armament from Boston appeared, and on the 28th the American troops were landed. The British picquets hastily fell back before them, with the exception of a single party of twenty men under the command of Ensign John Moore of Maclean's, a remarkably handsome lad of eighteen, of whom the British Army would see more. This young officer, though on that day he came under fire for the first time and had none but recruits with him, thought that the other picquets had retired too soon and held on stoutly to his post, until the general sent a party to bring him in, together with the thirteen of his twenty men that still remained unhurt.

That night General Maclean gave young Moore the command of a reserve of fifty men, with orders to fall on the flank of any attacking column with the bayonet, as soon as it should reach the ditch. But the men from Boston were not so enterprising as to attempt an assault, preferring the safer methods of sap and cannonade. For a full fortnight they played their guns upon Maclean's little handful of men, interrupted by occasional sorties which retarded their operations not a little; until on the morning of the 14th of August the garrison to its surprise found the American trenches deserted and the besiegers re-embarked. The appearance in the bay of a British squadron under Sir George Collier quickly explained the mystery; and then there ensued a very curious scene.

The American ships at first formed line as if for action, but before the shock could come they gave way, and every vessel sought safety for herself. Two put out to sea, but were promptly intercepted, one being taken and the other driven ashore. The rest fled up the river, transports mingled with men-of-war in panic and confusion, with the British in chase. A few were taken, but the greater number were driven ashore, where crews and troops took to their heels and fled into the forest, to find themselves a hundred miles from any base of supplies without a scrap of provisions. Soldiers and sailors soon fell to blaming each other for the disaster; from abuse they came to blows, and from blows to a pitched battle. Fifty or sixty were killed on the spot; a far larger number perished of hunger and fatigue; and only an exhausted remnant found its way back to the settled districts of the province. Of the American fleet every one of the nineteen armed vessels was taken or burnt, and twenty-four transports were likewise destroyed. The success, in a word, was very complete, and taught a most wholesome lesson to the city of Boston.

But this little affair could give small comfort to Clinton. Admiral Arbuthnot, with the reinforcements from England, arrived at New York simultaneously, (Aug. 25th), with Collier's return thither from Penobscot; but he brought also news that war with Spain was imminent, and a fresh suggestion from Germaine for an attack on New Orleans. (Germaine to Clinton, 25th June 1779).

Only five days earlier Clinton had written, (Clinton to Germaine, 20th August 1779), asking permission for the second time to resign his command and to make it over to Lord Cornwallis, who was just returning from a visit to England; and a glance at the embarkation returns could not but confirm him in his desire.

He was never more in need of reinforcements, for General Haldimand had written, (Haldimand to Clinton, 26th May 1779), from Canada that a change had come over the people since the war with France, and that he required two thousand men, which Clinton, though ill able to spare them, most loyally sent to him. Yet the long-expected succours from Europe, which Germaine had reckoned at four thousand recruits, besides two new regiments, (Macdonnell's—76th, Edinburgh—80th), now reduced themselves to fewer than thirty-four hundred men all told. Over one hundred men had died on the voyage and nearly eight hundred more were ill of a fever, which spread so rapidly through the garrison that within a month five thousand men, and within six weeks six thousand men were on the sick list in New York.

Simultaneously there came appeals for help from Jamaica, which was trembling under the presence of d'Estaing's fleet at St. Domingo, in ignorance that his true destination was Georgia; and Cornwallis was on the point of sailing for Jamaica with four thousand men, when the news of d'Estaing's appearance at Savannah arrived just in time to stop him. Clinton took the opportunity to evacuate Rhode Island, (Oct. 28th), and to concentrate all the troops in the northern colonies at New York; but he remained in cruel suspense as to the fate of Georgia until the middle of November, when the welcome news of d'Estaing's repulse left him free to form his plans for a campaign in Carolina. (Clinton to Germaine, 21st August, 4th, 26th, 30th September, 9th, 26th, 28th October, 10th, 17th, 19th November 1779).

Fortunate it was for him that Washington had as bad a master in Congress as he himself had in Germaine. All through the summer of 1779 the American general chafed against the paucity of numbers which kept him on the defensive and left him powerless to check the raids of Clinton; nor was he less annoyed at the waste of d'Estaing's power at Savannah, when the true point of attack should have been New York. Again, there was always the jealousy of the various provinces to contend with, and their selfish care for their own safety to the neglect of the common advantage.

It was vain for Congress to offer bounties to raise a Continental Army, since the different States would always outbid them to ensure levies for their own security. This same difficulty had borne hardly on Amherst when driving the French from the Continent twenty years before; but Amherst had all England at his back, and by her help had accomplished his task. Now Washington, who of all men least deserved it, was to feel the stress of the same trouble, and to discover that as his countrymen had left the expulsion of the French mainly to England, so they now purposed to leave the expulsion of the English to France, while they busied themselves in making money. The depreciation of the paper-currency issued by Congress had now become formidable, for the value of the paper in proportion to specie had sunk to forty and even fifty to one; and nearly the whole of the Americans had given themselves up to gambling and stock-jobbing. Washington wrote in December 1778:

> Speculation, peculation, and an insatiable thirst for riches seem to have got the better of almost every order of men.

He wrote again a year later, (*Works*, vi.):

> The depreciation of our Continental money is alarming, the only hope, the last resource of the enemy; and nothing but our want of public virtue can induce a continuance of the war. . . . Virtue and patriotism are almost extinct. Stock-jobbing, speculating, engrossing seem to be the great business of the multitude.

Such seem ever and in all countries to be the first-fruits of revolution, and it is remarkable that the issue of paper-money was a liberty very dear to the birthplace of revolution in America. In the early days of the seventeenth century the godly community of Boston had set up a mint and coined base money, but had been checked by the cancelling of her charter. Twice since that time, in 1751 and 1765, the British Parliament had been driven to intervene lest New England should defraud her creditors by paying her debts in depreciated paper. Now the gates of the temple of fraud, so carefully closed by Parliament, were flung wide open by Congress, and the multitude of worshippers formed the only hope, the last resource of Britain.

Truly the contest appears in a ludicrous aspect under such illumination, neither side seeing hope of success except in the divisions of the other. It is time now to return to the arena of faction on the other side of the Atlantic.

CHAPTER 9

The Carolinas

The withdrawal of d'Estaing's fleet after his repulse before Savan-nah, 1779, left the sea open to Clinton to transport troops whither he would. Pre vest's successes in Georgia had raised Germaine's hopes to an unwonted height, for their effect had been immediate. The southern provinces could no longer send remittances to France and to the West Indies; French merchants trading with them had become bankrupt, and American credit in France at large had been seriously shaken. (Germaine to Clinton, 5th May 1779).

The conquest of Carolina became, therefore, in his eyes an ob-ject of extreme importance, in order to reduce American exports and American credit still lower; nor was the design altogether without merit, provided that men enough were given to Clinton to execute it. But this was precisely the difficulty which had hampered the British operations throughout. Germaine's reckoning on a large enlistment of Americans had proved delusive during Howe's period of command, and promised to be little better realised under Clinton. (Clinton to Germaine, 15th December 1779).

At the end of 1779 the entire force at that general's disposal, in-cluding the troops in Florida and Georgia, did not exceed twenty-seven thousand rank and file fit for duty; and since the posts at New York and Long Island demanded from twelve to fifteen thousand men for their security, the balance remaining for service in other quarters was dangerously small.

It may be asked why, since the number of troops to hand was so scanty, they should not have been withdrawn altogether from the American Colonies, and Halifax made the headquarters for all naval operations. To this the answer is that in such a case the Americans would have been left free to turn all their force against Canada and the West Indies; and it is certain that Congress cherished no enterprise more closely at heart than the conquest of Canada. The presence of a considerable force at New York, in itself a standing menace to New England, was necessary to paralyse any such offensive movement of the Americans to the northward; and events showed that it did so effectually.

The same reasoning applies with equal force to another question, namely, whether the base should not have been shifted to the south, since the south had become the principal sphere of operations. It was of course certain that, wherever the main body of the British might go, Washington and his regular troops were bound to follow; but outside the Continental Army there was always that incalculable factor the American militia, a factor which could never be counted on by its friends, but equally could never be ignored by its enemies. It was therefore imperative that New York should be held; and, this being so, it was plain that any expeditions undertaken from thence, with the force at Clinton's disposal, could be no more than predatory.

It can hardly be doubted that raids upon the coast were the best means of harassing the Americans, of widening their internal divisions, and of keeping their forces apart; for the provinces were still far too selfish to help each other, or to use their own troops for any purpose but their own individual defence. Moreover, the British could be sure of working much mischief by such inroads, whereas the Americans could do nothing except by attack on New York, which implied a great and formidable effort. But if the British undertook serious operations to southward, or at any point remote from New York, the whole situation was altered, since each new British post offered to the enemy a fresh point for attack.

A new base must first be taken and held; and if any advance into the interior was to be effective, the captured territory and the lines of communication must be sufficiently guarded. In a word, two complete armies would be needed, one at New York to hold the forces of New England in check, and another in the south. The task set to Clinton was to make one army do the work of two, relying on the sea for communication between the different sections of the force. If the command of the sea were kept, the operations might be successful but could hardly be decisive; if the command of the sea were lost—and Clinton trembled night and day before the thought they could hardly fail to be disastrous.

On the 26th of December 1779 Clinton sailed with a force of

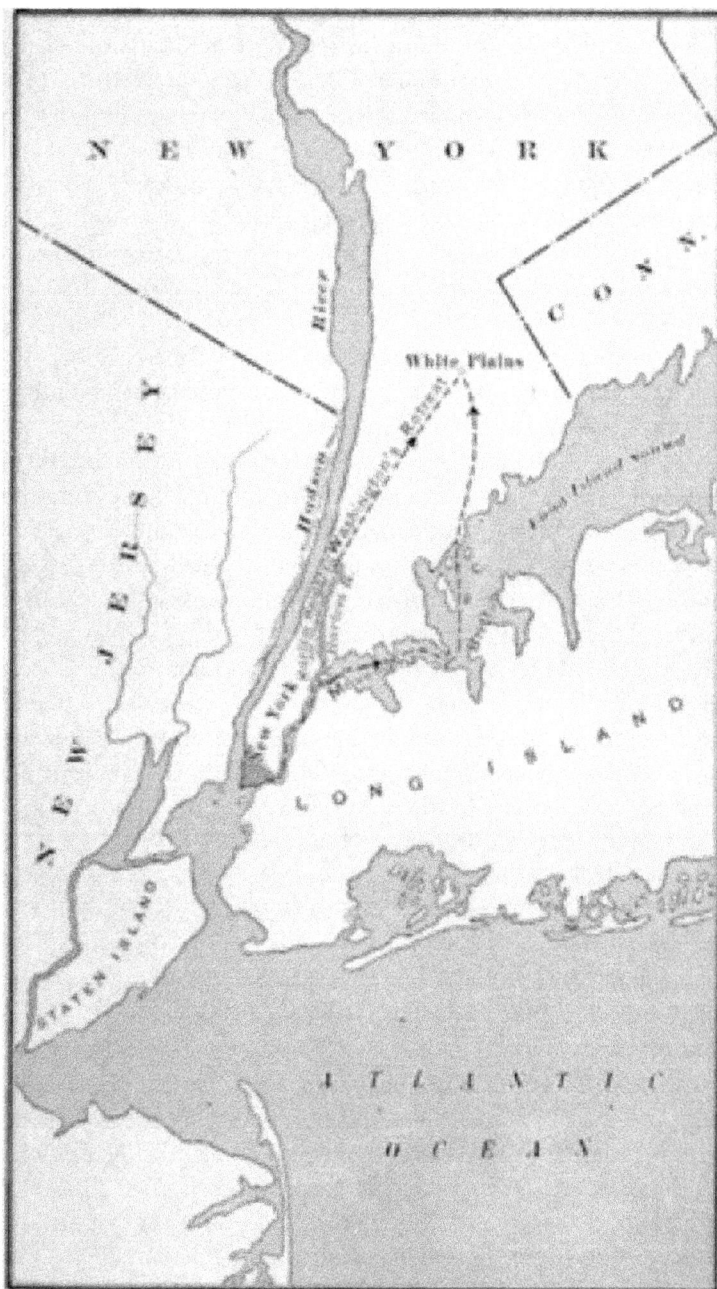

Map showing the movements of Washington and Howe to White Plains

seven thousand six hundred men, (1 batt. Light Infantry, 2 batts. Grenadiers, 7th, 23rd, 33rd, 42nd, 63rd, 64th, Queen's Rangers, 6 batts. of Germans), for the capture of his new base at Charleston, leaving General Knyphausen in command at New York. He was not in the highest spirits, having little trust in the service of the loyalists in Carolina. Many of his best officers were gone. Vaughan and Grey had sailed home sick; Campbell, the victor of Savannah, was dead; Francis Maclean, the hero of Penobscot, was dying at Halifax; worst of all, Lord Howe and Sir George Collier had gone to England, and the fleet was under command of Admiral Arbuthnot. He had, however, still Cornwallis, Rawdon, and other good officers of high rank, besides Simcoe of the Queen's Rangers and Banastre Tarleton of the "Legion," both of them fine leaders of irregular troops. In any case, he had no misgivings as to his ability to capture Charleston.

The voyage was exceptionally stormy, and the fleet was utterly dispersed. One vessel loaded with heavy cannon foundered, two or three more fell into the hands of American privateers, almost the whole of the horses perished, and it was not until the end of January 1780 that the transports arrived singly or in small groups at Tybee in Georgia. The delay gave General Lincoln time to improve the defences of Charleston and to receive from Washington reinforcements which raised the troops for defence of the town to about seven thousand men. Clinton, without waiting for any of the missing transports, summoned reinforcements from Savannah and New York and sailed again on the 10th of February for the Edisto River, where landing on John's Island he pushed forward slowly to James's Island, (11th).

Being inferior in numbers, he moved with extreme caution, fortifying his line of communication with the sea as he advanced, till at length he established himself on the south bank of the Ashley River over against Charleston. The city then stood at the tip of a tongue of land running, roughly speaking, east and west between the Cooper River on the north and the Ashley River on the south. To landward Charleston was defended by a chain of strong entrenchments and redoubts, covered by a double abatis; the line of fortifications extending from river to river except at certain points adjoining the Ashley, where a deep morass provided a sufficient natural protection. To seaward the entrance to the harbour was guarded on the south side by Fort Johnston on James's Island, and on the north side by Fort Moultrie on Sullivan's Island, by which latter the British squadron had been repulsed in 1776.

But more formidable than these forts to seaward was the bar beyond them, which was impassable by ships of the line and dangerous for frigates; while a patch of deep water just within it furnished a convenient anchorage from which the nine ships of the American squadron could play upon any British vessel that attempted the entrance.

However, at the first approach of the British squadron to the bar, (March 20th), the American commodore withdrew his ships to Cooper River, where he sank some of them to obstruct the navigation. Some of the British frigates then passed the bar, and nine days later Clinton, now strengthened by the arrival of his mounted troops from Georgia, moved twelve miles up the Ashley, crossed it unopposed, and on the next day invested the city from river to river.

On the 9th of April the British squadron ran past the batteries of Fort Moultrie with trifling loss, effectually isolating the city from the country to southward; and on the 10th Clinton summoned Lincoln to surrender, and was answered by the usual defiance.

The first thing needful, therefore, was to sever the communications of Charleston with the north, which were kept open by three regular regiments of American cavalry under General Huger, at that time encamped some thirty miles up the Cooper at Biggin's Bridge. On the 12th of April Tarleton with his Legion, (see note following), and Ferguson's Rangers surprised this corps at night, and dispersed it completely, with loss of all its stores and ammunition, four hundred horses, and one hundred prisoners.

★★★★★★

The Legion included both cavalry and infantry. The only regular troops attached to it were one troop of the Seventeenth Light Dragoons, who seem to have held the irregulars in some contempt, since they refused to wear the green uniform of the Legion, but stuck to their own scarlet.

★★★★★★

This brilliant little success, won at the cost of but three men wounded, was marred by a wanton brutality, too common among Tarleton's irregulars, which provoked Ferguson to such wrath that he was hardly restrained from shooting some of Tarleton's dragoons on the spot. The defeat of Huger effectually cleared the enemy from the ground north of the Cooper, which was now occupied by a strong force under Cornwallis.

Meanwhile, with the help of the reinforcements from New York, the besieging army pushed its trenches steadily forward, and on the

6th of May the third parallel was opened within two hundred yards of the abatis. This was a day of misfortune for the Americans. Fort Moultrie, heavily battered by sea and threatened by a strong force ashore, surrendered to the British, while Tarleton by a forced march of thirty miles northward to the Santee surprised the remnant of the cavalry that had escaped from Biggin's Bridge, killing or capturing one hundred men and carrying off the whole of the horses. Three days later Charleston surrendered, and Lincoln with his army of five thousand six hundred men, besides one thousand sailors, became prisoners of war. The losses of the British during the siege did not exceed two hundred and sixty-five killed and wounded.

Having thus gained his first great object, Clinton prepared at once to return with a portion of his army to New York, for he knew that a French fleet with reinforcements was on its way across the Atlantic, and he wished to be ready to meet it. He decided therefore to leave the completion of his task to Cornwallis, and meanwhile issued a proclamation, offering pardon to all Americans who should return to their allegiance, threatening confiscation of estates to those who should in future take up arms against the king, and inviting all well-disposed people to form a militia in order to suppress any further attempts at rebellion. Concurrently, he arranged for the advance of three separate columns into the interior, of which the first, under Cornwallis, was to move up the north bank of the Santee upon Camden, while the second should march to south-west of the Santee upon Ninety-Six, and the third up the Savannah River to Augusta.

Accordingly, on the 18th Cornwallis started with twenty-five hundred men, including Tarleton's Legion; and on the 27th, hearing that a Continental regiment of infantry under Colonel Burford, which had been ordered to march on Charleston, was now retreating in all haste before him, he sent Tarleton in pursuit. Taking with him only two hundred and thirty mounted infantry and dragoons of the Legion, and forty men of the Seventeenth Light Dragoons with one light gun, Tarleton hurried with all speed to the chase. Such was the rapidity of his march that many of his horses succumbed to fatigue and to the intense heat; but he impressed others on the road to take their place, and went on.

Reaching Camden next day, after traversing more than sixty miles, he learned that Burford had already left Rugeley's Mills, fifteen miles ahead, and was straining every nerve to join a corps that was on its way to him from the westward. After a short halt Tarleton started again at two in the morning, and by dawn was at Rugeley's Mills, where he obtained fresh intelligence of Burford, still twenty miles ahead.

He now sent forward an officer to summon Burford to surrender; but the American, far too shrewd to be delayed by such a trick, merely returned a defiant answer, and continued his march without halting for a moment. There was, therefore, nothing for Tarleton but to push on after him with exhausted men and exhausted horses. Many dropped to the rear unable to proceed farther, and the one British gun came to a standstill; but some of the men still rode on, and at three o'clock in the afternoon Tarleton's advanced party overtook Burford's rearguard and took four prisoners.

Then at last Burford faced about with his little body of infantry, less than three hundred and eighty men strong, and drew it up in a single line in an open wood, sending on his convoy and guns under protection of a small body of cavalry. Tarleton on his side sent one hundred and twenty men to open fire on Burford's left flank, selected thirty more to fall under his own leadership on his right flank and rear, and posted the remainder, including the men of the Seventeenth, in the centre, with orders to charge home. The centre moved rapidly to the attack; and the Americans with excellent discipline held their fire, by Burford's order, until the British were within ten yards of them.

The mistake though gallant was fatal. The volley was fired too late to check the rush of the horses, and in an instant the American battalion was broken up and the sabres were at work, the more fiercely since Tarleton, whose horse had been killed under him, was reported to have fallen. Over one hundred of the Americans were killed, and some two hundred more, together with two guns and all of their waggons and stores, were captured, at a cost to the British of three officers and sixteen men killed and wounded. Thus brilliantly closed an extraordinary march of one hundred and five miles in fifty-four hours. (Tarleton had once before covered sixty-four miles in twenty-three hours. Clinton to Germaine, 25th July 1779).

This success practically extirpated for the time the Continental forces in South Carolina. Cornwallis arrived at Camden a few days later, and on the 5th of June Clinton sailed for New York. His last act in Carolina was to issue a proclamation freeing all prisoners, except military men, from their paroles, but declaring also that unless they returned to their allegiance they should be treated as rebels. To this measure was ascribed much of the treacherous dealing that was shortly to follow. Meanwhile Cornwallis was left with about four thousand men to complete the recovery of South Carolina, and in due time to carry his arms into North Carolina also.

The inhabitants of South Carolina were of curiously diverse origin. Settled first by a handful of adventurers from England in 1669, the country received in succession between 1685 and 1763 immigrations of Protestants from France, of discontented Dutch from New York, of Swiss, of Palatines, and of Highlanders; while after 1763 the medley of immigrants was varied still further by the offer of bounties to all foreign Protestants who would settle in the province, and by the arrival of colonists from Virginia and Pennsylvania. The natural tendency of the different races was to segregate themselves into distinct communities; and, since inland communication depended chiefly on navigable rivers, the various settlements were distributed for the most part along one or other of the great waterways which, with their innumerable tributaries, cut their way down in parallel courses from the Blue Mountains to the sea.

The rivers with which the reader will be chiefly concerned are the Savannah, which forms the boundary between South Carolina and Georgia, the Edisto, the Santee, with its two tributaries of the Congaree and Wateree, the Peedee, and, across the border of North Carolina, the Cape Fear River. The sympathies of the people naturally varied according to the race to which they belonged, but it is noteworthy that the most prominent leaders both of loyalists and rebels bore, with a few exceptions, British or Irish names.

The Highlanders were almost to a man loyalists, as were also the Irish who had emigrated direct from Ireland; while the Irish who had moved down from other provinces were staunch for the revolution. The settlers in the hinder country were chiefly royalists, partly, as in the case of the Dutch, from a predilection for monarchy, and partly owing to the very sharp lesson against rebellion which some of them had received in 1771. In the majority of districts loyalists and revolutionists were pretty evenly divided; but there was one tract between the Broad and Saluda rivers on the upper forks of the Congaree, generally known as the district of Ninety-Six, which was a great stronghold of royalism and therefore a factor not to be ignored in any British general's plan of campaign.

In the course of the revolution South Carolina had in some respects led the rest of the Colonies in revolt. She first had shown the way towards united action, and had framed an independent provincial constitution; but the main encouragement to rebellion had been the failure of the British attempt on Charleston in 1776. Since that year until the invasion of Prevost the province had enjoyed extraordinary prosperity, the war having made Charleston the centre of supply for all the Colonies south of New Jersey. The loyalists had risen at least once in serious insurrection against the revolutionary government; but, their efforts being disjointed and uncombined, they had been put down with little difficulty, and had been forced in great measure to efface themselves.

All this was changed by the capture of Charleston. The loyalists began to come forth from their hiding-places and to take revenge for the sufferings which they had endured during the long ascendency of the revolutionary party. Both factions being made up in great measure of lawless, vindictive, half-civilised men, accustomed to settle all differences and to prosecute all feuds with the rifle, the contest between them could not but be of the bitterest.

It was in the midst of such a people, agitated with such passions, that Cornwallis found himself set down with four thousand men. His task for the present was so to canton his troops as to preserve order, while the militia was forming for the maintenance of royalist supremacy; for until the harvest should be gathered in and the heat of the summer should have passed away, active operations were impossible. His bases upon the sea were secured by garrisons at Savannah, Beaufort, Charleston, and Georgetown. Up the Savannah there was an intermediate post at Augusta and an advanced post at Ninety-Six, which latter was not only the controlling centre of the stronghold of loyalism, but dominated the upper waters alike of the Savannah and the Congaree.

Up the Santee the principal station was Camden, with a strong advanced post at Rocky Mount, on the eastern border of the loyalist district; the communication between Rocky Mount and Ninety-Six being secured by a moving column. On the Peedee the most important post was Cheraw Hill, communicating not only with Camden on the west but with Cross Creek, a settlement of loyal Highlanders on Cape Fear River, to the east. The entire area to be comprehended within these points was a tract of nearly one hundred and fifty miles square.

Having chosen these cantonments, Cornwallis returned to Charleston to settle the civil administration and to prepare for opening the campaign in September. The loyalists of North Carolina were in correspondence with him, and had been entreated to bide their time in patience until the British troops should enter the province; but with the precipitation of undisciplined men a party of them rushed into a premature and isolated insurrection,(June), which brought not only defeat upon themselves, but oppression upon all who sympathised with them, at the hands of the revolutionists.

Then the results of Clinton's second proclamation began to be revealed. Revolutionists who desired to remain neutral on parole, finding themselves compelled to swear allegiance to the king or to leave the country, took the oath with bad grace and bad faith, while the loyalists complained that notorious rebels needed only to take the said oath in order to receive as good treatment as the king's friends. The spirit of unrest was increased by the news that a detachment of two thousand men from Washington's army had reached Hillsborough, near the upper forks of Cape Fear River, (June 20th), and that reinforcements were on their way to join them. Finally, the hidden refugees of the revolutionary party reappeared from their lurking-places as guerilla bands, under leaders whose skill, activity, and daring were destined to change the whole face of the war in the Carolinas.

Thomas Sumter, a Virginian who had served with Braddock and had seen much fighting on the Indian frontier, was the first of these leaders to enter the arena, (July), midway between the upper waters of the Peedee and. Santee. Then the value of oaths was sufficiently tested. A rebel, who had sworn allegiance and obtained from Cornwallis not only a certificate of loyalty but a commission in the loyal militia, seduced his regiment from its colonel and led it to join Sumter.

Meanwhile, at the first menace of Sumter's advance Lord Rawdon had ordered the post at Cheraw Hill to be evacuated; and accordingly the sick men of the garrison were sent down the Peedee under escort of another body of loyal militia, which likewise rose against its colonel and carried the helpless invalids away as prisoners to North Carolina. Reinforced by these deserters, (July 30th), Sumter made two attacks, in quick succession upon the British posts at Rocky. Mount and at Hanging Rock, (Aug. 6th), which commanded the northward roads on the eastern and western banks of the Catawba; and though he was beaten off in both cases, it was not without heavy loss to the British. His advance was, moreover, sufficient to stir the entire district between the Santee and the Peedee to rebellion, while the revolutionary spirit was encouraged by the news, which had not yet reached Cornwallis, of the arrival of French reinforcements at Rhode Island, (July 10th).

Meanwhile the main body of the American Army still lay at Hillsborough, with Gates, the reputed conqueror of Saratoga, in command; and though no information as to his movements was obtainable from any quarter, (Rawdon to Clinton, 29th October 1780), there could be little doubt that he would advance upon Camden. Cornwallis was painfully embarrassed. The harvest was nearly over, but the magazines for his coming campaign were not yet ready at Camden; and yet he was convinced that active operations were an imperative necessity—that in fact the invasion of North Carolina, however imprudent, was the only alternative to the abandonment of South Carolina and Georgia and the withdrawal of the British troops within the walls of Charleston. (Cornwallis to Clinton, 6th August 1780).

Rawdon, who held command at Camden, was in an even more anxious position. He saw the necessity for contracting his posts and concentrating at Camden, but he dared not remove the garrisons from Hanging Rock and Rocky Mountain, lest Sumter should slip past him and either cut his communications with Charleston, or move rapidly westward and overwhelm his posts on the Broad River. He could, therefore, do nothing but wait and be vigilant; while Cornwallis wrote to Clinton, begging urgently that he would make a diversion in his favour on the Chesapeake, in order to draw Gates's army back to northward.

Gates meanwhile had marched from Hillsborough on the 27th of July. Two routes lay open to him for his advance on Camden, one of them following the arc of a circle by Salisbury and Charlottetown, but passing through a fertile country and a friendly population, and the other crossing the chord of that arc, which would lead him through a barren district wherein the few inhabitants were chiefly loyalists.

Notwithstanding that he was deficient in transport and supplies, he chose the latter route, rejecting the counsel of wiser men than himself; and, picking up sundry reinforcements on his way, he arrived on the 10th of August at Lynch's Creek, some fifteen miles north-east of Camden. To this same point Rawdon had already advanced with the few hundred troops, (23rd, 33rd, Fraser's Highlanders, Volunteers of Ireland), at his disposal, on the news of Gates's approach, and had taken up a position in rear of the creek in order to bar his advance; but he was only too painfully aware that a forced march of ten miles up the stream would enable the Americans to turn his left flank and to come down upon Camden by the road from Charlottetown.

Gates, however, instead of making this movement in force, remained for two days inactive with his main body and sent only weak detachments to his right; thus giving Rawdon time to withdraw the whole of his outlying posts to Camden, and to fall back in safety to join them. Gates then moved slowly westward, (Aug. 13th), to Rugeley's Mills, about fifteen miles north of Camden on the road to Charlottetown, and on the next day detached a party of his best troops to join Sumter in a raid upon the British communications.

Early on the same morning Cornwallis arrived at Camden from Charleston with a fixed resolution to attack Gates at all hazards.

******

Mr. Fiske assumes that Cornwallis brought reinforcements with him, but this was not the case, for he brought only his staff. This mistake in great measure vitiates Mr. Fiske's criticism of the operations.

******

He could indeed have retreated with ease to Charleston, but only at the sacrifice of some eight hundred sick men and of a vast quantity of stores at Camden, which he could not bring himself to abandon without a fight. His force was pitifully small, numbering but fifteen hundred regular troops, many of them Provincial corps, and from four to five hundred militia; but Gates, though he had thrice that number of militia, could muster no more regular troops than Cornwallis, and those of inferior quality.

At ten o'clock on the night of the 15th Cornwallis marched northward from Camden, for he had intelligence that Gates was meditating an attack, and had resolved to anticipate him. At precisely the same hour, by a ludicrous coincidence, Gates moved off to southward in the hope of surprising Cornwallis. By his own account he designed to take up a strong position on the road, about seven miles from his camp; but in this case Cornwallis outmarched him, for at two o'clock in the morning, when the British had traversed about nine miles, the advanced parties of the two armies came into collision.

The examination of a few captured Americans speedily satisfied Cornwallis that Gates was before him in force; and since the ground whereon he stood was narrowed by huge swamps on each flank, Cornwallis at once called in his advanced parties, halted, and made his dispositions to attack as soon as dawn should break. His line of battle, which extended from swamp to swamp, was made up of two brigades the Right Brigade, under Colonel Webster, consisting of three companies of Light Infantry, the Twenty-Third Fusiliers and Thirty-Third Foot, and the Left Brigade, under Lord Rawdon, of the Volunteers of

Ireland, the infantry of Tarleton's Legion, and a third Provincial corps. The whole were drawn up in the order here given, from right to left, with two six-pounder and two three-pounder guns. Two weak battalions of Fraser's Highlanders, each with one gun, stood as a support in rear of these two brigades, while the cavalry of the Legion under Tarleton was posted in rear of all. Gates formed his army into two lines, the right brigade in each line being composed of regular troops, and the left brigade of militia, with seven guns divided among the battalions. In all, his force numbered about fourteen hundred regular troops and sixteen hundred militia.

The action opened with an order from Gates to his militia to attack the British right. Addressed as it was to ill-disciplined and half-trained men, this command produced rather a confused wavering than a regular advance; and Webster promptly seized the moment to attack, while Rawdon engaged the regular troops opposed to him. The American militia thereupon flung down their arms and fled; and Webster, disdaining to pursue, at once wheeled up his brigade and fell full upon the flank of the American regular troops. So far these had held their ground against Rawdon with great steadiness and obstinacy, and even now they maintained a brave resistance for some three-quarters of an hour.

The day was so still and hazy that little could be seen through the smoke, and, the flight of the American militia being unknown to their regular troops, the latter never doubted but that the day was going well for them. But meanwhile Tarleton's cavalry, moving unseen round their flank, plunged down upon their rear; and then they broke and fled in all directions. The mounted troops promptly took up the pursuit; Tarleton pushed the chase relentlessly for twenty miles, and the rout was complete. About a thousand of the Americans were killed and wounded, and over a thousand prisoners, together with seven guns and the whole of their baggage, transport, and stores, were taken.

Baron von Kalb, a German officer of great ability in the American service, was killed, and Gates was swept away in the rush of fugitives, to find himself, when he drew rein, without an army. The loss of the British was three hundred and twenty-four of all ranks, killed and wounded, of whom one hundred belonged to the Thirty-Third Foot, (2 officers and 66 men killed; 18 officers and 238 men wounded).

The defeat was fatal to the spurious reputation of Gates, and, so far as it went, was crushing in itself. Yet it is noteworthy that on the day before the action, (Aug. 15th), Sumter had already passed to south of

DEATH OF DE KALB AT CAMDEN, S. C.

Camden, and had captured a British convoy with its escort, which was on its way to that place from Ninety-Six. There could, however, be no doubt that Sumter must retire when he heard of the rout of Gates; and accordingly Tarleton was at once sent north-westward with all speed to overtake him, while Cornwallis followed more leisurely in his rear.

Advancing up the eastern bank of the Wateree with three hundred and fifty men, (Aug. 17th), Tarleton learned from stragglers that, as he had expected, Sumter was in full retreat along the western bank; and on reaching Rocky Mount Ferry at dusk he descried the fires of Sumter's bivouac a mile away on the opposite shore. The boats on the river were at once secured, and all fires were forbidden; but at dawn it was discovered that the enemy had decamped. Tarleton forthwith crossed the river and resumed the chase, but at noon he had still failed to overtake his quarry, while his men, owing to the heat of the day and to incessant work since the action of Camden, were but few of them able to proceed.

Selecting, therefore, one hundred mounted men and sixty infantry from among them, Tarleton followed the tracks of Sumter with all possible caution, until the neighbourhood of the enemy was revealed by a shot from an American vedette, which killed one of Tarleton's dragoons. Both men of the vedette were at once cut down; and in the American camp, where there was no suspicion of the approach of the British, the shots were interpreted to signify nothing more serious than the slaughtering of cattle.

So Tarleton's handful of men stole quietly on, and were rewarded by finding the whole of Sumter's eight hundred men lying at ease about their camp, and Sumter himself but half dressed. Before the alarm could be given, Tarleton's men had secured the enemy's arms; and though some militia concealed among the waggons made some attempt at resistance, these were speedily overpowered. About one hundred and fifty of the enemy were killed and wounded, over two hundred were taken prisoners, two guns, together with the whole of their waggons and stores, were captured, and one hundred British prisoners were released, all at a cost to Tarleton of one officer killed and fifteen men wounded. Sumter in the general confusion made his escape, which was unfortunate, for so able a leader would have been a valuable prize. Tarleton was not destined again to catch him unawares.

This brilliant success, due entirely to the indefatigable energy of Tarleton, seemed at the moment to have crushed American resistance in South Carolina. The moment appeared propitious for pushing forward the invasion of North Carolina; and Cornwallis, sending emissaries to call the loyalists in the province to arms, hastened his preparations for an immediate advance on Hillsborough. Yet his situation was in too many respects disquieting. In the first place, the amount of sickness among all ranks of his army was positively alarming; in the second place, it was speedily manifest that Sumter, far from being killed, was hardly even scotched, and that besides him there were many other guerilla leaders in the field. Above all, it became more and more apparent that no trust whatever could be reposed in the local levies, miscalled loyal.

On the 19th of August, a small party of British was overwhelmed on the Broad River, owing to the desertion of its militia; and on the 24th a detachment of the American prisoners captured at Camden was actually betrayed, together with its escort, into the hands of the guerilla leader Marion, by a treacherous officer of this same militia. Cornwallis tried and executed several men who had voluntarily enrolled themselves with the British and had then turned against them; but, though without doubt he was justified in so doing, the revolutionists could always answer by reprisals. (Cornwallis to Clinton, 21st and 29th August 1780).

Lastly, as Cornwallis was aware, an invasion of North Carolina must depend for solid and permanent success on a diversion by Clinton in the north; and Clinton had long ago given warning that any such movement must be contingent on British supremacy on the sea. Nevertheless, an advance would benefit the health of the troops, not only by keeping them employed, but by moving them into a better climate; and Cornwallis determined to take the risk.

Accordingly, on the 7th of September, he advanced from Camden in two columns, the main body, (23rd Fusiliers, 33rd Foot, Provincial troops), under his own command moving up the eastern bank, and the light troops and cavalry up the western bank, of the Wateree. A third detachment under Major Ferguson at the same time moved up wide to the north-westward from Ninety-Six, with the object of raising recruits for the militia, in which Ferguson still reposed a confidence which no one else could share.

The progress of the main body was slow owing to scarcity of forage, and it was not until the 22nd that Cornwallis arrived and halted at Charlottetown. This district was a hotbed of revolution, and the British while they remained in it were harassed by incessant attacks on outposts and on convoys, while communication was rendered most difficult by the incessant waylaying or shooting of the British despatch-riders. Then, as usual, guerilla operations began again in rear of Cornwallis, and a fierce attack was made upon the post of Augusta, in Georgia, but was successfully repulsed with heavy loss to the Americans.

The officer in command at Ninety-Six at once conceived the hope of cutting off this American party on its retreat to northward; but finding that the chase led him too far afield, suggested the same idea to Ferguson. Eagerly embracing the project, Ferguson hurried to westward until he had placed at least seventy miles between his detachment and Charlottetown, when he suddenly found himself threatened by a new and wholly unexpected enemy in the shape of three thousand settlers from the extreme backwoods, rough, half-civilised men whom no labour could tire, and whose rifles seldom missed their mark. Realising his danger, Ferguson instantly sent messages for help to Charlottetown, and retreated towards that place with all haste. But every one of his messengers was shot down; and the backwoodsmen, sending forward fifteen hundred picked men to ride after him, made so swift a pursuit as to leave him no hope of escape.

On the 6th of October, therefore, he chose a strong position on a hill known as King's Mountain, and turned to bay. This hill was covered with tall forest, beneath which the ground was strewn with huge boulders, while on one side it was rendered absolutely inaccessible by a precipice; and Ferguson seems never to have dreamed that he could not hold it for ever. On the following afternoon the advanced party of the backwoodsmen arrived, about a thousand strong, and, having tied up their horses and divided themselves into three bodies, began to ascend the hill from three sides.

Creeping up in silence, every man confident in his skill as a stalker and a marksman, the central division made its way up to the crest, where Ferguson's men met them with a volley and a charge with the bayonet. The backwoodsmen then fell back slowly, keeping their pursuers in check by a biting fire from behind the trees and boulders, until a storm of bullets in Ferguson's flank showed that a second division of his enemies was lying in wait for him. Turning at once upon them, Ferguson found that the third division of backwoodsmen, which had been hidden on the opposite flank, was firing steadily into his rear.

Thus entrapped, the militia found the odds too many against them. Still they fought hard until Ferguson was killed; and nearly four hundred of them had fallen killed and wounded before the remainder, rather more than seven hundred, laid down their arms. The whole loss of the backwoodsmen was eighty-eight killed and wounded, and the only marvel is that it should have been so great, for their exploit was as fine an example as can be found of the power of woodcraft, marksmanship, and sportsmanship in war. The victors celebrated their success by hanging a dozen of their prisoners before they dispersed, in revenge for the execution at Augusta of certain militiamen who had been taken in arms against the British after accepting service with them. The victims were of course Americans, for it was not Mother Country and Colonies but two Colonial factions that fought so savagely in Carolina.

This unexpected blow shattered Cornwallis's whole plan of campaign at a stroke. The disaster fell the more hardly upon him since he had given Ferguson orders to retire, (*Cornwallis Correspondence*, i.), not wishing him to wander beyond reach of support on the other side of the Catawba; though it must be added that the very existence of such a force of backwoodsmen was unknown to him or to his staff. But none the less he acquitted his unlucky subordinate of all blame, and, as became a brave and chivalrous gentleman, took upon himself all responsibility for his defeat.

The loss of Ferguson himself, the most expert rifleman in the British Army and an admirable partisan leader, was a great misfortune; but that of his eleven hundred men was for the moment irreparable. There was nothing for it but to retreat; and accordingly on the 14th Cornwallis fell back on Winnsborough, his troops suffering much from scarcity of food and from exposure to incessant rain during the retreat. Sickness increased, and Cornwallis himself was among those that were stricken. He therefore committed his pen to Lord Rawdon, (Rawdon to Clinton, 29th October 1780), who wrote on his behalf to Clinton, setting forth with great ability the hopelessness of reliance on the loyalists of North Carolina, the certainty that a junction with them was not worth the risk of losing South Carolina, and his conviction that, whatever the difficulties and dangers of a defensive war, these were preferable to the perils of adherence to the original scheme of invasion. Beyond all doubt these views were wise and sound, though the reader before long will ask himself whether they were as much those of Cornwallis as of Rawdon. Still, for the present, further advance towards North Carolina was suspended.

CHAPTER 10

The Grinding Wheel

It is now time to return to Clinton, who had reached New York on the 17th of June, six months after his first departure for Charleston. During his absence the usual neglect of Congress, added to the rigour of a terrible winter, had done more than any operations of the British to dissolve the American Army. The country near New York had been exhausted of all supplies; transport, owing to the depth of snow on the roads, was extremely difficult; and finally the depreciation of the American paper-money was such that the people would not accept it in payment for provisions. Washington wrote in January 1780 that his army had never been in so distressing a state since the beginning of the war; and in fact he was compelled to levy contributions lest his troops should disband themselves from sheer want of food. (Johnson's *Life of Greene*, i.).

In April things had improved but little. The officers of the Continental regiments had never been so much dissatisfied; the men were constantly on the point of starving from dearth of victuals and forage, and the patience of both was very nearly exhausted. (Washington, *Works*, v.; vi.).

At length Lafayette appeared on his return from a flying visit to France, with the news that French reinforcements would arrive shortly, together with a sufficient fleet; and Washington was not a little comforted, for Clinton's successful attacks on points remote from each other had forced him to confess that such a system, if continued, might be fatal. In May, however, his former troubles began again. His army was once more reduced to extremity by want of provisions; and the insubordinate and seditious spirit within it finally culminated in the mutiny of two Continental regiments.

Yet still the revolted provinces remained insensible and indifferent, and there was little hope of a change for the better; on the contrary, there was rather new danger ahead in the rapidly and deservedly declining power of Congress. There is no more ruthless commentary on the glowing narratives of the struggle of the Colonies for independence than the letters of Greene and of Washington.

On the 10th of July the French Admiral de Ternay arrived off Newport, Rhode Island, with seven ships of the line, three frigates, and transports containing six thousand troops under Count de Rochambeau. This squadron, however, gave the French supremacy at sea for only three days, since on the 13th Admiral Graves arrived from England with a reinforcement for Admiral Arbuthnot; but it should seem that Graves, if he had done his duty, would have arrived on the coast before de Ternay and enabled Arbuthnot to gain a signal advantage. (Germaine to Clinton, 4th October 1780).

Nevertheless, since British supremacy at sea was established, the British commanders determined to attack the French in Rhode Island forthwith; and on the 27th of July Clinton, having embarked the necessary troops, sailed with them into Long Island Sound. Washington thereupon at once marched upon Kingsbridge with twelve thousand men, a force which compelled Clinton, weakened as he was by the detachments in Carolina, to turn back on the spot; so that Arbuthnot sailed with the fleet alone to blockade the French in Newport.

This was a bitter disappointment to Clinton, whose complaints against both Admirals seem to show that dissension between the two services, rather than Washington's movements, was responsible for the collapse of the enterprise. None the less, the blockade of Narragansett Bay sufficed to neutralise every effort of the French and Americans on the side of New York; for a second division of French troops and ships, which should have joined de Ternay, had been shut up in Brest by the British Channel Fleet.

Thus for the third year in succession the French alliance had accomplished nothing for the Americans; and Washington was almost in despair. His levies came in but slowly, provisions were still scarce, and patriotism was almost extinguished, while the depreciation of the paper-currency was such that his troops absolutely declined to receive it. He wrote in August:

To me it will be miraculous if our affairs can maintain themselves much longer in their present train.

The news of Gates's defeat at Camden could not but increase his discouragement. De Ternay wrote at this time:

> The fate of North America is still very uncertain, and the revolution is not so far advanced as has been believed in Europe.

Which is a singular confirmation of former expressions of French officers, as to the comparative enthusiasm over the revolution in Paris and on the American continent. At his wits' end, Washington wrote to Admiral de Guichen, who commanded a French squadron in the West Indies, setting forth his situation and entreating for help; but de Guichen, as shall presently be explained, was busy enough over his own affairs. Meanwhile the intrigues of unscrupulous men in Congress, Samuel Adams among them, had driven Greene, one of Washington's best officers, to resign his post as quartermaster-general.

Greene had written so far back as in April:

> I have lost all confidence in the justice and rectitude of the intentions of Congress.

He now added with yet fiercer indignation, (Washington, *Works*, vii.; Johnson's *Life of Greene*, i.):

> Honest intentions and faithful services are but a poor shield against the machinations of men without principles, honour, or modesty.—

Such machinations, though powerless to provoke so upright a man as Greene to reprisals, were not without effect upon another more brilliant but less scrupulous character among the American generals. After the great American success at Saratoga, Benedict Arnold, to whom it was principally due, had been placed by Washington in command at Philadelphia, since a wound for the time disabled him from further service. It is a singular fact that luxury and extravagance never reigned with such unbounded licence in Philadelphia as in the years when the Americans, according to the narratives of their historians, were struggling to throw off the chains of despotic England. Arnold, penniless though he was, outdid all others in Philadelphia in ostentation, particularly in the matter of his stable; for he was a great lover of horses, and indeed had at one time been a horse-dealer, which is a calling not usually associated with scrupulous honesty or with loftiness of principle.

Naturally he ran into debt, and as naturally he resorted to speculation to clear himself; nor is it difficult to believe that he may have abused his high position to further the success of his ventures. Further, he betrothed himself to the most beautiful girl in the city, who happened to belong to a loyal family; and thus he brought himself into closer relation with loyalists, whom possibly he may have found to be pleasanter company than the contrary party. Having thus tasted the pleasures of peace and quietness, he announced his intention of leaving the army, of obtaining a grant of land near New York, and of retiring into private life.

But a man who in virtue of natural military genius has outshone incapable superiors in the field, who keeps the best table and the best horses at a time when ostentation is most fashionable, who enjoys and uses peculiar facilities for making money by crooked methods when the competition in that particular field is at its keenest, and who finally carries off the loveliest woman of his society for his wife—such a man cannot fail to make enemies. Thus when Arnold went to New York with a view to acquisition of the land which he desired, his back was no sooner turned than the Council of Pennsylvania formulated a series of accusations against him, and published them far and wide in all the provinces.

After long delay, due to much tortuous dealing on the part of the Council, he was tried by court-martial and acquitted of all but two very trivial charges; but meanwhile he had entered into anonymous correspondence with Clinton, (April), in order to be revenged upon his enemies. With the same object he abandoned all idea of leaving the army, and sought and obtained from Washington, (July), who was anxious to give proof of his confidence in him, the command of the fortress of West Point on the Hudson River.

The correspondence with Clinton, always conducted through his adjutant-general, Major Andre, now became more frequent and more definite; and it appeared pretty certain that Arnold was the correspondent when proposals were put forward to betray West Point, a new stronghold which secured to the Americans the command of the Hudson, and which, it was reckoned, could not be taken by a smaller force than twenty thousand men. The plot thickened; and most opportunely, though unexpectedly, on the 16th of September there arrived from the West Indies not de Guichen, as Washington had hoped, but his opponent, Sir George Rodney, with half of his squadron.

Clinton at once embarked troops, spreading everywhere the report that they were bound for the Chesapeake; and on the 18th Washington started for Rhode Island to consult with Rochambeau as to this unlooked-for complication. Advantage was at once taken of his absence for Andre and Arnold to meet; and the former accordingly went up the river in a frigate and arranged with Arnold the final details for the capture of West Point. But by the merest accident the American batteries opened fire on the frigate and compelled her to drop down the stream, so that André was compelled to return to the British lines disguised as a countryman.

On his way he was stopped by a party of *banditti*, and, betraying himself by sheer bad luck to be a British officer, was arrested and carried into the American lines. The report of his arrest was in due course reported to Arnold, who with marvellous presence of mind effected his escape; but André was tried by court-martial as a spy, and, on the damning evidence of certain documents found in his boots, was sentenced to be hanged.

Beyond all doubt this sentence was perfectly justified by the rules of war, but equally beyond all doubt it was pronounced in the hope that Clinton, in order to save André, would surrender Arnold. Indeed, it was covertly whispered to Clinton that if Arnold were allowed to slip into the hands of the Americans, Andre would be set free. Moreover, the Americans at large had not shown themselves particularly scrupulous in the observance of the rules of war, and Washington himself little more scrupulous than others.

He had indeed discountenanced the use of split bullets by his men, as well as wholesale breach of parole by his officers; and he had strongly reprobated the sale of British medicines, which had been supplied for the benefit of American prisoners, by American doctors for their own profit. (Washington, *Works*, iv.). Yet we find him suggesting of his own motion that a party of an American regiment, which happened, unlike other corps, to be dressed in scarlet, should be furnished with the buttons of some English regiment, in order that they might pass for English soldiers and kidnap General Clinton. (*Ibid.*, v.).

Now, had these American soldiers, thus attired, been caught in the act, Clinton would have been perfectly justified in hanging every one of them; and their blood would have been upon Washington's head. It seems to me, therefore, unquestionable that the rigorous execution of Andre's sentence was employed chiefly as a means of putting pressure of a peculiarly cruel kind upon Clinton; and it was for this reason and for no other that it was so much resented by the British Army, (see Simcoe's *Queen's Rangers*), and the British nation.

Meanwhile, the fact remains unshaken that Washington acted

within his right in confirming the sentence. Any charges of ungenerosity against him are entirely beside the mark; for it is not the business of a general to show generosity to his enemies, rather it is his duty to withhold it if he think generosity impolitic. André therefore, having petitioned in vain to be shot, went to the gallows without flinching, as became a British officer and a British gentleman. He had done his duty with full knowledge of the risk, so could not be dishonoured in his death.

The failure of Arnold's treachery and the arrival of Rodney's squadron left Clinton free to comply with Cornwallis's request for a diversion on the Chesapeake, for which Arbuthnot had declared himself unable to spare ships. (Clinton to Germaine, 30th August 1780).

Not that Clinton viewed inland operations in Carolina with any favour, for he was persuaded that all hopes founded upon the loyalists were visionary. He wrote to Germaine, (*Ibid.*, 25th August 1780):

An inroad is no countenance and to possess territory demands garrisons.

Nevertheless, Cornwallis's situation appeared so critical that he embarked between two and three thousand troops, (Guards, Maclean's— 82nd, 1 German batt., 2 Provincial corps; in all a nominal 2500 men), under Major-General Leslie, with orders to sail to the Chesapeake, thence to proceed as far as possible up James River, destroying any magazines at Petersburg or elsewhere, and, after establishing a post on Elizabeth River, to gain touch with Cornwallis. By these means he hoped to sever the American communications between Virginia and Carolina, and to ruin at any rate some of the enemy's chief depots of supplies.

Leslie accordingly sailed for his destination on the 16th of October, just two days after Cornwallis's retreat from Charlottetown; but, very soon after arriving in the Chesapeake, he received a letter from Rawdon in Cornwallis's name, (Nov. 9th), which altered for him the whole aspect of the situation. The document simply showed that the tranquillity of South Carolina, upon which the whole plan of a diversion had been based, was illusory, and begged Leslie, if his instructions permitted him, to move his force to Cape Fear, where his co-operation would really make itself felt. (Rawdon to Leslie, 24th October 1780).

Clinton approved of this, thereby committing himself more deeply to inland operations in Carolina, towards which he now further engaged himself to contribute another diversion on the Chesapeake.

It was an unfortunate time for such a decision, since Washington had just submitted to Congress a scheme for reorganising the American Army, which measure could not but modify the whole of Clinton's plans. Arnold was for meeting Washington's new designs with a counter-stroke, which would probably have defeated them. He wrote to Germaine, (Arnold to Germaine, 28th October 1780. *S.P. Col. America and West Indies*):

The troops of the enemy engaged for the war have received a promise of half-pay for seven years after its close, of one hundred acres to every private and eleven hundred acres to every general. Why not offer to make good to them all arrears, equal to about £400,000, to give half-pay for seven years, two hundred acres to every private and ten thousand acres to every general, as also a bounty of twenty guineas to every deserter who enlists for the king? It would be cheaper than importing men from England. Authorise me to do this, and I have no doubt of recruiting two or three thousand of as good soldiers as there are in America. Money will go farther than arms in America.

There was shrewd worldly knowledge, whatever the cynicism, in these proposals; nor were Arnold's plans for a future campaign less sensible:

There are two ways of ending the war. The first is to collect the whole army and beat Washington, secure the posts which command the Hudson, which could be done in a few days by regular approaches, and cut off the Northern from the Southern Colonies. The supplies of meat for Washington's army are on the east side of the river and the supplies of bread on the west; were the Highlands in our possession, Washington would be 1780. obliged to fight or to disband his army for want of provisions. The second way is to concentrate the whole army, except the garrison of New York, to the southward; but instead of marching three or four hundred miles from South Carolina to Virginia, we ought to seize Baltimore, which would overawe Virginia and Maryland, and proceed thence to Pennsylvania and New Jersey. But an army of fifty thousand men, wherever placed, will do nothing without energy and enterprise.

Other soldiers besides Arnold had long striven to din the principle of concentration into the deaf ears of Germaine.

Such, therefore, was the position in America at the close of 1780. Cornwallis had been forced back to Winnsborough in South Carolina, with his communications everywhere threatened, and with his whole plan of invasion wrecked by the defeat of Ferguson; while Clinton, always apprehensive as to the movements of Washington and of the French at Rhode Island, was weakening his force by constant detachments to the south, for inland operations which at heart he disapproved. So far superiority at sea had enabled him to carry on the war on these terms; but how long that superiority might endure was another question.

It is now necessary to turn to the West Indies, in 1779. order to trace the course of events which brought Rodney so unexpectedly to New York. General Grant sailed from St. Lucia for Europe in August 1779, leaving General Prescott at St. Kitts to command the troops in that island and in Antigua, and Brigadier Calder at St. Lucia. His departure was followed by a general confusion of all military arrangements to windward. Troops there were in abundance, for British inferiority at sea had prevented the return of four battalions to Clinton at New York; but the sickly season was at its height.

At St. Lucia the soldiers began to fall down fast from want of proper shelter; for the planters, directly that Grant's strong hand was withdrawn, refused to spare their negroes to repair the temporary barracks, doubtless in the hope of hastening the recapture of the island by the French. (see list following).

Calder to Germaine, 19th September, 26th October 1779.

Returns of troops—19th September, 1137 fit for duty, 510 sick; 29th October, 933 fit, 500 sick; 30th December, 685 fit, 576 sick. The gradual diminution of numbers is of course due to deaths.

In St. Kitts and Antigua, though sickness was less prevalent, there was almost more danger owing to the disloyalty of the population and the encroachment of the civil governor, Mr. Burt, on the province of the military commander. St. Kitts itself is an island on which, from the multitude of practicable landing-places, it was impossible to prevent an enemy from disembarking and laying waste the country. The island, further, so far differs in conformation from its sisters that the mountains, instead of extending to the sea on all sides, are surrounded by a belt of plain, with but one position that offers advantage to a defending force of inferior numbers.

196

This position, famous in the annals of West Indian warfare, is an isolated eminence called Brimstone Hill, which lies near the south-western corner of the island, fully nine miles from the chief town of Basseterre and therefore of no protection to it. Here accordingly Prescott resolved to make his citadel for final resistance in case of a French attack, but found himself thwarted at every turn by the ignorant and conceited interference of Governor Burt. The relations between the two were strained almost to rupture when Burt, as a climax of folly, ordered two battalions to be moved from Antigua to St. Kitts, that is to say, from windward to leeward, leaving the whole of the naval stores and the only good harbour in that group of islands exposed to capture by any enemy. (Prescott to Germaine, 30th August, 29th December 1779; 17th January 1780).

Happily this state of things was presently ended. In December 1779 Major-General Vaughan, who had just returned from America with high commendations from Clinton, was appointed commander-in-chief in 1779. those islands and ordered to sail to the West Indies with Rodney's squadron. He sailed accordingly in January 1780. with two complete regiments, (Keating's/88th, Gary's/89th), and drafts of recruits; and while Rodney defeated the Spanish fleet and threw succours into Gibraltar, as has been already narrated, Vaughan proceeded with the transports to Barbados, and on arriving there, (February 14th), found Sir Hyde Parker awaiting him with a fleet of sixteen sail of the line.

Germaine had left Vaughan a free hand, but had recommended the recovery of Grenada and St. Vincent as objects of prime importance; only suggesting further, in his usual airy fashion, that an attack should be made on Porto Rico, though without a word as to the means whereby that island should be held, if captured. (Germaine to Vaughan, 7th December 1779).

Meanwhile the policy of dispersion, enforced by Germaine in the face of Grant's advice, had produced its inevitable effects. Scattered as they had been all over the islands, the troops had been practically useless for purposes of defence, and now they were found to be useless also for attack; while want of transports made concentration a work of great difficulty. Having first despatched a part of his reinforcements to Jamaica, Vaughan sailed without delay to Antigua, and found the regiments there and at St. Kitts sickly, spiritless, and lifeless.

If troops are not kept together in the West Indies the best of them will soon cease to be soldiers.

Such had been Grant's warning to Germaine in the previous year; and Vaughan had now to pay for Germaine's perversity. With great difficulty he contrived to embark the majority of the men, and, leaving twelve hundred only at St. Kitts, sailed with the remainder to St. Lucia, (March 10th). The voyage of two hundred and fifty miles against the trade-wind occupied ten days, from which the reader may judge of the risks incurred by Germaine's insane policy of scattering troops to leeward.

Vaughan arrived in St. Lucia only just in time; for on the 22nd of March a strong reinforcement for the French fleet and army reached Martinique under Count de Guichen, and on the 23rd a powerful force, escorted by twenty-two ships of the line, came before Port Castries to attempt the recapture of St. Lucia. Sir Hyde Parker had but sixteen ships; but so skilful were his dispositions at his anchorage, and so strong were Vaughan's defences on Morne Fortuné and Vigie, that de Guichen put back into Martinique without venturing to attack.

Here, however, was the command of the sea lost to the British, while five precious weeks, which might have been turned to good account before de Guichen's arrival, were wasted in the concentration of troops which ought never to have been dispersed. Meanwhile Rodney, having finished his work in the Mediterranean and sent home the bulk of his fleet, had arrived at Barbados with four ships only; Germaine having promised that he should be reinforced by three of Arbuthnot's ships from the North American station. Since, however, these ships never appeared, the British fleet necessarily remained inferior in strength; and Vaughan, seeing that offensive operations were out of the question, reinforced the garrisons of Antigua and St. Kitts and prepared to stand on the defensive, (April 17th).

A month later Rodney gallantly engaged de Guichen with twenty ships against twenty-three. Vaughan was on the flagship with him, and large numbers of troops were serving as marines in the action, which, notwithstanding the disparity of force, bade fair to be a brilliant victory for the British. But the unfortunate misinterpretation of a signal deprived Rodney of his reward; and the battle was indecisive. Correct reading of a few fluttering rags of bunting might have altered the whole course of history; but such is the fortune of war.

The failure of this engagement extinguished all hopes of an active and successful campaign to windward. Fragments of four regiments,

(St. Leger's/86th, Clinton's/87th, Tottenham's/90th, Acland's/91st), had begun to drop into various ports of the West Indies, the intention having been that they should do service first in that quarter and pass on during the hurricane season to New York. But the transports had been dispersed by a gale off the Lizard, and, since by some extraordinary oversight no port of rendezvous had been indicated to the masters before they sailed, fully a quarter of them put into Cork, about half went to Barbados, and the rest sailed to Antigua. (Germaine to Vaughan, 20th January; Vaughan to Germaine, 22nd and 23rd March 1780).

Thus, when there were ships enough for an attack there were no troops to act with them, and when there were troops enough to act there were no ships to escort them. The arrival in June of a Spanish squadron, which raised the allied fleets in the West Indies to a strength of thirty-four ships against Rodney's eighteen, threatened destruction to the whole of the British islands, the more so since there was alarming sickness among the troops in St. Lucia. (882 men out of 2086 on the sick list. Vaughan to Germaine, 31st May 1780).

But on the ships of the Allies also there raged a terrible epidemic, and after some weeks of delay and vacillation they broke up about the middle of July. In August de Guichen sailed to Europe with fifteen ships, which had been badly shattered in the action of the 17th of April; and the danger for the present passed away. Ignorant, however, of de Guichen's destination, Rodney sailed, as has been seen, to New York. He was in no amiable temper, and had already sent a letter to Arbuthnot to tell him that, but for his omission to reinforce the West Indian fleet, both the French fleet and the Spanish auxiliary squadron would have been destroyed. (Rodney to Arbuthnot, 18th June 1780). Yet, as shall be seen, Arbuthnot was by no means to blame.

How Rodney was employed at New York has already been told, nor for the present need we follow him farther; but it is remarkable that his proverbial good luck, by drawing him to America, saved him from a great disaster. On the 10th of October a hurricane of appalling violence broke over a part of the Windward Islands and wrought frightful destruction. In Barbados, where the fury of the storm was fiercest, the whole island was laid waste, four thousand inhabitants, over nine thousand horned cattle and horses, and smaller stock without number were killed, and the damage to property was reckoned at over a million sterling.

In St. Lucia, where close on six hundred soldiers had died during

June, July, and August, every building was unroofed, the sick were lying in pools of water, most of the ammunition was spoiled, and the whole of the transports were driven ashore. Nor was the mischief to be reckoned only by damage to property and shipping. Over and above the terrifying influence of the hurricane itself, there was the danger of a large servile population suddenly freed from all restraint and let loose to plunder and destroy; and the task of restoring order, which necessarily fell chiefly on the troops, bore heavily on bodies already weakened by sickness and now further enfeebled by exposure.

So miserably ended the campaigning season in the Windward Islands for the year 1780. Yet, strangely enough, the hurricane proved to be a blessing in disguise; for the levelling of the tropical forest by the storm converted St. Lucia by magic from a deadly into a healthy station.

To leeward matters went little better than to windward. Pursuant to the grand scheme for drawing a chain of posts across the Central American isthmus from ocean to ocean, a force of four hundred regular troops, (detachments 60th, Liverpool Regiment/79th, and of Dalrymple's Jamaica Corps), under Captain Poison of the Sixtieth had sailed from Port Royal on the 3rd of February for the Bay of Honduras. Poison's orders were to make first for Cape Gracias a Dios in order to pick up a contingent of Indians, who were supposed to be disaffected towards Spanish rule, together with a flotilla of small sailing craft which was expected from the English settlement at Black River.

On arriving at his destination, (Feb. 14th), however, he found that Spanish agents had been tampering with the Indians and that the flotilla was not arrived. Three weeks passed away before the boats came in, when the expedition continued its voyage southward, stopping at Sandy Bay and at Pearl Cay lagoon to collect more Indians, which involved a stay of four or five days at each of these places. Finally, when Poison at length arrived in St. John's Harbour, Nicaragua, there was more delay, owing to unskilful loading of the small craft, so that April was come before the flotilla could start up the river for the Lake of Nicaragua. For a week the little force, urged on by the impetuous energy of Nelson, moved from five to ten miles a day against a rapid current in stifling heat; and then it was found that further progress by water was impossible.

The troops were accordingly landed, (April 10th), and warily drawn round Fort St. Juan, the work which guarded the outlet from the lake to the river. One officer, whose enterprise could not be subdued even by sweltering heat in a pestilent climate, offered to lead a storming party against the fort on the spot; but it was thought expedient to proceed to a cannonade in form. Accordingly, with immense labour the heavy ordnance was brought up, and fire was opened on the 13th; but so low was the strength of the party reduced that almost every gun was laid either by Nelson or by Lieutenant Despard, the chief engineer. At last, after six weary days, the garrison was reduced by want of water to capitulate, (April 29th).

Governor Bailing wrote grandiloquently from Jamaica, but to what advantage he did not explain:

Thus the door to the South Seas is burst open.

Owing to constant delays, which must be attributed to blind faith in the stories of Indians and to profound ignorance of the country to be traversed, the expedition had occupied three entire months instead of the four weeks which had been thought sufficient for it; and the rainy season was drawing dangerously near. Dalling had sent a reinforcement of three hundred and fifty men close on the heels of the first detachment; but sickness was so general and so deadly among the troops that Colonel Kemble, who had now assumed command, had no energy to continue the advance to the lake, where the climate was said to be healthier.

The very Indians were sickly and began to desert in numbers. By the middle of May there were not men enough to do the duty of the camp, and the guards remained unrelieved for forty-eight hours. (Poison to Dalling, 30th April 1780. Kemble to Dalling, 19th May 1780).

Kemble, therefore, left a garrison at Fort St. Juan, and sent the rest of the force back to St. John's Harbour. But the troops were as sickly by the sea as on the river, and at the end of June but ten men out of two hundred and fifty were fit for duty. (Sir Alex. Leith to Dalling, 26th June 1780).

Still, Dalling continued to pour in such reinforcements as he could, though he could send few except privateersmen from Jamaica, unruly and insolent fellows who gave a great deal of trouble and were useless for any military purpose. Altogether some fourteen hundred men of one kind and another seem to have been sent to Nicaragua; but by the end of September only three hundred and twenty of them, blacks and whites, were left alive, while of these not one-half were fit for duty. (Captain Clarke to Dalling, 27th September 1780).

Officers who were sent out to report on the situation declared that with greater activity the object of the expedition might have been accomplished, (Sir Alex. Leith, enclosed in Dalling to Germaine, 2nd November 1780), but they did not mention how the garrisons at each end of the isthmus were to be maintained.

Finally, on the 8th of November, Dalling ordered Fort St. Juan to be blown up and Nicaragua to be evacuated; and so ended this disastrous enterprise, which is remembered chiefly by the fact that Nelson took part in it and came out of it alive. (Judging by the medical certificate upon which he was invalided, it was almost a miracle that Nelson recovered).

While Dalling, faithful to the example set by Germaine, was thus frittering away the lives of his men, the Spaniards had not been idle. In March a Spanish force of no great strength appeared at its leisure before Mobile, escorted by a single armed vessel, and swept away the little garrison of three hundred men. Pensacola only narrowly escaped the same fate through the timely arrival of the British squadron; yet the warning of the mishap at Mobile was not laid to heart. A feeble little force was still maintained at Pensacola, as a standing invitation to the Spaniards and a perpetual source of anxiety to the Commodore at Jamaica.

Unfortunately, also, Jamaica during this season was proving itself little less deadly to the troops than Nicaragua. Four of the newly raised regiments, (Harrington's/85th, Jas. Stuart's/92nd, M'Cormick's/93rd, Dundas's/94th), in England had been ordered to the West Indies in February, but through some mismanagement had not arrived at St. Lucia until July, just at the opening of the sickly season.

From thence they sailed to Jamaica, arriving there on the 1st of August, by which time out of twenty-three hundred men one hundred and sixty-eight were dead and seven hundred and eighty on the sick list. (Governor Dalling to Secretary of State, 12th August. Major-General Garth to same, 11th August 1780).

The mortality rapidly increased; and between the 1st of August and the 31st of December 1780 eleven hundred men out of seven and a half battalions in Jamaica died outright, while half of the three thousand that remained were sick. The cause was easily to be traced. The barracks were built on low and unhealthy ground, and were continued there because neither the Assembly of Jamaica nor the British Government would be at the expense of reconstructing them in the higher and more salubrious districts of the island. Yet the outlay would have recouped itself within a year by the saving in the cost of transporting recruits. Dalling wrote, in a sentence of terrible bitterness:

> Considered only as an article of commerce, these eleven hundred men have cost £22,000, a sum which if laid out above ground might have saved half their lives.

Here then for the present let us leave the army in the West Indies, little injured by the enemy, but so much reduced by disease as to be powerless, both to windward and to leeward, for offensive movement. Cornwallis also we have left in Carolina, too weak to move, and Clinton in New York likewise. It is necessary now to return to Europe before entering upon the fateful year 1781.

CHAPTER 11

Florida

On the 1st of September 1780 Parliament was suddenly and unexpectedly dissolved, with the result that the elections as a whole turned greatly in favour of the government. At the meeting of the new Parliament October 31, the speech from the throne was more cheerful than for some sessions past, owing to the successes in Georgia and Carolina. Thanks were voted to Clinton and to Cornwallis; and even Fox, though predicting fresh disasters to follow the success at Camden, thought that the victory might be made the foundation of an honourable peace with the Colonies.

But meanwhile the past year had been marked by a new sign of hostility on the part of the European powers, namely, by a declaration to the effect that "free ships made free goods," that neutral vessels had the right to maintain the coasting trade of a belligerent, and that no articles were contraband except arms, equipments, and ammunitions of war. This declaration, issued first by Russia, was very soon subscribed by Sweden and Denmark, and later by all the powers of Europe; and, since the contracting parties bound themselves to uphold their principles by a combined fleet, the agreement received the name of the Armed Neutrality.

This convenient euphemism, however, could not conceal the fact that the declaration was a threat directed at England only; and England answered by retaliation upon Holland, the power that had used her rights as a neutral most unscrupulously to the prejudice of the British arms. St. Eustatius, as has already been told, was neither more nor less than a depot and arsenal for the Americans and French.

The Dutch flag had been used from the first to cover French and American goods, and Dutch men-of-war had been employed to convoy American privateers. In September 1780 the capture of an American packet revealed the fact that a formal treaty between Holland and the United Colonies, greatly to the prejudice of Britain, had long been in progress and was now on the point of conclusion. This line of conduct on the part of the Dutch was due to the influence of France and of the French faction in the Netherlands; while France in her turn had been stirred to increased bitterness against England by Frederick the Great, who rejoiced alike to damage the English and to hurry the French on their road to ruin. An open enemy being always preferable to a secret one, the British Government demanded satisfaction of Holland, (Dec. 20th), and, when this was refused, without further delay declared war.

Though the number of England's overt enemies was thus increased, the establishment of the military forces showed little augmentation, the only addition being that of forty independent companies, which were raised in Ireland at the private cost of individuals, and which brought the nominal total of the British troops, including embodied militia, to about one hundred and eighty-two thousand men, besides twenty-five thousand foreign troops hired on the Continent.

More troops were undoubtedly wanted, and in March orders were issued for the raising of six new regiments in Ireland, which, however, do not all of them seem to have come to birth. (Cunningham's, Ross's, Rowley's/102nd, Douglass's/104th, Burgoyne's/23rd Light Dragoons, Maunsell's. *S.P. Ireland*. Secretary of State to Lord Lieutenant, 22nd March 1781. Only those which are numbered were ever formed).

In truth, the drain of men was so heavy in North America, in the West Indies, and in the East Indies, that it was difficult to keep the ranks filled. Nevertheless, in the face of the European coalition, the country still held her head high. The eagles might be gathered together, but the carcase was not yet at their mercy.

It was just at this time, significantly enough, that the Spaniards, after a blockade of seventeen weeks, gave signs of more serious attack on Gibraltar. For several months they had been employed in drawing fortified lines of great strength across the isthmus, erecting batteries, and mounting guns; but on the 23rd of November they at last broke ground in earnest, and began to carry their trenches forward against the Rock. Eliott had worked unceasingly to strengthen his defences, but in December he wrote that victuals were running short and that he needed two thousand more men. The reply of the Secretary of State was ominous; he promised supplies immediately, but said plainly that not a man could be spared.

Even more serious to the besieged was the fact that the Spanish Government had outbid the British for the favour of the Emperor of Morocco, thereby cutting off supplies of provisions which hitherto had frequently found their way into the fortress. The distress of the garrison was thus greatly increased. Scurvy broke out and food rose to famine prices, till at length, on the 12th April 1781, Admiral Darby's fleet sailed safely into Gibraltar Bay with a convoy of nearly one hundred store-ships.

On that very day the Spanish batteries opened a furious bombardment, which was thenceforth continued without intermission for thirteen months. But though from that moment the attack upon Gibraltar entered upon a new phase, the fortress was safe for twelve months against starvation; so the reader need only bear in mind for the present that throughout the year 1781 the rain of projectiles upon Gibraltar was ceaseless, though its effect was remarkably small upon either the batteries or the nerves of the garrison. Of Minorca there is no more to be said than that Murray, though still without reinforcements, continued with all diligence his preparations for defence.

One more incident alone need detain us before we leave Europe to follow the operations on the other side of the Atlantic, namely, a French attack upon the island of Jersey. For this service about two thousand French troops were embarked under the command of Baron de Rullecourt, who put to sea in dark and stormy weather with the hope of descending upon the island by surprise. Half of his transports were blown back to France, and some of his vessels were wrecked upon a shoal; but about eight hundred troops seem to have reached Jersey in safety, (Jan 6th).

Of these the larger portion landed at Bane du Violet, about four miles from St. Heliers, marched straight up to the town under cover of night, and, having surprised two outlying posts, occupied the marketplace, with its avenues, and took the Lieutenant-governor, Major Corbet, prisoner. The alarm, however, was quickly given; and though Corbet, under threats of burning and massacre, had signed a capitulation for the whole island, the senior officer, Major Pierson, refused to recognise it. Assembling his troops round the town, Pierson quickly drove the French into the market-place and there surrounded them. Rullecourt dragged Corbet with him into the midst of the fire, but was quickly shot down, while Corbet escaped with two bullets through his hat.

The French in the town then surrendered; two detachments which had been disembarked at other points were also overpowered, and the entire force of the French was captured with no greater loss to the British than eighty men killed and wounded. Among the slain was Pierson; and it is probably to a well-known picture of his fall in the moment of victory that the majority of Englishmen owe their knowledge of this futile descent upon Jersey.

Let us now pass to operations across the Atlantic, and first to the windward group of the West Indian Islands. After two months' stay on the American coast Rodney sailed for St. Lucia, where he arrived at the beginning of December 1780. On. the 16th he opened the campaign by escorting a force under General Vaughan to St. Vincent, where, however, the enemy was found to be too strongly posted to warrant an attempt to recapture the island.

Shortly afterwards a reinforcement consisting of the First, Thirteenth, and Sixty-Ninth Foot arrived at Barbados; and a fortnight later, (Jan. 27th), came the news of war with Holland. Without a moment's delay Vaughan embarked a sufficient force and sailed, (Feb. 3rd), under Rodney's escort for St. Eustatius, which, with the adjacent islands of Saba and St. Martins, at once surrendered. Then for the first time the value of St. Eustatius to the enemies of England was fully realised.

The whole island was one vast store of French, Dutch, and American goods, the very streets being piled with bales for want of space in the warehouses. Over one hundred and fifty sail of merchantmen and six men-of-war were taken in the bay, thirty more merchantmen with their armed escort were also pursued and taken, and, the Dutch flag being kept flying for some time over the island, yet more vessels were decoyed into the familiar roadstead and captured likewise. The total value of the captured goods was reckoned at four millions sterling.

The capture of the island was regarded by many as a deathblow to the American rebellion; and there arose not only from the Americans, but from all quarters in the West Indies and in England, a storm of impotent rage, which even after a century and a quarter has not yet wholly died away.

★★★★★★

See, for instance, the pages devoted by that usually impartial writer, Mr. Fiske, to what he describes as the work of robbery, treachery, and buccaneering. It is really inexplicable why the destruction of a great depot of stores of war by the British should always be stigmatised as an act of wanton barbarity. The capture of St. Eustatius was as legitimate an operation of war as the capture of Ticonderoga, and the confiscation of the goods by no means an extreme measure considering the provocation. Washington could never find language hard enough for Americans who helped the English, and did not spare them when he caught them in the act. Why Rodney and Vaughan should not have meted out like measure to English who helped not only the Americans, but the enemies of their country generally, is to me an insoluble problem. The truth seems to be that such strictures as Mr. Fiske's are an echo of the ravings of Burke over the affair; but Burke, though a very great man, allowed himself a lamentable latitude in the matter of talking nonsense.

★★★★★★

For the capture of St. Eustatius was a stab to the heart of the contraband trade in the West Indies. Thither it was that Franklin from the first had consigned munitions of war from Europe, that the Colonists of St. Kitts had exported provisions and ammunition for French and American privateers, that the Bermudians had sent their famous schooners which could outsail all craft on the sea, that the enterprising traders of Holland, France, and Portugal, and the greedy, traitorous merchants of Barbados, Jamaica, and of London itself, had consigned every kind of supplies that could benefit the enemy.

So enormous were the profits of these gentry, that the annual rents of the lower town in St. Eustatius—that is to say, of a space not greater than eighteen hundred yards long by two hundred yards broad—exceeded a million sterling. Rodney wrote:

> But for the treasonable practices of these people, I am convinced that the Southern Colonies of America would long ago have submitted.

And he confiscated the whole of their goods with the less mercy, since the merchants of St. Eustatius, though nominally neutral, had refused to sell him naval stores, while vending them freely to the French and Americans. It need hardly be added that Burke and Fox raved like madmen in Parliament against Vaughan and Rodney for this stroke against their country's enemies; but since it was revealed in the course of debate that over six score merchants of Liverpool, including at least one member of Parliament, had lost very heavily over St. Eustatius, the source of their indignation is not very difficult to trace.

However, those merchants comforted themselves by plaguing Vaughan and Rodney considerably by litigation; and inasmuch as there was hardly a British trader in the West Indies without some venture in St. Eustatius, it may be guessed that the West Indian prize-courts raised many difficulties as to the condemnation of the prizes.

The captured islands were secured by a small garrison; and very shortly afterwards the Dutch settlements of Demerara and Essequibo were captured by a squadron of British privateers. These, since they had given no such provocation as St. Eustatius, were treated by Rodney with all possible gentleness and liberality. Meanwhile, at the end of March, the Count de Grasse sailed from Brest for the West Indies with twenty-one ships, and, despite all the efforts of Admiral Sir Samuel Hood, contrived, (April 29th), to effect his junction with the French squadron of four ships at Martinique.

Though he had thus twenty-five ships against the British eighteen, de Grasse declined to come to an action with Rodney. A partial engagement was, however, forced upon him, after which he retired to Fort Royal, while the British bore away to Antigua to refit, and from thence returned to Barbados. Taking advantage of their absence, de Grasse, on the night of the 10th of May, landed troops on three different points of St. Lucia, and even captured a few sick men at Gros Islet; but General St. Leger's dispositions for defence were such that he re-embarked his troops on the following day, and abandoned the attempt to recapture the island.

A few days later, May 23, however, de Grasse despatched a small squadron with twelve hundred troops to Tobago, where they effected their landing unopposed. The governor, who had but one hundred and eighty regular soldiers, (5 cos. Duke of Rutland's Foot/86th, of which 116 men were sick), and about twice that number of militia and armed negroes, at once took up a strong position on the hills, and sent a message to Rodney at Barbados for help. Rodney thereupon despatched six ships of the line, (May 28th), and some smaller vessels under Rear-admiral Drake to the relief of the island; but meanwhile de Grasse had moved to the assistance of the attacking force with his whole fleet, so that Drake had no option but to retire to Barbados.

The Governor of Tobago, wholly undaunted by the display of force by the French, withdrew his garrison to a yet stronger position which defied attack; whereupon the French general began to burn the plantations, and the colonial militia, unable to endure the trial of seeing their houses in flames, prevailed upon the governor to surrender, (June 2nd). Two days later Rodney appeared on the scene with his whole fleet; but it was too late. Altogether the affair was vexatiously unlucky, for the garrison might very well have held out for several days longer; and the mishap was the more exasperating to Rodney since de Grasse, notwithstanding a superiority of five ships, still refused to come to a general action. Shortly afterwards the French Admiral sailed to Haiti, where he found despatches awaiting him from Washington, of which the purport will soon be too plainly seen. Rodney, for his part, sent fourteen ships under Sir Samuel Hood to the American coast, and himself returned to England for the recovery of his health. So ended the campaign of 1781 to windward.

To leeward affairs presented a still more unpromising aspect. The safety of Jamaica was seriously endangered by the behaviour of the Assembly, which, though always clamouring for military stores, refused to make any provision for housing them, and would not vote a penny even for repair of the fortifications. (Dalling to Germaine, 16th February; Brigadier general Campbell to Germaine, 27th September 1781).

Herein there was treachery as well as faction, with greed of gain, as usual, at the root of both. Again, most of the merchants had ventures in privateers, American as well as British, and spared no pains to seduce sailors from the Royal Navy to man them. It was vain for the admiral to invoke the protection of the law, for the judges and juries on the island, being all of them interested parties, never failed to decide against him. (Admiral Sir Peter Parker to Admiralty, 23rd September 1780).

In fact, in Jamaica, as in the rest of the islands, the military measure which was most sorely needed was the hanging of half a dozen members of Assembly. Meanwhile the troops had dwindled to such weakness through disease that Governor Dalling had been compelled to apply to Cornwallis for some of his local levies from Carolina, and even to send an officer to enlist American prisoners for service against the Spaniard. Nor were these efforts without success, for the whole of the Continental soldiers captured at Camden, after a little hesitation, took service under the flag of the brutal oppressor, and became part of the garrison of a British Colony. (Dalling to Germaine, 10th August, 10th October 1781). The fact forms a curious comment on the zeal of the Americans for the revolution.

Dalling's anxiety, however, was not only for Jamaica but also for Florida, for he knew the defencelessness of Pensacola and yearned to relieve it, if possible, by the capture of New Orleans. With this object he embarked a regiment of American loyalists in February, but was unable to despatch it, since the admiral could not spare him a single man-of-war for an escort. His apprehensions proved to be well founded, for on the 9th of March a Spanish squadron appeared before Pensacola, and on the following day a Spanish Army began to disembark. Then, proceeding in their own leisurely fashion, the Spanish forces by land and sea increased, until at last from eight to ten thousand men were encamped around the forlorn British post. The British garrison, under command of Brigadier Campbell, numbered no more than nine hundred men, but defended itself so stoutly, that on the 28th of April the Spaniards actually broke ground in form, and a few days later opened fire For a week afterwards the siege made little progress, until the Spanish gunners, guided by a deserter from one of Campbell's American regiments, succeeded in dropping a shell into the principal magazine. The explosion, (May 8th), killed or disabled over a hundred men, and utterly demolished one of the principal redoubts; whereupon the Spaniards at once advanced to the assault.

The garrison met them gallantly and repelled the first attack; but the enemy, despite all their efforts, succeeded in establishing themselves in the ruined fortifications, whence they could shoot down any man who attempted to work the British guns. With his defences thus paralysed, and his garrison reduced to six hundred and fifty men, Campbell capitulated, (May 9th); and Florida passed once more into the hands of Spain.

Leaving now the West Indies, where, both to windward and to leeward, the British had suffered loss through their inferiority on the sea, let us return to Clinton at New York. There we discover at once the secret of Rodney's weakness in the West Indies.

Arbuthnot had received Rodney's orders to detach ships to strengthen his squadron; but Clinton had pointed out that his own communications with Cornwallis depended entirely on the command of the sea, and that if de Ternay's fleet and de Rochambeau's army, which still lay at Rhode Island, were left free to act in Long Island Sound, the safety of New York itself might be endangered. The remonstrance was so unanswerable that Arbuthnot could not but submit; but the incident shows how fatally Germaine's policy of dispersion reacted upon operations in every quarter.

Meanwhile, though Rawdon had pointed out that the whole plan of a diversion in the Chesapeake had been based by Cornwallis on a fallacious trust in the loyalists of Carolina, Clinton, partly in deference to his instructions, partly from morbid fear of seeming disloyal to Cornwallis, now fulfilled his promise to send a detachment to that quarter. Accordingly, about fourteen hundred men, chiefly Provincials and irregular troops, were embarked under command of Benedict Arnold, who was instructed to make Portsmouth, at the mouth of Elizabeth and James Rivers, his base, and to prepare a flotilla in Albemarle Sound for the destruction of the enemy's shipping, and for the impediment of the navigation.

Notwithstanding a stormy passage which cost him the loss of more than half of his horses, Arnold duly made his way up James River to Richmond, and in three weeks returned to Portsmouth, (Jan. 20th), having captured several vessels, destroyed a cannon-foundry and vast quantities of stores, and inflicted generally much damage on the enemy, with trifling loss to himself. Arnold, indeed, could be trusted always to do his work in the field with ability; but at the same time Clinton, by setting him down permanently in isolation with a mere handful of men, was giving him as a hostage to fortune, for the British squadron on the coast was little if at all superior to the French.

Washington, for his part, had opened the new year in the face of frightful difficulties. The discipline of his regular troops had been shaken by two serious mutinies, (Jan. 1st-20th), which were due not to any fundamental disaffection, for the mutineers refused to enlist with Clinton, but to resentment against the ill faith kept with them by Congress. The execution of a few ringleaders sufficed to quell the rising, and Washington seized the opportunity to ask Congress to extend his powers of flogging to the infliction of five hundred lashes. (Washington to Congress, 3rd February; *Works*, vol. vii.). Thus the irony of fate retorted upon the American soldier the name of "bloody back," doubtless with great benefit to his discipline.

Having thus restored order, Washington despatched Lafayette to Virginia by land with twelve hundred men; and on the 8th of March the French fleet and army sailed from Rhode Island to the Chesapeake in order to make an end of Arnold. Clinton, who had full information of the design, likewise embarked three thousand men under Major-General Phillips; while Admiral Arbuthnot's ships sailed to encounter the French squadron. The admiral was so slow in getting under way that Clinton trembled for Arnold's safety; but, albeit late in starting, the British ships arrived before the French off the capes of the Chesapeake, and, though they gained little if any advantage over them in the action which followed, cut them off from the entrance to the bay, and so delivered Arnold. (Clinton to Cornwallis, 5th March 1781).

Washington was bitterly disappointed at the failure of this stroke, for the fortunes of the revolutionists seemed at the moment to be desperate. His troops were naked through neglect, and starving because transport was no longer to be purchased with paper-money; his hospitals were without medicines, and all public undertakings were at a stand. He wrote on the 4th of April, (Washington, *Works*, viii.):

> If France delays timely aid now it will avail us nothing if she attempt it hereafter....We are at the end of our tether, and now or never our deliverance must come.

Beyond all doubt the capture of St. Eustatius was a thrust that had sped home; and yet, when we glance at the little group of the British Isles, torn by faction and insurrection, beset by enemies on every side, fighting desperately against overwhelming odds in Europe, in the West Indies, in America, and in India, we are tempted to ask, on meeting with this despairing lament of Washington, whether there was ever much real life at the heart of the American Revolution.

The French having been driven from the Chesapeake, the detachment under Phillips sailed at its ease on the 26th to join Arnold at Portsmouth. The operations prescribed for it by Clinton were only of a desultory nature, such as the destruction of magazines and stores, with the primary object of taking some pressure off Cornwallis; but, since Leslie's detachment had long since gone to Carolina, Phillips was instructed if possible to establish a post, which could be held by a small force, to command the mouth of the Chesapeake. (Clinton to Phillips, 10th and 24th March 1781; to Germaine, 5th April 1781).

Clinton had no idea of entering upon solid operations in that quarter until reinforcements should arrive from England; and indeed the report of a great success, presently to be narrated, of Cornwallis, inspired him with the hope that not only Phillips's troops but Cornwallis's also would shortly be free to return to New York. Meanwhile, so long as the British retained superiority at sea, he felt no anxiety over the temporary dispersion of his force. (Clinton to Phillips, 10th and 24th March 1781; to Germaine 5th April 1781).

Everything, as he wrote alike to Germaine, to Cornwallis, and to Phillips, depended on the command of the sea; and Germaine had held out every hope that it should remain in the hands of the British.

CHAPTER 12

Cowpens & Guildford Court-house

We left Cornwallis at Winnsborough, of one mind with Lord Rawdon to remain for the present in a position which should secure the frontier of Carolina without dividing his force. Since he had taken that resolution, events had conspired to strengthen rather than to weaken it. The partisan Marion had roused the entire district between the Santee and the Peedee to arms; and it was necessary to despatch Tarleton to check him. But Tarleton had only just begun to press him hard, when he was recalled by news of a mishap in another quarter. Sumter was lying about forty miles north of Winnsborough, to cover the movements of certain marauding bands which were murdering and plundering the loyalists to westward, between the Tiger and Pacolet Rivers; and it was important, if possible, to crush him. Accordingly, Major Wemyss, thinking that he saw a good chance of surprising Sumter, obtained leave from Cornwallis to march against him with the Sixty-Third Foot, which had been converted for the nonce into Mounted Infantry.

The attack was well planned and was not wholly unsuccessful, but Wemyss was unfortunately wounded early in the action, and the command devolved upon a very young officer, who, knowing nothing of his plans nor of the numbers of the enemy, abandoned the whole enterprise. Wemyss and a few more wounded men having been left behind in a house, the Americans at once proclaimed the fact as evidence of a great victory; and the whole country rose to join Sumter, who now moved southward upon Ninety-Six.

He was on the point of overwhelming a small post about fifteen miles from that garrison, when he learned from a British deserter that Tarleton, having marched with his usual secrecy and swiftness, was close upon him. Sumter at once retreated, hoping to place the rapid

River Tiger between himself and his pursuers; but finding escape impossible, took up a strong position on the bank, (Nov. 20th), of the river by Blackstock House. Soon afterwards Tarleton came up with his mounted troops only, having made a long and fatiguing march. Since his infantry were several miles in rear, he dismounted his little party, fewer than three hundred men all told, within sight of the enemy, doubtless hoping to overawe Sumter by this parade of boldness.

Sumter, however, quickly perceived the true state of affairs, and advancing his riflemen against Tarleton compelled him to deliver his attack against superior numbers in a strong position. By sheer skill and audacity Tarleton contrived to escape disaster till darkness came to deliver him, though he lost a fifth of his men; but fortune so far favoured him that Sumter was severely wounded, and his force for a time dispersed for want of a leader. Yet, in its general result, this little skirmish was damaging to the British, since it interrupted the sequence, hitherto unbroken, of Tarleton's successes.

★★★★★★

English and American accounts differ very greatly as to this action of Blackstocks, each party claiming a victory with heavy loss to the other. As usual, there is probably much exaggeration on both sides.

★★★★★★

Mishaps such as these could not but be disquieting to Cornwallis; and now he found himself confronted with a new commander, aided by several able subordinates. Nathaniel Greene, who had been appointed by Washington to replace Gates, arrived at Charlottetown on the 2nd of December, and was presently joined by his engineer Kosciusko, the Pole, by Daniel Morgan, who had so greatly distinguished himself against Burgoyne, and by Henry Lee and William Washington, the latter a kinsman of the great George, both of whom enjoyed great reputation as leaders of cavalry.

At his base in Virginia Greene possessed a very able Prussian officer, Baron Steuben, for the superintendence of transport and supplies; and there were yet more good men to whom he had committed the task of surveying the upper waters of the great rivers of North Carolina and Virginia, hitherto little explored, for purposes of navigation. On arriving at Charlottetown, Greene found that not more than eight hundred men of his army were properly armed and fit for duty, though by the energy of Lee, Steuben, and others he was soon reinforced to a strength of two thousand. But for the present it was plain that the chief hope of the Americans in Carolina rested on the guerilla-bands which, under the leadership of such men as Marion and Sumter, never ceased to threaten Cornwallis's communications.

Meanwhile a change had come over the spirit of Cornwallis himself. So far he had worked well and loyally with Clinton, while Clinton on his side had granted to him all possible latitude, permitting him to correspond directly with Germaine and supporting him to the fullest of his power by diversions and reinforcements. In December Cornwallis's *aide-de-camp*, Captain Ross, who had carried home the news of Camden, returned to him from England; and from that moment Cornwallis's tone and bearing towards Clinton were completely altered. The fact was that Germaine, always crooked and purblind, and now dazzled by the success of Cornwallis at Camden, had decided virtually to give him an independent command and to make Clinton's operations subservient to those of his subordinate. In a word, since neither Howe nor Clinton would act upon his insane schemes of conquest without garrisons and of invasion without communications, he took advantage of the ambition and comparative youth of Cornwallis to thrust these disastrous designs upon him.

On the 14th of December Leslie's detachment arrived at Charleston from the Chesapeake, and shortly afterwards began its march up country to Winnsborough; but before he had even seen these troops, (the Guards, a German battalion, six companies of Maclean's/82nd, and two Provincial regiments). Cornwallis wrote to complain of their quality in a letter of unbecoming and patronising tone, (Cornwallis to Clinton, 22nd December 1780). He then sent a detachment under Major Craig to occupy Wilmington on Cape Fear, so as to secure the transport of his supplies into North Carolina; ordered the fortifications of Charleston to be dismantled, which was directly contrary to Clinton's orders; and on the 7th of January 1781, without a word to the commander-in-chief of his intentions, began his advance northward with some two thousand men, (see list following).

★★★★★★

His force (including Leslie's detachment, which joined him on the 18th) consisted of the brigade of Guards, 7th Fusiliers, 3 companies of the 16th, the 23rd, 33rd, 2nd battalion of Fraser's Highlanders, 450 Germans, 700 Provincials, and Tarleton's Legion. It thus numbered about 4000 men.

★★★★★★

Greene meanwhile had divined with quick penetration the only scheme of operations from which he could hope for success. Though too weak to oppose a front to Cornwallis's advance, he could keep the guerilla-bands of Marion and Sumter playing on his flanks, and he now resolved to divide his army so as to second them. Accordingly, he himself moved, (Dec. 20th 1780), with eleven hundred men to Haly's Ferry on the Peedee, some eighty miles north-east of Winnsborough, to support Marion, and sent Morgan with nine hundred men across the Catawba to join with Sumter's troops in harassing Cornwallis's left flank.

Thus Cornwallis could not march with his whole force against Greene, for fear of exposing the posts at Ninety-Six and Augusta to attack by Morgan, nor could he attack Morgan in real strength without leaving Greene free to march on Charleston. The situation was not only embarrassing but extremely irritating, owing to the incessant raids of the guerrilla-bands; and Cornwallis saw no other course open to him than to divide his own force. He therefore sent Tarleton with about a thousand men to the west of the Broad River to drive back Morgan, and, advancing himself along the western bank of the Catawba, ordered Leslie's detachment to march upon Camden along the eastern bank, so as to guard his right flank.

Tarleton quickly gained touch of Morgan and forced him back northward before him. Then keeping himself well to westward, he urged Cornwallis to hug the eastern bank of the Broad River, in the hope of driving Morgan into his arms. Following up the enemy with his usual diligence, Tarleton on the 17th January overtook Morgan, whom he found posted on a grazing ground, not yet wholly cleared of trees, which was known as the Cowpens, with the Broad River in his rear cutting off all hope of retreat.

The position was not such as is generally favoured by military critics; but Morgan said boldly that he preferred to have an impassable river in his rear, since his militia would then understand that it was useless for them to run away. With excellent judgment he had posted the said militia, who were all of them good marksmen, in his first line, with strong exhortations not to give way until they had fired at least two volleys "at killing distance." On an eminence one hundred and fifty yards in their rear were drawn up his regular troops, few in numbers but of excellent quality; and behind a second eminence about the same distance in rear of these was concealed his cavalry under Colonel Washington. (The militia numbered 600, the regulars 290, the cavalry 80. Total, 970. Johnson, *Life of Greene*, i.).

The whole force numbered just under one thousand men. Tarleton, always eager for action, decided to attack forthwith, though his men were weary with marching for half the night along bad roads and wading through swollen creeks. His line was soon formed. A small body of Light Infantry stood on his right, and next to them in succession were the Legion Infantry and the Seventh Foot, with two three-pounder guns. A troop of fifty dragoons was posted on each flank of the infantry of the first line; and two hundred more cavalry, together with Fraser's Highlanders, formed the reserve. The entire force amounted to about eleven hundred men.

Without any delay the infantry advanced rapidly in double rank at open files till, at a range of about forty yards, they received the fire of the militia, who, safely posted behind trees, picked off officers, sergeants, and corporals with unerring aim. After a short struggle, however, the militia, having made a very creditable resistance and wrought much havoc, gave way and retired round the left of Morgan's second line. Tarleton at once let loose his troop of the Seventeenth Light Dragoons upon them from his own right, but Washington's horse coming forward drove back the Seventeenth by sheer weight of numbers; and the American militia, on reaching the second hill in rear of Morgan's position, speedily rallied and re-formed.

Meanwhile the British infantry continued their advance against Morgan's regular troops, but in no very good order, for the men were out of breath and a great number of their officers had fallen. Tarleton, hoping to bring the action to an end by a decisive stroke, now brought up Fraser's Highlanders to the left of the Seventh, and directed the squadron posted on that flank, together with his reserve of cavalry, to incline still farther to the left, so as to threaten Morgan's right.

Morgan therefore ordered his right-hand battalion to wheel back at right angles to the line, in order to repel this flanking attack; whereupon the rest of his first line, seeing this battalion turn about, followed its example and retreated likewise, with perfect steadiness and discipline. This quite unpremeditated and accidental movement decided the issue of the action. The British infantry, confident that the day was won, hurried forward in ever-increasing disorder, with the Americans still retiring before them; when Colonel Washington, whom the pursuit of the British cavalry had carried to some distance in advance, sent a messenger to Morgan with the words:

They are coming on like a mob; give them a fire and I will charge them.

BATTLE OF COWPENS.

At this moment the rallied militia reappeared on the American right; and Morgan gave the word for the whole line to halt and fire. The Continental troops with perfect coolness turned about, the British being then within thirty yards of them, and delivered a destructive volley, which was the more demoralising because it was unexpected. Panic seized upon Tarleton's whole line. The Seventh was made up chiefly of recruits, the infantry of the Legion had never been well disciplined, the Light Infantry had suffered heavily; one and all were spent by a long march and breathless after a rapid advance; and after this staggering volley there was no spirit left in them. Fraser's Highlanders, in spite of heavy losses, fought hard for a time, but being presently attacked in front and on both flanks gave way like the rest.

Tarleton in vain tried to save the day by a charge of the cavalry of the reserve. The dragoons of the Legion, ill disciplined at the best of times, and spoiled by the easy successes which Tarleton's energy had gained for them, were not the men to face so desperate a venture. They turned and galloped headlong from the field; and not a fraction of Tarleton's force showed a front except a tiny handful of British artillerymen who stuck indomitably to their two three-pounders, and the solitary troop of the Seventeenth Light Dragoons, which had rallied from its first repulse by Washington's horse. At the head of this troop, now reduced to forty soldiers, Tarleton and a dozen mounted officers charged forward to extricate the artillery, but too late to save either the guns or the gunners, who had fallen almost to a man. There was then nothing left for Tarleton but to retreat with this little body of dragoons, the only men that retired from the field in order.

So ended the action of Cowpens, small in scale but momentous in result. The numerical superiority was slightly on Tarleton's side, but the quality inclined to the side of Morgan, whose militia were veterans in partisan warfare as well as practised marksmen, and fought, as violators of their oath, with halters round their necks. To Morgan, however, belongs the credit of making the most of their excellences while avoiding the dangers of their defects; and it is certain that the heavy slaughter of British officers by these marksmen at the beginning of the action contributed greatly to Morgan's ultimate success.

Yet the turning-point of the whole engagement was the fortuitous retrograde movement of the American second line, which manoeuvre was crowned with such success that, had not Morgan been too honest to claim praise for a mere accident, he might have credited himself with one of the most daring stratagems ever practised in war. (Chastellux, ii. Chastellux, however, had never heard of Bouquet's action at Bushy Run).

Blame is attached to Tarleton for making an attack when his men were wearied by five hours of arduous marching, whereas his opponent's troops were perfectly fresh and had breakfasted at their ease. But, on the other hand, Morgan's situation with an impassable river in his rear certainly invited attack, and the flanking movement whereby Tarleton strove to snatch the victory was well and boldly conceived, since, if successful, it must have driven Morgan across the line of Cornwallis's advance. It seems to me, therefore, that Tarleton deserves no blame, for the fortune of war was his chief enemy; though, looking to the behaviour of the dragoons of the Legion, there can be little doubt but that the better men won the day.

The American loss did not exceed seventy-two killed and wounded: that of the British was close upon eight hundred killed, wounded, and prisoners, a very large proportion of those that fell being officers. Two British guns and the colours of the Seventh were also captured; and Tarleton's column, although he collected the best part of his fugitive cavalry on the day after the action, was to all intent annihilated. Morgan halted no longer in the field than was necessary to secure his prisoners, but crossed the Broad River on the same evening and hurried eastward, lest Cornwallis should cut off his retreat.

But Cornwallis, anxious for Leslie's detachment, which by an unfortunate error of judgment he had ordered to march on the east bank of the Catawba, had halted in order to enable it to join him; so that on the day of the action he was still at Turkey Creek, twenty-five miles south-east of Cowpens. Moreover, Leslie's march had been so much delayed by the passage of the swamps of the Catawba that he could not unite with the main army until the 18th. Tarleton had reckoned, (Tarleton's *Campaign*), not without reason, that Cornwallis would have been parallel with him at King's Mountain on the day of the action, and had regulated all his movements according to that calculation; and since he had received no message from Cornwallis since the 14th, he had no reason to suppose that he was wrong in so doing. The General's action after learning of Tarleton's defeat was also questionable, for he hastened north-westward in the hope of intercepting Morgan, though by marching due north he would have taken the chord instead of the curve of the arc along which Morgan was retreating. The celerity of Morgan's movements and the swelling of the creeks by heavy rain defeated his object, and on reaching Ramsour's Mills, twenty-five miles north-west of King's Mountain, Cornwallis came to a halt, (25th).

It is not difficult to conceive of his embarrassment and mortification. He was now in exactly the same position as after Ferguson's defeat at King's Mountain, when, with Rawdon at his side, he had declared that the invasion of North Carolina must be abandoned. Like a good and chivalrous commander, he now acquitted Tarleton, as he had before acquitted Ferguson, of all blame; but the repetition of disaster, involving as it did the loss of the whole of his light troops, was sufficient to convince him of the peril of further advance. Nevertheless, the influence of Germaine seems to have been overpowering; and on the day after the fatal action Cornwallis wrote to Clinton that nothing short of the most absolute necessity should induce him to abandon his project for the winter's operations. (Cornwallis to Clinton, 18th January 1781).

He had already committed himself deeply by ordering the destruction of the fortifications at Charleston, and by dragging up under Leslie's escort the entire material necessary for a campaign. He now resolved to destroy the whole of his superfluous baggage, to follow up Morgan and Greene, and to end the campaign at a blow.

Meanwhile Greene, on learning of the success at Cowpens, had set his army in motion at once, (Jan. 28th), to march from Haly's Ford north-eastward to Salisbury, while he himself galloped for a hundred miles across country to take personal command of Morgan's force. In spite of the recent victory his lack of regular troops forbade him to be sanguine, though, to use his own words, he was not without hopes of ruining Lord Cornwallis if he should persist in his mad scheme of pushing through the country. (Johnson, *Life of Greene*, i.).

Unfortunately Cornwallis had every intention of persisting in it, for he too had marched eastward on the 28th, and on the 30th had reached the western bank of the Catawba, eighteen miles below the camp occupied by Greene on the opposite bank. Greene, on ascertaining the fact, gave up his former idea of checking Cornwallis's advance at the River Yadkin, and altered the destination of his main army from Salisbury to Guildford, in order to draw his adversary deeper into the country. (*Ibid.* i.)

Meanwhile for two days the hostile armies lay separated by the swollen waters of the Catawba, until on the 1st of February the flood subsided; but the fords along a length of thirty miles were still guarded by the American militia, though Morgan with his light troops had already retired. Accordingly, at dawn of the 1st, Cornwallis with one division of the army began the passage of the river at Cowan's Ford, sending the other division under Colonel Webster to another ford six miles above it. Webster was not opposed; but the Guards, who led Cornwallis's column, were not more than halfway across the river when they were met by a biting fire.

The American guide thereupon fled, and the Guards were left in the darkness, in the middle of a river five hundred yards wide and so rapid as to sweep even horses off their legs, with the bullets cutting the water into foam all round them. Yet still they advanced without heeding or returning the fire, Colonel Hall making his way at their head through an unknown depth of water towards the opposite bank. The flight of the guide was, as it happened, a piece of great good fortune, for the Guards finally emerged from the river at an unprotected point, and the Americans were dispersed without difficulty. The British then continued their advance, but the roads proved to be so bad that Cornwallis on that evening made a further sacrifice of waggons and baggage so as to double his teams and increase his force of mounted men.

Heavy rain had warned Morgan to push on with all speed to the Yadkin, the next river to eastward, where Greene, with admirable foresight, had collected every obtainable boat at the principal ford. Cornwallis's mounted troops made a rapid advance, (Feb. 3rd), to cut off his army, but succeeded only in intercepting his rearguard, the main body being already safe on the opposite bank.

Cornwallis was now compelled to halt for two days at Salisbury to collect provisions, after which he turned north to a ford ten miles up the river; but he was so long detained by swollen creeks and bad roads that he did not pass the Yadkin until the 8th. With a start of five days, the Americans seemed unlikely to be overtaken; but Cornwallis, deceived by false information that the next river, the Dan, was impassable in winter and that few boats could be collected on it, hurried on in the vain hope of penning Morgan's force between the Dan and the Yadkin. He was, however, still twenty-five miles astern when Greene, on the 10th, effected his junction with his main army at Guildford.

None the less, judging his numbers to be too weak for a general action, Greene continued his retreat to the Dan, and crossed it at Boyd's Ferry in boats which he had caused to be collected several weeks before. Cornwallis, pursuing in hot haste, had the mortification, as usual, to see the last detachment pass over safely to the northern side of the river just as he arrived on the southern bank, (Feb. 15th).

So often had this incident been repeated during the retreat that it is impossible not to attribute it to deliberate and well-calculated design on the part of General Greene.

Cornwallis now fell back by easy marches, (Feb. 20th), to Hillsborough, where he hoisted the royal standard; but the loyalists of North Carolina had lost heart through long suffering, and Greene took care to keep his light troops hanging perpetually upon Cornwallis's rear. Thus it was never safe for large bodies of loyalists to join the British; and indeed one unfortunate party, which mistook the American cavalry for Tarleton's Legion, was surrounded and cut to pieces, (Feb. 25th).

Cornwallis described his position as lying among timid friends and adjoining to inveterate enemies; but in the hope of giving better protection to his unlucky friends he now turned southwestward from Hillsborough to the country between the Deep and Haw Rivers, which he had appointed to them as a place of assembly. There he encamped at the junction of the roads from Salisbury, Hillsborough, Cross Creek, and Guildford, thus at once bestriding the line of his own retreat to Wilmington and commanding the avenues whereby he could take advantage of any opportunity that Greene might give him.

Once he thought that he saw his chance, and with great readiness and skill made a spring upon an isolated American column; but fortune did not favour him, for Greene was able to concentrate in the nick of time. Meanwhile reinforcements had joined the Americans from Virginia, and Greene, being now strengthened to a force of fifty-five hundred men, pushed westward to Guildford Court-house, within twelve miles of the British Army, and offered battle.

Cornwallis hastened, (March 15th), to seize the chance of closing with his redoubtable adversary. Leaving three hundred and fifty men to guard the baggage, he marched at daybreak with the remainder of his force, now reduced by fatigue, sickness, constant skirmishes, and desertion to about nineteen hundred soldiers.

★★★★★★

There is much controversy as to the number of British engaged at Guildford. Cornwallis wrote to Clinton that he had but 1360 regulars and 200 volunteers, but this he contradicted himself in a letter to Germaine of 17th March, wherein he said that these volunteers and 120 more men were detached to guard the baggage. A return of his troops of 1st March (Stevens, *Clinton-Cornwallis Controversy*, i.) gives his total numbers (without artillery) as 2213 rank and file fit for duty, or, allowing for artillery, say 2300 fit for duty. Deduct from these the volunteers (given in the return of 1st March as 232) and the rest of the baggage-guard, in all 352, and there remain 1950 men. But there were several petty skirmishes between the 1st and the 15th of March, wherein the losses may be reckoned as reducing the number to 1900; and since a field-return sent to Germaine gives the numbers at 1924., I think that 1900 may be taken as the likeliest figure. Stedman, however, quotes the Adjutant-general's return for the day, which states the force at 1445 exclusive of cavalry, or 1600 in all. For the American force I accept the careful computation of Johnson (*Life of Greene*, ii.), which gives the numbers at 4300. Greene's regular troops of all arms were 1715, his militia 2600.

★★★★★★

The men started fasting, for provisions were scarce; but though the numbers of the enemy were stated to be seven or eight thousand, they felt confidence in their leader and tramped cheerfully on, westward, until they struck into the road from Salisbury and then north-eastward upon Guildford. About four miles from Guildford the advanced cavalry of both armies met, and the Americans were driven back; but no information could be obtained from the prisoners, while the accounts given by the people of the country were extremely inaccurate.

Continuing his advance along the road, Cornwallis presently found himself in a narrow defile with thick copses on either hand, which continued unbroken to within half a mile of Guildford Court-house. At this point the ground had been cleared on both sides of the road, leaving an open space, broken only by fences, about five hundred yards square. Ahead of this first clearing the woods again closed upon the road for another half-mile, at the end of which there came another open space of cultivated ground, seamed by hollows, around the Court-house itself.

When the British reached the southern skirt of the first clearing, two American guns opened fire upon them, whereupon Cornwallis deployed his troops into line, resolving that since the woods on the right of the road were less dense than those on the opposite side, he would attempt to turn the American left. It was perhaps a weak foundation whereon to base the plan of a general action, but there was none firmer to be discovered; and it is impossible not to admire the nerve of a man who would thus enter the lists, as it were blindfolded, against an enemy of twice his numbers, trusting to his own skill and to the discipline of his troops to tear the bandage from his eyes in sufficient time.

His three guns he posted on the road itself, since they could not move elsewhere, to answer the American artillery; and the remainder of his force he disposed in the following order:—

The right wing, under Major-General Leslie, consisted of Rose's Hessian regiment and Fraser's Highlanders in first line, with the first battalion of the Guards, (drawn from all three regiments, but sorted into two mixed battalions), in support; and the left wing of the Twenty-Third and Thirty-Third under Colonel Webster in first line, with the Grenadiers and second battalion of the Guards under Brigadier O'Hara in support. A small corps of German *Jägers* and the Light Infantry were stationed in the wood to the left of the guns, while Tarleton with the cavalry remained in rear on the road.

The dispositions of Greene, at which Cornwallis could only guess, were made with his usual ability. His first line, consisting of the North Carolina militia, was extended in the wood on the northern skirts of the first clearing, with two corps of picked riflemen thrown forward on each flank, the whole comprehending in all nearly sixteen hundred men. Immediately in rear of these riflemen were two small bodies of cavalry, each of about eighty men, under Lee on the eastern and under Washington on the western side; and in advance of them upon the road were two field-guns.

Three hundred yards in rear of this first line was a second line of Virginian militia, numbering about one thousand men, the right brigade being commanded by General Lawson, the left by General Stevens. These were deftly hidden in the woods on each side of the road, with picked marksmen behind them ready to shoot any man who should run away. Three hundred yards in rear of this second line, and rather to westward of the road, was a hill that formed a salient angle in the midst of the clearing round the Court-house; and here Greene had drawn up his regular troops in conformation with the ground, two Virginian brigades on his right and two Maryland brigades on his left, numbering together about fourteen hundred and fifty men, with two six-pounder guns in the salient angle between them. One point of vantage only was unsecured by Greene, namely, a height rising on the eastern side of the road, just at the point where the forest ended and the clearing about the Court-house began. It will be seen that he paid dearly for the oversight.

At about half-past one in the afternoon the action opened with the advance of the British across the first clearing, amid a storm of bullets from the invisible enemy in front and flanks. Perfectly unshaken, the redcoats pressed on to within close range and charged with the bayonet; but the North Carolina militia was not there to receive them, having fled away in panic, while Greene's two advanced guns had retired, in obedience to orders, to take post near the road with the American third line. But though the militia in front had disappeared, the American riflemen in the flanks of their first line still poured in a most destructive fire; whereupon the British line was halted, in order that the flank-battalions might turn outwards to meet them. Bose's regiment accordingly wheeled off to the right flank, the first battalion of Guards moving into the line to take their place next to the Highlanders; while on the other wing the Thirty-Third, with the *Jägers* and Light Infantry on their left, wheeled off in like manner to the left flank, and the Grenadiers and second battalion of the Guards advanced to the left of the Twenty-Third in their room.

★★★★★★

The order of the British line, from right to left, was now as follows: Bose's Regiment, 1st battalion of Guards, Fraser's Highlanders, 23rd, 2nd battalion of Guards, Grenadiers, 33rd, Jägers, Light Infantry.

★★★★★★

Gradually the American sharpshooters were forced back from tree to tree before the bayonet's point, Lee and Washington falling back likewise with their cavalry behind them; and thus the British fought their way forward to the Virginian militia in Greene's second line. These held their ground with a stubbornness which contrasted very favourably with the panic of their brethren from Carolina, and, being most of them armed with rifles, did great execution among the British. But the redcoats were not to be denied, and gradually Lawson's brigade on the American right began to give way before the Light Infantry and *Jägers*, who were almost their peers in bush-fighting.

Farther and farther Lawson's brigade retreated, though Stevens's brigade on their left stood firm; and Webster's men bringing up their left shoulders pressed them on and on till at last, on reaching the road, Lawson's militia fairly broke and retired in disorder through the wood to Greene's third line. They were, however, protected from pursuit by Washington's cavalry, which had retired with them to the edge of the forest.

Webster now caught up the Thirty-third, Light Infantry, and Jägers, and led them, thinned as they were by their losses and wearied with hard marching and hard fighting, against Greene's third line on the hill by the Court-house. Selecting the nearest point for his attack, he encountered, as it happened, the finest battalion in the American Army, the First Maryland, which awaited his assault with perfect steadiness, poured in its volley at close range, and, charging with the bayonet, drove the British back in disorder with very heavy loss.

Had Greene followed up this stroke effectively, he might have made it fatal to Cornwallis, but he did not; and Webster, though severely wounded, drew off his men to the shelter of the forest, where they speedily rallied. Meanwhile, the three British three-pounders had advanced along the road, and were unlimbered with admirable judgment by Lieutenant Macleod on the rising ground at the edge of the forest, from which they kept up a steady and well-directed fire.

Moreover, General O'Hara, observing that there were already troops enough to deal with Stevens's brigade of Virginian militia, now led the second battalion of Guards and the Grenadiers against the Maryland brigade in Greene's third line, while Leslie, finding the resistance of the Americans in the wood failing steadily before him, presently sent the Twenty-Third and Highlanders to support him. The Second Maryland Regiment, however, gave way instantly before O'Hara's attack, and the second battalion of Guards was pressing on in triumph after them, when Washington with his cavalry galloped up from the wood and crashed into their rear, while the First Maryland Regiment also fell full upon their left flank. The Guards fought fiercely, but were utterly broken; and Cornwallis, who had come forward to rally them, was fain to hurry back to Macleod and bid him open with grape-shot upon the American horse. The fire checked Washington's onslaught, but dealt terrible destruction among the Guards, who were still mingled with his cavalry.

There was now a pause, during which Cornwallis reformed his line. The Highlanders and Twenty-Third were halted; O'Hara, though very severely wounded, rallied the second battalion of Guards on their right, where the first battalion also joined them; and Webster again led up the Thirty-third, Jägers, and Light Infantry on their left. Bose's regiment was still hotly engaged with Stevens's brigade of militia on the American left; but these now began to retire in small parties, while Lee withdrew also his cavalry and a portion of his sharpshooters.

Cornwallis therefore brought up Tarleton to make an end of the

American resistance on his right, which was done by an effective charge of cavalry, delivered under the smoke of a volley. Bose's regiment and Tarleton then pressed upon the Americans' left flank, while the remainder of the British line engaged them in front; and Greene, seeing that the day was lost, gave the order to retreat, abandoning his four guns, together with their ammunition. There was little pursuit, for Cornwallis's troops were spent with long marching and heavy fighting; and thus came to an end the action of Guildford.

Never perhaps has the prowess of the British soldier been seen to greater advantage than in this obstinate and bloody combat. Starting half-starved on a march of twelve miles, the troops attacked an enemy, fresh and strong, which not only outnumbered them by more than two to one, but which was so posted, by Greene's excellent judgment, as to afford every possible advantage to its natural superiority in bushcraft, armament, and marksmanship.

Yet, though heavily punished, they forced the Americans from the shelter of the forest and drove them from the field; while the Thirty-Third and Guards, though at one moment absolutely shattered—the latter indeed rent to pieces by Washington's well-timed charge—rallied at once and came forward again to the attack. American writers point with just pride to the fine behaviour of the First Maryland Regiment, and the still finer performance of Stevens's militia; but while doing justice to the valour of the British, they forget that the Guards and Thirty-third had already broken through two lines of Americans before they reached the Marylanders.

★★★★★★

Thus Johnson puts down the 33rd at the moment of attacking the Maryland Regiment as 322 strong. But this was their strength on the 1st of March, since which day they had been frequently engaged, to say nothing of their previous losses on the 15th. He also sets down the Second Battalion of Guards, with its Grenadier Company, as far exceeding the First Maryland (which he reckons at 285 men) in numbers. The Guards went into action 481 of all ranks, including brigadier and staff, and were divided into two battalions, a Grenadier Company, and a Light Infantry Company; so that one battalion and one company could not have exceeded 240 of all ranks at most, even supposing them to have suffered no loss (which is incredible) before they closed with Greene's third line.

★★★★★★

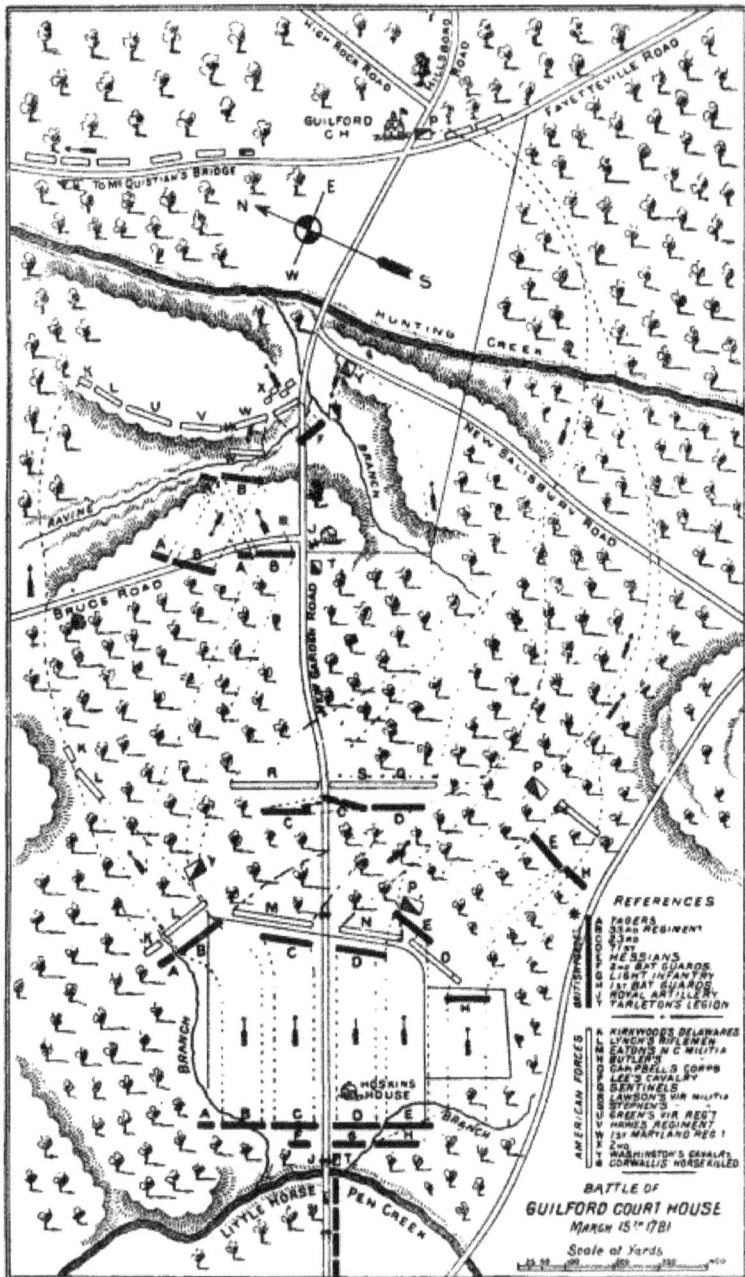

■ SITE OF THE MARYLAND MONUMENT.

The losses of the victorious army were very severe. The Guards went into action with nineteen officers, including brigadier and staff, of whom four were killed or died of wounds, and seven more were wounded; while of four hundred and sixty-two men, thirty-seven were killed and one hundred and sixty-nine wounded. Colonel Webster died of his hurts; Brigadier O'Hara was long disabled, and his son, Lieutenant O'Hara of the artillery, was killed.

In all twenty-eight officers fell, killed or wounded; and the total casualties of the army amounted to ninety-three killed and four hundred and thirty-nine wounded, making five hundred and thirty-two in all more than a fourth of the whole number engaged, at the highest computation; more than a third, if the adjutant-general's return be correct. Want of food for not a man received a morsel until the following afternoon and pouring rain during the night increased the sufferings of the injured, of whom no fewer than fifty expired before the morning came.

In truth, the victory, though a brilliant feat of arms, was no victory. Greene did indeed retreat, and the most part of his militia deserted to their homes, so that his losses were never actually ascertained; but Cornwallis had gained no solid advantage to compensate for the sacrifice of life, and he was now too weak farther to prosecute his mad design. Clinton, on hearing the first rumours of the action, wrote that Cornwallis seemed to have finished his campaign handsomely, but he was speedily undeceived by fuller intelligence; and Phillips truly described the engagement as the sort of victory that ruins an army.

Cornwallis's troops had undergone hardships, fatigue, and starvation with cheerfulness, since the officers, and most notably the general himself, fared in every way as they did; but they were now terribly reduced in numbers, and almost destitute of provisions. Cornwallis had no choice but to accept the inevitable; and on the third day after the action, (March 18th), he turned southward, and retreated down the Cape Fear River through the Highlanders' settlement at Cross Creek. But he found there neither provisions nor forage; while the navigation of the river, on which he had counted for transport, was found to be impracticable, the stream being narrow, the banks high, and the population hostile.

Greene, who had followed him almost to Cross Creek, now struck eastward upon Camden; but Cornwallis even so would not change his line of retreat. He merely sent a message of warning to Lord Rawdon at Camden, and then, leaving his sick and wounded to the care of the inhabitants, with many assurances that he would speedily return to them, (Cornwallis to Germaine, 18th April), he retired down the river from Cross Creek, and on the 7th of April arrived at Wilmington.

CHAPTER 13

The End of the Tether

Throughout the time since Cornwallis had advanced from Winns-borough, there had been practically no communication between him and Clinton. Frigates, in spite of Arbuthnot's repeated remonstrances to the Admiralty, were scarce in the fleet; and, since the departure of Lord Howe and Sir George Collier, there had been sufficient friction between the naval and military commanders to compel the general to organise his own service of despatch-vessels, (Stevens, i.).

Clinton was therefore quite in the dark as to the real scope and intention of Cornwallis's movements; and, though the force which he had sent to the Chesapeake under Arnold had diverted most of the Virginian troops from joining Greene, (*ibid*), yet, as we have seen, it had itself only narrowly escaped capture by the French fleet from Rhode Island. Of the disaster at Cowpens Cornwallis had indeed informed his chief, though the news had taken a full month to reach New York; and Clinton had written without reserve that he dreaded the consequences, that he was even then trembling for the safety of Arnold's detachment, and that without reinforcements from England and assurance of superiority at sea he should not undertake solid operations in the Chesapeake. (*Ibid.* i., 2nd 10th March 1781).

These letters reached Charleston on the 6th of April, but were not at once forwarded by the commandant, Colonel Balfour, to Wilmington. For what reason they were delayed it is not easy to explain; but it seems only too probable that Germaine's attitude towards Cornwallis had encouraged general disloyalty among subordinate officers towards the commander-in-chief.

The confusion caused by this tardiness of communication was incredible. Everyone was working at cross-purposes. Clinton, with no information except from American sources, which could not conceal the fact of a British victory at Guildford, not unnaturally assumed that Cornwallis really had accomplished the subjugation of the Carolinas, and began to think of withdrawing all troops from the Chesapeake. In this intention he was strengthened by Phillips and Arnold, who pointed out that with their present strength they could do little except destroy tobacco, though with a small reinforcement they thought it might be possible to overwhelm a small force under Lafayette which lay at Baltimore.(Phillips to Clinton, 15th to 19th April 1781).

Cornwallis, on the other hand, chose without the least warrant to assume that the presence of Phillips and Arnold in the Chesapeake signified solid operations in Virginia, to which he knew Germaine to be inclined. Germaine, (Germaine to Clinton, 7th March 1781—received by Clinton, 27th June 1781), for his part, though Clinton as yet knew it not, had airily assumed that the Carolinas had been reconquered by Cornwallis months before, and that Washington could now be driven to the eastern bank of the Hudson. Meanwhile, in these same first weeks of April, there came a messenger from Germaine to say that six regiments had been embarked to reinforce Clinton; whereupon Clinton, on the 13th of April, wrote to Cornwallis to come and meet him at the Chesapeake as soon as his arrangements for the security of the Carolinas were complete, in order to concert plans for the future.

But at just about the same time Cornwallis was writing to Clinton to tell him, (Cornwallis to Clinton, 10th April 1781), not that he was on the point of abandoning the Carolinas altogether, which was actually the case, but that any hold upon those provinces must be precarious unless Virginia were first reduced, for which reason he advocated vigorous operations in the Chesapeake, even at the cost of evacuating New York.

Having written thus to Clinton, he sat down to urge a serious attempt on Virginia upon Germaine, (Cornwallis to Phillips, 18th April 1781), rather, it must be feared, to justify his previous recklessness than from reliance upon any well-conceived plan of operations. Finally, ignoring Clinton's instructions on no account to imperil Charleston, and forgetful of his promise to the loyalists at Cross Creek, he wrote to Phillips, (ibid. 23rd April 1781), that he saw no prospect of reaching Camden in time to relieve Rawdon, and should therefore march for the Roanoke, hoping that Phillips would be able to advance as far as Petersburg to join him, without exposing his army to ruin.

In plain words, while fully conscious of the immense danger to which he would subject Rawdon and every garrison in Carolina, he resolved deliberately to abandon them, and this although Colonel Balfour had prepared a flotilla to carry his army down the Waccamaw River to the mouth of the Santee and so to Charleston. Accordingly, on the 25th of April, without awaiting instructions from Clinton, he started on a march of two hundred miles to the north, perfectly aware that by so doing he was risking the safety of Phillips's force as well as of his own, but lulling himself with the false comfort that Greene might perhaps leave Carolina to follow him.

Greene, meanwhile, after pursuing Cornwallis as far as Ramsay's Mill to eastward, had turned south upon Camden, (April 7th), detaching Colonel Lee to join with the partisan Marion in attacking some of the intermediate posts between Camden and Charleston. Moving with great rapidity, Lee appeared first before Fort Watson, about sixty miles north-west of Charleston. This post consisted merely of a stockade on the top of a mound which rose forty feet above the plain, and was held by a garrison of one hundred and twenty men.

Neither side had any artillery, and Lee despaired of mastering the fort until one of Marion's officers suggested that a tower, after the classical model, should be constructed out of the forest hard by. Such was the expertness of the American axe-men, that in five days the trees were felled and shaped, while the tower itself was erected in a single night. In the morning the garrison, finding themselves commanded by rifles on every side, surrendered; and by this very ingenious expedient a first gap was made in Rawdon's communications with Charleston. Marion then moved northward to join Greene, who on the 19th had already appeared with his main body before Camden.

Greene had hoped to capture this very important post by surprise, and he was not a little chagrined to find that Rawdon, though unable to produce more than nine hundred men, was quite ready for him in a position which was unassailable except by means of heavy artillery. Having no heavy cannon, and judging himself too weak either to assault or to invest, Greene retired two miles northward to Hobkirk's Hill, where he took post astride of the northern road on rising ground covered with forest.

His force numbered something over twelve hundred men, five-sixths of them regular troops, (850 regular infantry, 40 artillery, 90 cavalry, 250 militia); and with the accession of Marion's detachment he might hope for a superiority which would enable him to deal decisively with Rawdon. But Rawdon had no intention of allowing the junction to come to pass unhindered. At nine o'clock on the morning of the 25th he marched out with every soldier that he could spare, about eight hundred men in all, and, making a wide circuit through the forest, came upon the picquet that covered the American left.

Greene's force thereupon at once took up its allotted position, two Maryland and two Virginian regiments in first line, and the militia and cavalry in reserve. His three guns were concealed in rear of his first line, for Rawdon, thinking that Greene possessed no artillery, had brought no cannon against him and Greene was not the man to undeceive his adversary. Rawdon then formed his own troops for action, the Sixty-Third Foot occupying the right, the New York Volunteers the centre, and the King's American Regiment, (Provincial corps raised by Colonel Fanning, New York, 1776), the left of his line. Rawdon's own corps, the Volunteers of Ireland, stood in support of the right, a detachment under Captain Robertson in support of the left, and in rear of all stood a party of sixty Provincial dragoons. Taking a lesson from his enemies, Rawdon also sprinkled his flanks with loyalist marksmen to pick off the American officers.

Since his entire force did not number as many men as Greene's first line, Rawdon's line of battle necessarily presented a far narrower front; and Greene, coolly allowing the British to advance within close range, suddenly shifted his two centre battalions to right and left so as to unmask his guns, and poured in a heavy shower of grape. Then, seeing the British recoil under the unexpected rain of shot, he in one breath ordered his cavalry to move round upon Rawdon's rear, the flank battalions to close upon his flanks, and the two battalions of his centre to charge with the bayonet. But Rawdon was not so easily to be caught. Extending his supports to right and left of his first line, he allowed the Americans to advance, and then, closing in upon them in flanks and rear, caught them neatly in their own trap.

The fall of one or two American officers under the bullets of Rawdon's riflemen shook the First Maryland Regiment, which occupied Greene's left centre, and caused it to retire in panic. The Second Maryland Regiment having lost its Colonel, retreated likewise, and in a very short time only one battalion of Greene's first line was holding its ground. Greene at once gave orders for it to cover the retreat, which it did with creditable steadiness, and then bestirred himself to save his guns; but it was not until he dismounted and laid hand to the drag-ropes himself that his men would look to them.

A resolute little party of Americans kept Rawdon's cavalry at bay while he did so, and Washington, who had been busy with the task (rather strange in a leader of cavalry) of capturing the British medical staff, at last came up hurriedly to save the guns from jeopardy. Greene then ordered a retreat to Rugeley's Mills, his men being still too unsteady to renew the action; and Rawdon, at the age of twenty-six, had won his first victory. He had lost two hundred and seventy officers and men in the fight, which was a heavy price to pay for it, but he had captured one hundred prisoners and, most important of all, had gained a moment's breathing time.

Greene was much depressed by this reverse, (Johnson, *Life of Greene*, ii.), which, though all praise must be given to Rawdon for his skill and boldness, was anything but creditable to the American troops. But Marion, Sumter, and other partisan-leaders were still active in attacking the posts on the British lines of communication, and it was evident to Rawdon that he must fall back. A reinforcement of five hundred men of the Sixty-Fourth, which had made its way to him in contempt of the American guerillas, did indeed tempt him to advance to Greene's position; but finding it unassailable he turned back, evacuated Camden on the 9th of May, and retired rapidly to Monk's Corner, thirty miles from Charleston.

Within the same week the British posts of Fort Granby and Fort Motte on the Congaree, and of Orangeburg on the North Edisto, fell in quick succession after a short resistance. Meanwhile Greene on the 10th marched eastward to the Saluda, and on the 22nd invested Ninety-Six, while Lee and one of the partisan-leaders moved with astonishing rapidity to the Savannah River and laid siege to Augusta. This latter post was held by a body of Provincial troops under one Colonel Browne, a loyalist whom the revolutionists in the days of their ascendency had striven unsuccessfully to convert to their opinions by roasting his feet at a slow fire. He had since taken his revenge upon his enemies without mercy, and, being not only a desperate but a really brave man, he now made a very fine defence; but the erection of a wooden tower again enabled the enemy's riflemen to shoot down all his gunners, and on the 5th of June he was forced to surrender.

Within two days one of his officers was murdered and another badly wounded while under confinement. The American officers were simply powerless to prevent such outrages, which indeed seem to have been as frequent on the part of loyalists as of revolutionists among these half-savage people of Carolina. Nor is the fact surprising, looking to the nature of the arguments first employed by the revolutionary party.

Nothing beyond Charleston now remained to the British in Carolina except Ninety-Six, the centre of loyalism, which was held by Colonel Cruger with rather more than five hundred loyal Americans, chiefly recruited in New York and New Jersey. Before he left Camden, Rawdon had sent orders for the post to be evacuated and for the troops to be withdrawn to Charleston; but every one of his messages had been intercepted, and the garrison, hating the revolutionists, was very well content to try conclusions with them.

The defences of Ninety-Six consisted of a stockade strengthened by an earthen parapet and abatis, which enclosed the village on all sides, and of a star-fort adjacent to it. To this latter Greene, with the assistance of Kosciusko, laid siege in form, adding the now celebrated wooden towers to the ordinary resources of the engineer. The siege progressed slowly, not without heavy loss to the besiegers; but on the 17th of June the garrison was compelled to evacuate the stockade, and matters would have gone hardly with them but for a strange accident. This was nothing less than the arrival at Charleston of three, (3rd, 19th, 30th Foot), of the six regiments which had been sent to reinforce Clinton from England, and which, but for the interception of Cornwallis's orders by an American privateer, would have sailed straight to New York.

Rawdon at once marched with them to relieve Ninety-Six; whereupon Greene raised the siege, leaving Rawdon to withdraw the garrison in all haste to Orangeburg, (June 29th). So terrible was the heat during this retreat that fifty of Rawdon's men dropped dead on the march. Both parties then went into summer quarters, Greene retiring to the high hills of Santee, some forty miles north-west of Orangeburg. Broken in health, Rawdon was now obliged to hand the command to Lieutenant-Colonel Stuart of the Buffs, and to return to England. Fortunate it was that a commander of such talent, constancy, and resource as Rawdon had been at hand to take charge of the scattered posts in Carolina after Cornwallis's reckless abandonment of them, and to bring at any rate a great part of them into Charleston.

Greene now awaited the arrival of reinforcements, which were slow in coming; but on the 22nd of August he marched up to Camden, being unable to cross the Santee lower down, and moved from thence upon the Congaree. Stuart thereupon fell back from that river to Eutaw, to await the arrival of a convoy, while Greene marched down slowly towards him, collecting his guerilla parties as he went.

It speaks ill for the vigilance of Stuart, who was only just arrived in the country, and well for the activity of the American patrols, that the British commander had little or no information as to Greene's movements; for it was only by the warning of two American deserters that he learned, on the morning of the 8th of September, that Greene was actually on the march to attack him.

So deeply was he lulled in false security that he had actually allowed a party of one hundred unarmed men, with only a slender escort of cavalry, to go three miles forward to gather sweet potatoes, which, since the army was without bread, were in great request. The whole of this party was cut off and captured, while the cavalry, galloping back in panic, threw the entire camp into consternation. Stuart's force, which numbered fewer than eighteen hundred effective men, lay in a cleared space amid high forest, with a house and garden in rear of the camp. He now drew up his troops in a single line somewhat in front of the clearing, and astride of the road by which Greene was advancing. His right flank rested on a creek, with a body of three hundred men under Major Marjoribanks thrown slightly forward on the extreme right, at an obtuse angle to the line.

In echelon to his left rear he posted his small body of cavalry to guard his left flank, and in the road he stationed his three guns. Greene, according to sound rule, formed his first line of militia, about four hundred and fifty strong, with two small bodies of light troops echeloned in rear of each flank, and two guns in the centre. The second line consisted of three brigades of regular troops, rather over twelve hundred strong, with two more guns; and in rear of all came a reserve of cavalry and infantry under Colonel Washington. In all his force numbered about two thousand men.

The action opened with a slow advance of the Americans, during which the artillery on both sides carried on a duel of peculiar obstinacy, with the result that one of the English and both of the American guns were dismounted. The American militia behaved with great gallantry, many of them being paid substitutes who had served in the regular army and would fight well when led by officers whom they admired and trusted. They gave way at length before the British fire; and in an evil hour the battalions of the British left rushed forward in pursuit. They were met by Greene's regular troops with a heavy volley and a charge of the bayonet which drove them back in utter confusion; and Greene seized the favourable moment to order a general charge of his second line, while the British left was still uncovered.

The British right and centre stood firm for a time, notably the Sixty-Third and Sixty-Fourth Regiments, which had fought all through the war; but being assailed on front and flank, and embarrassed by the crowd of fugitives, the whole line, with the exception of Marjoribanks's detachment, gradually gave way and fell back in disorder into the clearing where the British camp stood. Stuart, however, had instructed one of his officers to occupy the house in rear of it immediately in case of mishap; and this was now promptly done, while several companies rallied and took post in the garden to make further resistance.

It now remained for Greene to sweep away Marjoribanks, who with troops strongly posted and skilfully handled still held his own upon the extreme right. Washington accordingly brought up his cavalry from the rear and charged with great gallantry, but was repulsed with very heavy loss and was himself wounded and taken prisoner. A renewal of the attack with infantry met with no better success, for Marjoribanks only fell back to a stronger position at the edge of the garden and maintained himself as stoutly as ever.

Meanwhile Greene's victorious infantry poured into the British camp, where all tents were still standing, hurrying their two guns along with them; but while the officers ran on to storm the garden, the men stopped to plunder the camp, and, finding liquor in the tents, soon became unmanageable. The British in the house and garden quickly perceived their opportunity, and, having picked off most of the American officers, poured a most destructive fire upon the disorderly plunderers in the camp.

Greene therefore ordered a retreat, and directed a party of cavalry to advance up the road in order to cover the movement. Stuart's small body of horse came forward to encounter this party, but, being borne back, drew the American troopers under the fire from the garden, by which they were almost annihilated. Marjoribanks snatched the moment to fall upon the American guns, which, together with two captured from the British, had been brought up to the garden, and carried the whole of them into a place of safety. Then collecting men from the house and garden, he attacked the Americans who hung about the tents, and drove them out, though he did not venture to pursue them into the forest; and so ended the very bloody and desperate action of Eutaw Springs.

Both sides vehemently claimed the victory, as is usually the case when neither has much to boast of; the only creditable features in the action being the steadiness of the American militia during the first onset, and the admirable skill and tenacity of Marjoribanks. The British captured two guns and the Americans one; and the losses on both sides were very heavy. Those of the British amounted to twenty-nine officers and six hundred and sixty-four men killed, wounded, and prisoners. (3 officers and 82 men killed; 16 officers and 335 men wounded; 10 officers and 247 men missing).

Those of the Americans, according to Greene's own account, numbered sixty officers and four hundred and ninety-four men killed, wounded, and missing; but the return is incomplete, and it is reasonable to assume that Greene lost at least as many men as Stuart.

★★★★★★

Stuart's despatch says that over 200 dead Americans were left on the field; but, apart from this, Greene returned only 8 men missing, which, considering that the greater part of his force was dispersed among the British tents, plundering and drinking, is incredible. Moreover, the totals in his casualty list do not tally with the details.

★★★★★★

In any case, both armies were for the present crippled. Greene fell back some seven miles forthwith, while Stuart on the 9th also withdrew to Charleston Neck, leaving seventy of his wounded behind him. Greene made a show of following him, but in a few days, (12th), retired to the high hills of Santee, keeping the river between himself and the British. The action of Eutaw being the last serious engagement in the south, it is unnecessary to linger in Carolina. From the moment when Cornwallis marched northward, the recovery of the province by Greene was assured; and it was only through the courage, skill, and energy of Rawdon that Greene's advance was checked for so long. It is now, therefore, time to follow once more the fortunes of Cornwallis.

That officer, in accordance with his own design, had marched from Wilmington on the 25th of April with sixteen hundred men, (Guards, 23rd, 33rd, 2nd batt. Fraser's Highlanders, Bose's Hessians, L. I. companies of Maclean's/82nd and of Hamilton's Provincials, and R. A. with four guns), and four guns.

Taking part of the garrison with him he ordered Major Craig to withdraw the remainder to Charleston as soon as he should himself have passed the Roanoke. Travelling almost due north, he encountered little resistance; and on the 14th of May his advanced parties met those of the British force in Virginia, a little to northward of the Nottoway River. On the 20th of May the junction of the two armies was completed at Petersburg, and Cornwallis took command of the whole, though with Arnold, not Phillips, for his second; for Phillips had died just a week before, leaving a gap which was not easily to be filled. A few days later there arrived a reinforcement of seventeen hundred men, (17th, 43rd, two German battalions), from New York; for Clinton, on hearing of Cornwallis's retreat to Wilmington, had determined to sacrifice all other objects to the furtherance of his operations in Carolina, (Clinton to Phillips, 26th April 1781).

Not until after Cornwallis had entered Virginia did rumours reach the commander-in-chief that Carolina had been abandoned. These reports caused him the greatest uneasiness. When Cornwallis was within two days' march of Petersburg he wrote:

I hope Cornwallis may have gone back to Carolina. . . . . If he joins Phillips I shall tremble for every post except Charleston, and even for Georgia.

On the following day, May 21, he received a letter from Cornwallis, dated at Wilmington, which confirmed his worst fears; but yet he wrote:

I still hope that Cornwallis may not join Phillips, for I doubt if he will affect Greene's movements.

Whatever Clinton's merits or demerits, his calculation of the result of Cornwallis's manoeuvres showed no little sagacity. (Clinton to Germaine, 18th, 20th, 22nd May 1781).

Now, however, he stood face to face with the fact that Cornwallis, without the slightest regard for his orders, had abandoned Carolina for Virginia; but though he did not fail to censure the proceeding, (Clinton to Cornwallis, 29th May 1781), he left Cornwallis a free hand for further operations instead of ordering him to return forthwith to Charleston.

Meanwhile his own position in New York was an extremely anxious one. Though Germaine had long ago promised to remove Arbuthnot, the old admiral still remained in command of the fleet, constantly changing his plans and hampering the general in a fashion which kept Clinton in terror of losing supremacy at sea, (Clinton to Phillips, 30th April).

Moreover, Cornwallis set at naught all projects that had been previously concerted for operations in the Middle Colonies. Phillips and Arnold had recommended an attack first on Baltimore and then on Pennsylvania; but Cornwallis would hear of nothing but a campaign in Virginia, and announced his intention of marching against Lafayette, who was then lying with a small force at Richmond. Accordingly, he crossed the James River with that object; whereupon Lafayette at once crossed the Chickahominy and, retiring rapidly northwestward, defied the British general to overtake him. Finding that pursuit was hopeless, Cornwallis turned abruptly westward, and, having destroyed a quantity of arms and ammunition at Charlotteville, doubled back down James River through Richmond to Williamsburg.

Meanwhile Lafayette, returning directly that he found himself unpursued, hung continually on Cornwallis's flanks and rear during the march. At Williamsburg, however, Cornwallis's wanderings were abruptly ended by the receipt of new orders, (June 26th), from Clinton. Enclosing an intercepted letter from Washington to Lafayette, the commander-in-chief directed Cornwallis to establish a defensive post at Williamsburg or Yorktown, and to send back to New York every man that he could spare, as soon as the operations then in train should have been completed.

This letter from Washington, which was destined to exert a strange influence on the coming campaign, pointed to a design for a great attack upon New York, to which end he had, at the close of May, written to de Grasse at Haiti entreating him to bring the French fleet to his assistance. There can be no doubt that Washington at that time centred all his hopes in the capture of New York, and that the garrison of the city was then so weak as to justify Clinton's alarm for its safety. Cornwallis, however, received these orders at Williamsburg in no loyal nor kindly spirit. Some allowance may be made for the facts that he had long enjoyed practically independent command, that he had passed through a very arduous campaign with great strain to mind and body, and that he must have felt misgivings as to the absolute failure of his plans.

But, be that as it may, he now deprecated the establishment of a defensive post in the Chesapeake, and begged, though rather late, for permission to return to Charleston in order to look to the safety of Rawdon. (Clinton to Cornwallis, 30th June 1781). Then, deciding that his force, after sending a detachment to New York, would be too weak to hold Yorktown together with the supplementary post of Gloucester on the opposite side of York River, he retired from Williamsburg to James River and prepared to cross it in order to fall back to Portsmouth. Lafayette at once followed him up with twenty-five hundred men, and Cornwallis with great skill contrived to draw him into an action, (July 6th), which cost the marquis a number of men and two guns.

It was thought by some with the army that Cornwallis might have followed up this success and annihilated Lafayette's detachment without prejudice to his other arrangements; and it is certain that the troops destined for New York might very well have been embarked in York River without retiring to James River at all, (Tarleton). No sooner had Cornwallis crossed the James River than there arrived a second letter from Clinton, (July 8th), ordering him to send him forthwith from two to three thousand troops, since he wished to make a raid upon Philadelphia and to destroy all the stores accumulated there. (Clinton to Cornwallis, 28th June 1781).

Then, on his arrival at Portsmouth, he found yet more letters from Clinton, (Clinton to Cornwallis, 11th and 15th July 1781), evidently written with the design of burying all unkindness and restoring the cordial relations that had once reigned between them. These last gave Cornwallis to understand that he was at liberty to keep the whole of his troops, but that it was the opinion both of Clinton and of Admiral Graves, who had lately superseded Arbuthnot, that a defensive post must be established at Old Point Comfort in York River, for the protection of the British cruisers.

If the reader be weary of this tangle of contradictory orders, he can the better understand the feelings of Cornwallis; and yet the blame for this confusion does not lie with Clinton. His own idea was not unsound, namely, to establish a post at the mouth of Chesapeake Bay, which would serve at once as a refuge for the British ships employed in guarding the great waterways of Maryland and Virginia, and as a base for operations on a greater scale so soon as reinforcements should enable him to undertake them. No doubt he would have insisted on his first orders to Cornwallis, had he not just received positive commands from Germaine, (Germaine to Clinton, 2nd May 1781), that not a man was to be withdrawn from the Chesapeake, but that conquest should be pushed from south to north.

This was nothing less than the rejection of the commander-in-chief's scheme in favour of his subordinate's; yet by the irony of fate Clinton had hardly received this order before Germaine repented of it, and wrote again, though of course too late, to approve of Clinton's original plan, (Germaine to Clinton, 7th and 14th July 1781).

The truth was that Clinton, Cornwallis, and Germaine were all of them in favour of a campaign in the Middle Colonies. Clinton, as has been seen, wished to await the arrival of reinforcements and of a covering fleet, and meanwhile to secure a naval base. Cornwallis was for evacuating New York, transferring the principal base of the British to the Chesapeake, and opening the campaign there at once. Germaine desired to combine both designs after some incomprehensible fashion of his own, with the result that he ordered the principal operations to be carried on from some vague external point inward towards the base, instead of from the base outwards upon some given objective.

This ill-timed interference of Germaine was in every respect fatal. Not only was Clinton forced to abandon his own plans, but, being irritated beyond endurance by Germaine's disloyalty, he kept Cornwallis close at hand in order to resign the command to him, instead of sending him back, as he should have done, to Carolina.

Cornwallis now proceeded to examine Old Point Comfort; but this station being condemned by his engineers, he returned again to York River, seized Yorktown and Gloucester, and began to fortify them both. The evacuation of Portsmouth meanwhile proceeded gradually, though not a man except Benedict Arnold was sent back to Clinton, and on the 22nd of August the whole of Cornwallis's force was concentrated in these two new posts.

Meanwhile, on the side of New York all had been quiet. At the end of June Washington took post at White Plains, where on the 6th of July he was joined by the French force from Rhode Island under de Rochambeau. There the two commanders impatiently awaited news from de Grasse, making occasional demonstrations against the British posts at Kingsbridge. Clinton for his part was perfectly aware that de Grasse was expected, but felt little anxiety, since he had been assured that the French fleet would be followed by Rodney with a superior force. At the beginning of August two thousand German recruits reached New York from Europe; and Clinton at once conceived the design of dealing a sudden blow at Rhode Island before de Grasse should arrive. Admiral Graves was cruising to intercept a convoy at the time, but when he returned to New York, (Aug. 16th), there was still ample time for the execution of the project, which Clinton broached to him with great eagerness.

Nevertheless, to the general's great disappointment, Graves declared that the condition of his ships forbade any such operation; and the design was abandoned. (Clinton to Graves, 16th August; Graves to Clinton, 18th and 21st August). Meanwhile Washington, having received intelligence that de Grasse was sailing for the Chesapeake with his whole force, withdrew on the 19th behind the Crotton, and, crossing the Hudson four days later, advanced southward as if to take up his old position at Morristown in New Jersey.

Clinton was puzzled, for he knew that Washington would not dare to move to Virginia without command of the sea, and he had long been assured that naval superiority would be on the side of the British, (Clinton to Cornwallis, 27th August 1781). Then there came to him a message, dated the 25th of August, from Sir Samuel Hood, saying that he had arrived off the Chesapeake with fourteen ships of the line, that he could neither see nor hear anything of de Grasse, and that he was sailing for New York to join Admiral Graves. He duly arrived on the 28th of August; and since there was intelligence that Admiral de Barras had sailed from Rhode Island with eight ships of the line and a convoy on the 27th, Graves on the 31st put to sea with eighteen ships to intercept him.

Unfortunately de Grasse had already arrived in the Chesapeake on the previous day with twenty-eight ships of the line, had surprised two frigates at anchor, which should have been on the watch for him, and had captured the one and driven the other up York River. His appearance in such overwhelming strength was a surprise to every English commander, and upset all calculations. De Grasse lost no time in detaching four ships to convoy the troops which he had brought with him up James River to Lafayette, and anchored with the rest in Lynhaven Bay, just within the southern cape of Chesapeake Bay. There, on the 5th of September, Graves found him with twenty-four ships instead of de Barras with eight ships, as he had expected. An indecisive action followed, wherein Graves showed little skill; but after five days of manoeuvring de Barras passed safely within the Capes, while Graves sailed to New York to repair damages.

It was not until the 2nd of September that Clinton realised that Washington was actually on the march for Virginia, but still he felt little anxiety. He wrote to Cornwallis that Admiral Digby's squadron was expected shortly, and that he himself would send reinforcements and make a diversion from New York, adding, in tragic ignorance of the true state of affairs, that, as Graves had sailed, Cornwallis need fear nothing. (Clinton to Cornwallis, 2nd, 6th, 8th September 1781).

True to his promise, he sent an expedition under Benedict Arnold against New London in Connecticut, which captured Sept. 6. two forts and a number of ships; but the loss of men was disproportionate to the object attained, and as a diversion the enterprise was absolutely ineffective. Cornwallis, meanwhile, knew more of the true situation than Clinton, who had no idea, until Graves's return to New York, of the enemy's superiority at sea; and it must have been clear to him that Clinton's promises were dependent on the movements of the British naval force. Cornwallis had about seven thousand troops, for the most part of excellent quality, while Lafayette lay at Williamsburg with no more than five thousand, many of whom, having been just imported from the West Indies, were sickly and inefficient.

Obviously, Cornwallis could have attacked this force and beaten it before the arrival of Washington's army; and indeed, by his own account, he only refrained from the enterprise in the expectation of speedy relief, though he was fully aware that the French had thirty-six ships against the British twenty-one, (Cornwallis to Clinton, 16th and 17th September 1781). There lay open to him also the alternative of retreat into Carolina, which would no doubt have been hazardous, and must have led to great sacrifices, though to far less than the loss of his whole army. He decided, however, to hold his hand, and busied himself with the strengthening of his position. Meanwhile, on the 14th, Washington and his staff arrived at Lafayette's headquarters. Four days later the first division of his army marched in, and by the 26th the whole of it, some sixteen thousand strong, was assembled at Williamsburg. On the 28th Yorktown was invested, and the siege began.

The defences of the place were by no means contemptible. The little town was covered both to east and west by swamps, and the half-mile that lay in the centre between these two natural protections, as also the passages over the swamps themselves, were commanded by strong redoubts. Within this outer line was an inner line of defence drawn about the town itself, consisting of a stockade and a parapet of earth with redoubts and batteries; but the space included within this internal line did not exceed twelve hundred yards in length by five hundred in depth.

On the 29th a messenger arrived from Clinton saying that Admiral Digby had arrived with three ships, and that he had every hope of sailing to his assistance with five thousand troops and twenty-six ships of the line on the 5th of October. Thereupon, for no apparent reason, Cornwallis abandoned the outer line of defences and retired within the works of the town, though these were actually commanded by the

DEATH OF COLONEL SCAMMELL AT THE SIEGE OF YORKTOWN.

outer line.

Accordingly, on the night of the 30th, the enemy broke ground on the eastern front, advanced their first parallel on the 6th of October, and on the 9th opened fire at a range of six hundred yards. Within two days the enemy's batteries had approached to within three hundred yards, their fire telling heavily, since, by Cornwallis's own confession, most of the inner defences could be enfiladed from the outer line. On the 14th the capture of two advanced redoubts made the British position almost hopeless. A gallant sortie on the 16th, though not wholly unsuccessful, was of little help, and an attempt to retreat across the river to Gloucester was defeated by a sudden storm of wind.

There was no sign of Clinton's coming; and on the 19th, with a large proportion of his force disabled by wounds or sickness, and with hardly a gun able to fire, Cornwallis capitulated. On that same day Clinton, after long delay due to the defects of the fleet, sailed to his relief, but on his arriving found that he was come five days too late, and sailed back, sick at heart, to New York.

The losses of the garrison during the siege were five hundred killed and wounded. The number that surrendered was six thousand six hundred and thirty men, of whom twenty-five hundred were Germans and the remainder British; and it is noteworthy that no fewer than two thousand men were in hospital. (Tarleton's list gives the total at 7247, including hospital staff and non-combatants. The above figure is from a return of 18th October 1781).

The blow was, on the whole, perhaps the heaviest that has ever fallen on the British Army, and to all intent it put an end to the war in America. There was, indeed, occasional petty fighting from time to time in Carolina; but it was recognised that the contest was hopeless; and aggressive hostilities had long been abandoned in every quarter before Charleston was finally evacuated in December 1782. The story of the War of American Independence therefore ends practically with the surrender of Yorktown.

The immediate cause of the disaster was of course the arrival of de Grasse in such immense strength. No one dreamed that he would carry all his ships with him to America. Rodney reckoned that he would take at most ten, and supposed that by sending fourteen ships with Hood, and ordering six more, which for some reason never came, from Jamaica, he had made ample provision against all contingencies. The more credit is due to de Grasse for his energy and decision; and he was favoured, as he deserved, by the fortune of war. With the British admirals everything went amiss.

Apart from many mishaps which they could not have prevented, they made mistakes, and, worst of all, mistakes for which fortune exacted the utmost penalty. For in the conduct of war, as in the world at large, those sins only are unpardonable which are found out. But, setting the naval operations wholly aside, it seems to me that, judged by purely military standards, Cornwallis emerges by no means altogether with credit from this last phase of the campaign. Undoubtedly he contributed more than any one man, except only Germaine, to the final catastrophe by his mad invasion of North Carolina after Cowpens, and by his equally mad advance into Virginia from Wilmington.

But even if this be forgiven to him, his behaviour at Yorktown seems to have been singularly weak. He knew that he was in a most perilous situation, and his better instinct prompted him to strike at Lafayette before Washington could arrive; but he resisted this impulse and abstained. Even so, all might have been well had he held fast to his outer line of defence, in which he could almost certainly have prolonged the siege for another week; whereas he knew that, by abandoning them, he rendered his inner line untenable. This proceeding has never been satisfactorily explained, and I confess that to me it wears no very pleasing aspect. Nevertheless, it is perfectly intelligible that Cornwallis, who at his best was certainly a good, skilful, and gallant soldier, might have been practically broken down by incessant anxiety and strain; and it is probably not less just than charitable to ascribe his shortcomings in great degree to physical causes.

But the readiness of disloyalty with which he turned against his commander-in-chief, the ill-temper which he showed when Clinton very properly called him to account for disobedience of orders and for the prosecution of unwise and unsound operations, and above all the impatience which he evinced at every stage in the miscarriage of his foolish campaign—these characteristics do not strike me as those of a good commander or of a well-conditioned officer.

At the same time, he showed some very fine qualities. He shared every hardship with his men, he never hesitated to take the blame for any mishap that befell his subordinates, and he was rewarded by a devotion in his troops which gained for him the astonishing victory at Guildford, and kept his little force in heart through weeks of untold hardship, fatigue, and want.

As to Clinton, who was made the scapegoat for every misfortune that occurred during his period of command, it seems to me that no general was ever worse treated. With fewer troops than Howe, and with a French fleet constantly on the coast, he was expected to do fully as much as his predecessor. Had he been left to himself he might have won better success, for his letters show considerable insight into the realities of the situation, and he had a radical distrust of all operations based on the support of loyalists. Knowing his weakness in numbers, he would have relied on a system of raids on the coast, occasionally hazarding a heavier blow when he saw opportunity, but never attempting to conquer country which he could not hold.

He could strike hard and swiftly, as he proved by his capture of Forts Clinton and Montgomery; but it was his misfortune, after brief and perfectly cordial intercourse with Lord Howe and Sir George Collier, to find himself harnessed with admirals who were neither good yoke-mates nor efficient commanders. Twice he was about to swoop upon Rhode Island and make it a Yorktown for the French, and twice he was thwarted by the admiral. His views as to the conduct of the campaign were always sane, and he recognised, as Cornwallis did not, that the naval operations far exceeded the military in importance. Altogether he was an unlucky man, unlucky above all in the mistakes which were forced upon him by the minister at home.

For it is to Germaine, if to any one man, that the disaster of Yorktown as of Saratoga is to be ascribed: to Germaine with his blindness to facts, his deafness to wise counsel, his jealousy of commanders in the field, his appalling ignorance of the elements of war, his foolish ambition to direct all operations from Whitehall. In the matter of failure to furnish the recruits, supplies, and ships required by the generals, very much may be forgiven to one who had to deal with such a multitude of enemies in all quarters; but nothing can excuse the encouragement of disloyalty in a subordinate towards his commander-in-chief, nor deliberate insult offered to a commander-in-chief by ostentatious quotation of a subordinate's opinion against him. (See Germaine to Clinton, 6th June 1781; a most insulting letter).

He knew that Clinton would have resigned the command at once if the king would have permitted him, and therefore he took a cowardly delight in thwarting him. Then when he had driven him, as he had already driven Burgoyne, into disaster, he turned upon them both and rent them. There is, in fact, a malignity in the behaviour of Germaine towards all the principal commanders in America which bears very strong marks of personal vindictiveness. The man had never forgotten the court-martial after Minden.

Yet, in spite of Germaine in office, of Fox and Richmond in opposition, of Ireland on the verge of insurrection, and of all Europe armed against Britain, the fact remains that the American Revolution at the moment of its final triumph was on the eve of collapse. Washington wrote in April 1781:

> We are at the end of our tether .

"Great Britain desisted from the contest exactly when she ought most to have pressed it," writes the biographer of General Greene, (Johnson, ii.), who gives abundance of facts to show that the Southern Colonies could not have maintained another campaign. Nor is the reason difficult to discover; for it is abundantly evident from the testimony of the Americans themselves that there was little enthusiasm in the Colonies over the quarrel. Unless their homes were invaded the people of America were unwilling to fight themselves, and except with paper money they were unwilling to pay others to fight for them. Everybody wanted to make money out of the war, but few wished to take any other share in it.

Hence, dull to all sense of shame and honour, Congress violated the Convention of Saratoga and maltreated the prisoners simply in order to drive them into the American service. Joseph Galloway, a renegade member of Congress, averred that scarcely one-fourth of the American regular troops were natives, one-half being Irish and the remainder British. Evidence from such a source should not, I think, be hastily accepted, for Galloway did not put forward such statements without purposes of his own; but, whether his calculations be exaggerated or not, there can be no doubt that they contain a strong leaven of truth.

Again, it cannot be denied that desertion assumed extraordinary proportions at different periods of the war, chiefly of Germans from the British side and of Irish from the American. Greene was often heard to say that at the close of the war he fought the enemy with British soldiers, and that the British fought him with those of America, (Johnson, ii.); and it seems certain that the Provincial troops in British pay exceeded, on an average, the permanent force of Washington. "Money will go further than arms in America," wrote the cynical Benedict Arnold, who knew his countrymen.

It is in view of these circumstances that the history of the war seems most remarkable. There were two great blows struck on each side, by the Americans at Saratoga and Yorktown, and by the British at New York and Fort Washington in 1776 and at Charleston in 1780. Minor successes on both sides, such as the repulse of the British before Charleston in 1776, and of the Americans at Penobscot and Savannah, leave little advantage to the credit of either. But in pitched battles the British were almost invariably successful; and though this is easily accounted for at Bunker's Hill and Brandywine, it is less easily explained after 1777, when the best part of the veteran troops sent from England had been used up in the campaigns of Howe and Burgoyne.

Such of them as survived marched with Cornwallis through the Carolinas, but there can have been few of them left after the Battle of Camden; and yet the remnant contrived to win the action of Guildford, when beyond doubt there must have been many Provincials in the ranks. Rawdon, again, won his action of Hobkirk's Hill almost entirely with Provincial troops, which, by hypothesis, should have been no better than Greene's. Even at Eutaw, Stuart's Provincial troops rallied after their first defeat, whereas Greene's broke up to plunder before their work was half done. Cowpen's was the one exception, for the action of King's Mountain was unique of its kind, and Cowpens was won, as many actions are, principally by an accident. Speaking generally, it seems to me certain that the British made far better troops of their Provincial recruits than the Americans themselves.

Regular pay was no doubt a principal cause of this, together with the better system of discipline which goes necessarily with an army of long standing and great traditions. No slur can be cast upon the gallantry of American officers, as their losses at Eutaw can testify; but even so they had rarely the hold possessed by English and loyalist officers over their men. The reason for this I believe to be that the loyal party was far more enthusiastic for its cause than the revolutionists. The most gallant feat of the whole war was the work of a little party of loyalists in one of the posts about New York, who, though no more than seventy strong and without a single cannon, held a block-house for three hours against several hundred of the enemy with seven guns. One face of the block-house was pierced by no fewer than fifty-six cannon shot, and the losses of this noble little garrison amounted to twenty-one killed and wounded; yet they held their post indomitably, beat the enemy off with heavy loss, and even took some of them prisoners. (This happened on 21st July 1780. The king sent them his special thanks).

Clinton also bore repeated witness to the excellent behaviour of his Provincial regiments; and I am driven to the conclusion, despite the presence of many brave and excellent officers in the American Army, that the better class of American generally preferred the King's Commission to that of Congress, partly from a natural leaning to the side of loyalty, partly because, in Washington's phrase, the Americans regarded their officers, as such, no more than a broomstick. Nor is this in the least surprising when we reflect on the jealous and unclean intrigues of the self-seeking body named Congress.

Had the British Government at the beginning of the war offered the inducements to enlistment which were afterwards suggested by Arnold, Washington's source of recruits would have been in great measure dried up. The fact is, as I must repeat, that the revolution was the work of a very small but busy and ambitious minority, which but for the support of unscrupulous partisans in the British Parliament, would probably have dwindled away to nothing. Had the Americans really cared seriously about the quarrel with England, they would have raised the hundred and fifty thousand men of whom Conway spoke, and driven the British from the Continent in two campaigns. As it was, they left their work to be done mainly by the French.

How then, it will be asked, did the Americans contrive to achieve such successes as Saratoga and Yorktown? The answer is, that in the first instance they had their militia with them, and in the second a force of French troops in addition to the French fleet. It was, in fact, only when the militia came forward that the Americans achieved any important success apart from their allies; but the militia was an extremely uncertain element, both to friend and foe. Washington wrote, (*Works*, vii.), in 1781:

> The collecting of the militia depends entirely on the prospects
> of the day; if favourable, they throng to you; if not, they will
> not move.

This was strictly true, as the fate of Burgoyne can prove; and it was the knowledge of the fact that made the British commanders so extremely cautious and so adverse as a rule to operations far inland, where the militia could waylay detachments or overwhelm posts on the lines of communication without going far from their homes. It was doubtless this consideration which prompted Amherst and Lord Harrington to urge that the war should be a naval war only. Against it there was of course the objection that the militia was of value for the intimidation of loyalists; but as this terrorism soon degenerated into indiscriminate robbery and violence, it would necessarily have provoked retaliation, and would have brought about, as it actually did in Carolina, a civil war of unsurpassed ferocity. (The process had begun in Pennsylvania. Washington, *Works*, iv. New York also was full of brigands).

By allowing Congress to work its will inland, while cutting off all communications by sea and making occasional raids on the ports which sheltered privateers, the British fleet would probably have brought the Americans back to the Crown without the expense of large forces from England and Germany; while if a Montrose had chanced to appear among the loyalists he might have shortened matters considerably. Even as things fell out, when the American war was a matter of but secondary importance in England's gigantic struggle with the powers of Europe all over the world, there was not vitality enough in the revolution to support it; and but for foreign assistance the whole movement would have collapsed.

In truth, as an eminent historian has written, the general aspect of the American people during the contest was far from heroic or sublime; and it is pleasanter to turn from it to the gallantry of their troops in the field, and to the indomitable steadfastness and constancy of their leaders, Washington and Greene. Of their strictly military talents it is not easy to speak, for it is impossible to say how far Washington's earlier operations may have been marred by Congress. His fame as a military commander rests on the surprise of the German posts at Trenton, and on his march from the Hudson to the Chesapeake in 1781. The former, though a very brilliant and skilful feat, which led to great results, can hardly be rated more highly than a dozen similar exploits of the war; while the march to the Chesapeake was unopposed by Clinton, less from any skill of Washington's in feint or manoeuvre than from Clinton's reliance on Rodney's word that British supremacy at sea would be maintained.

As a matter of fact, Washington would never have attempted this march with American troops only, since, by his own confession, they would have melted away on the road. (Washington, *Works*, viii., 15th July 1781). On the other hand, there were very grave flaws in his campaign of 1776 about New York, while he was completely outmanoeuvred by Howe in Pennsylvania in 1777. From that time onward until 1781 he practically had no army with which to take the field, but was compelled to sit quietly on the defensive. It was in those long months of waiting in entrenched positions, and most notably in that bitter and desperate winter at Valley Forge, that Washington's finest qualities were displayed his constancy, his courage, and his inexhaustible patience. Yet though every Englishman must admire him as a very great man and a brave and skilful soldier, it is, I think, doubtful whether he has any claim to be regarded as a really great commander in the field. He was not, it is true, a soldier by profession, but neither was Cromwell; and I take it that few would venture to rate Washington, as a general, so highly as Cromwell.

Greene's reputation stands firmly on his campaign in the Carolinas, his luring of Cornwallis into a false position, and his prompt return upon Camden after the retreat of Cornwallis to Wilmington. His keen insight into the heart of Cornwallis's blunders and his skilful use of his guerilla troops are the most notable features of his work, and stamp him as a general of patience, resolution, and profound common sense, qualities which go far towards making a great commander. One gift he seems to have lacked, namely, the faculty of leadership, to which, as well as to bad luck, must be ascribed the fact that he was never victorious in a general action.

Washington's ascendency over his men was remarkable, but Washington had the advantage of being a gentleman. I am aware that this is now supposed to be no advantage; but Washington considered it to be essential to a good officer, and I am content to abide by his opinion. Saving this one small matter, Greene, who was a very noble character, seems to me to stand little if at all lower than Washington as a general in the field.

But in natural military genius neither Washington nor Greene are to my mind comparable with Benedict Arnold. The man was of course shallow, fickle, unprincipled, and unstable in character, but he possessed all the gifts of a great commander. To boundless energy and enterprise he united quick insight into a situation, sound strategic instinct, audacity of movement, wealth of resource, a swift and unerring eye in action, great personal daring, and true magic of leadership. It was he and no other who beat Burgoyne at Saratoga, and, with Daniel Morgan to command his militia, Benedict Arnold was the most formidable opponent that could be matched against the British in America.

In justice to the Americans, too, it must be remembered that the British generals, taken altogether, were good and able officers. Howe and Clinton were fettered by Germaine, but Howe's brigadiers were all of them capable—some of them, indeed, such as Grey, Grant, and Vaughan, of unusual capacity. Many detachments were made in the course of the war, but few of them failed to do their work with success. Burgoyne and Cornwallis, for all their misfortunes, were excellent officers; so also were Cornwallis's brigadiers, O'Hara and Webster. Major Craig showed very great ability in his difficult post at Wilmington; and Ferguson, Tarleton, and Simcoe, though they had experience of mishaps, won deserved reputations as partisan-officers.

But the ablest of all was Lord Rawdon, who received his baptism of fire at twenty-one, on Bunker's Hill, and at twenty-six contrived with great skill to save the position abandoned by Cornwallis. With him, together with James Craig and Ensign John Moore of Maclean's, among its officers the British Army would fair better in the future.

LEONAUR

ALSO FROM LEONAUR
AVAILABLE IN SOFTCOVER OR HARDCOVER WITH DUST JACKET

THE 9TH—THE KING'S (LIVERPOOL REGIMENT) IN THE GREAT WAR 1914 - 1918 *by Enos H. G. Roberts*—Mersey to mud—war and Liverpool men.

THE GAMBARDIER *by Mark Severn*—The experiences of a battery of Heavy artillery on the Western Front during the First World War.

FROM MESSINES TO THIRD YPRES *by Thomas Floyd*—A personal account of the First World War on the Western front by a 2/5th Lancashire Fusilier.

THE IRISH GUARDS IN THE GREAT WAR - VOLUME 1 *by Rudyard Kipling*—Edited and Compiled from Their Diaries and Papers—The First Battalion.

THE IRISH GUARDS IN THE GREAT WAR - VOLUME 1 *by Rudyard Kipling*—Edited and Compiled from Their Diaries and Papers—The Second Battalion.

ARMOURED CARS IN EDEN *by K. Roosevelt*—An American President's son serving in Rolls Royce armoured cars with the British in Mesopatamia & with the American Artillery in France during the First World War.

CHASSEUR OF 1914 *by Marcel Dupont*—Experiences of the twilight of the French Light Cavalry by a young officer during the early battles of the great war in Europe.

TROOP HORSE & TRENCH *by R.A. Lloyd*—The experiences of a British Lifeguardsman of the household cavalry fighting on the western front during the First World War 1914-18.

THE EAST AFRICAN MOUNTED RIFLES *by C.J. Wilson*—Experiences of the campaign in the East African bush during the First World War.

THE LONG PATROL *by George Berrie*—A Novel of Light Horsemen from Gallipoli to the Palestine campaign of the First World War.

THE FIGHTING CAMELIERS *by Frank Reid*—The exploits of the Imperial Camel Corps in the desert and Palestine campaigns of the First World War.

STEEL CHARIOTS IN THE DESERT *by S. C. Rolls*—The first world war experiences of a Rolls Royce armoured car driver with the Duke of Westminster in Libya and in Arabia with T.E. Lawrence.

WITH THE IMPERIAL CAMEL CORPS IN THE GREAT WAR *by Geoffrey Inchbald*—The story of a serving officer with the British 2nd battalion against the Senussi and during the Palestine campaign.

www.ingramcontent.com/pod-product-compliance
Lightning Source LLC
Chambersburg PA
CBHW032039080426
42733CB00006B/138